David Gregg

Makers of the American Republic

A series of patriotic lectures

David Gregg

Makers of the American Republic
A series of patriotic lectures

ISBN/EAN: 9783337308209

Printed in Europe, USA, Canada, Australia, Japan

Cover: Foto ©Suzi / pixelio.de

More available books at **www.hansebooks.com**

MAKERS
OF THE
AMERICAN REPUBLIC.

BOOKS BY REV. DAVID GREGG.

MAKERS OF THE AMERICAN REPUBLIC.

Historical Studies of Colonial Times; portraying pen pictures of the Virginia Colonists, the Pilgrims, the Hollanders, the Puritans, the Quakers, the Scotch, and the Huguenots, with chapters on the influence of the Discovery of Columbus, the Life and Times of Washington, and the Christian Church as a moral uplift in the formation and development of the Nation. 405 pages. Cloth, - - - $1.50.

OUR BEST MOODS.

Soliloquies and Other Discourses; eloquently addressing the every day hearer, and encouraging him to higher aspirations.

"The Themes chosen are of practical moment and in their treatment the preacher never loses sight of his purpose to stimulate men to realize the highest ideal of character and life."—*The New York Observer.*

362 pages, Frontispiece Portrait. Cloth, - $1.25.

THE HEAVEN LIFE;
Or, Stimulus for Two Worlds.

The whole idea of the book is the comfort and stimulus of those who wish to live their best in two worlds, and a consolation to those who are in bereavement. 168 pages. Cloth, - - - 75 Cents.

IDEALS FOR BOTH;
Or, How to make Life Beautiful.

A Series of Addresses to Young People on Ideal Manhood and Ideal Womanhood, republished from the Treasury Magazine. A pastor writes: "Can you do a better thing than to publish them in a book. I speak for six copies in advance to lend to young men and women." 114 pages. Cloth, - - - 50 Cents.

TESTIMONY OF THE LAND TO THE BOOK;
Or, The Evidential Value of Palestine.

Chautauqua Lectures on The Fascination of the Land; The Voices from Above Ground; or, The Land in its Physical Features and Argument; and The Voices from Underground; or, The Land in the Light of Modern Discovery.

"This work presents the arguments of the Bible derived from topography and explorations. It is a work up to date, and is as interesting as a novel."—*New York Tribune.*

Neatly bound in boards, imitation leather, 35 Cents.

E. B. TREAT, Pub., 5 Cooper Union, N.Y.

MONUMENT TO FAITH.
PLYMOUTH, MASS.

MAKERS

OF THE

AMERICAN REPUBLIC

A SERIES OF PATRIOTIC LECTURES

BY

DAVID GREGG, D.D.

PASTOR OF THE LAFAYETTE AVENUE PRESBYTERIAN CHURCH
BROOKLYN, N. Y.

NEW YORK

E. B. TREAT, 5 COOPER UNION

OFFICE OF THE TREASURY MAGAZINE

1896

Copyright, 1896, by
E. B. Treat.

THE NEW YORK TYPE-SETTING COMPANY.

PUBLISHER'S NOTE.

THIS series of popular lectures is full of historical data and pioneer incidents of colonial times, vividly portraying pen-pictures of the Virginia colonists, the Pilgrims, the Hollanders, the Puritans, the Quakers, the Scotch, and the Huguenots, with chapters on the influence of the discoveries of Christopher Columbus, and the work of George Washington as a factor in American history, and the effect of the growth of the Christian church in the formation and development of the nation.

The book embodies the results of a large historical research. It sets forth in a vivid and attractive light the races, the personalities, the principles, and the occasions entitled to credit in the construction of the American Republic. It is highly suggestive of American history yet to be written. The book pleads for the broadest and purest type of Americanism, and is outspoken and fearless in advocating the highest interests of our nation.

The American citizen will find in it enlightenment and stimulus for his patriotism.

Our young people, as they shall be taught in the universities, public schools, and Chautauqua, Christian Endeavor, and other societies, will find it a veritable thesaurus in their preparation to write or speak upon " Christian citizenship."

The preacher will find abundant and helpful material for his pulpit ministrations, and learn how an occasional patriotic service can be made attractive to the people, as well as a power for God and country.

The statesman will here find facts and data for the equipment of argument and illustration, giving strength to and lighting up his patriotic, historical, and political addresses.

All of these historic lectures have been delivered with great acceptance to audiences of thousands, and on this account carry with them a telling indorsement of their life and power. This fact should weigh with those who wish to possess effective patriotic literature. It is the teachings of such patriotic recitals that assure us of a future for our Republic. Their legitimate product will be intelligent Americans, on fire with a holy enthusiasm to make ultimate America the realization of the brightest visions of the great men of the different races who lived and died for the Republic.

CONTENTS.

		PAGE
I.	THE OLD DOMINION; OR, THE VIRGINIA COLONISTS	17
II.	THE PILGRIM FOREFATHERS	53
III.	THE PURITAN FOUNDERS	75
IV.	THE HOLLANDERS IN THE NEW NETHERLANDS	103
V.	THE SCOTCH	133
VI.	THE HUGUENOTS	169
VII.	THE QUAKERS; OR, IDEAL CIVILIZATION	209
VIII.	COLUMBUS: THE RESULTS OF HIS LIFE	249
IX.	GEORGE WASHINGTON: A FACTOR IN AMERICAN HISTORY	279
X.	THE CHURCH AND THE REPUBLIC	311
XI.	AMERICA FOR CHRIST	341
XII.	THE HONOR DUE TO OUR PATRIOTIC DEAD	371

I.

THE OLD DOMINION; OR, THE VIRGINIA COLONISTS.

I.

THE OLD DOMINION;

OR, THE VIRGINIA COLONISTS.*

A GREAT statesman of olden times, in speaking to his countrymen, gave them this advice: *"Take ye therefore good heed unto yourselves;"* i.e., *"Go to school to self."* The advice is good counsel for the American Republic. We are to learn from ourselves; we are to study our own history. This is not a narrow study nor an uninteresting study nor an unprofitable study. Our Republic has made history rapidly, and it has made it on lines altogether different from the other nations of the world. As a nation our Republic has sprung to the head of nations, and has led them toward a newer civilization and a more abundant liberty.

We have a large history, for we have grown phenomenally. No nation on the earth can match us for growth; we have grown like the wheat in

---

* Delivered in Lafayette Avenue Presbyterian Church, Brooklyn, at a Forefathers'-day service.

our harvest-fields. Humboldt informs us that a follower of Cortez sowed the first wheat in America. He found just three kernels in his supply of rice. They got into the rice accidentally. These three kernels he carefully planted. The dividends of this planting in 1895 were millions on millions of bushels. In the month of May, 1607, when the first American colony of Englishmen was planted at Jamestown, Va., there were only one hundred and two souls; now we number sixty-five millions. What is crowded into the history between then and now? The overrule of God; the noble struggles and sacrifices of our civil fathers; the planting of everlasting principles and the growth of the same into magnificent institutions; the play of the forces and events which has made us what we are as a body politic—these things are crowded into our history, and to know them is to know where our strength lies and where our duty lies and where the source of our national perpetuity lies.

Do we understand our own institutions? We cannot serve our country intelligently and effectively if we do not. Our national greatness will inevitably go down before a wide-spread national ignorance of these. As the great white dome of our federal capitol at Washington rests upon a circle of giant pillars, even so our national greatness rests upon the vast circle of our civil institutions. These are the pillars of our Republic, and we should so know them as to be able intelligently to guard them. I believe that there is something to be learned from each individual fact pertaining to us as a nation. For example, we are territorially one—solidly one. Our dominion is not fractional. With the exception of Alaska, it lies in one undivided body, animated practically by one blood, using one national language, and living under one law enacted at one center. And yet for all this practically the sun never sets on our territory. On the short summer night the light of the sunset does not cease to gleam on the shining spears of the seal-fishermen of Alton off Alaska before the sunshine commences to flash on the glinting axes of the woodmen in the forests of Maine. We differ from England in this: we are territorially one. The British empire is scattered about the world in no less than forty-one different parcels. Now I believe that the fact that we are one territorially teaches us that we should be and should ever remain one in government, and that every attempt to sever our national union should be treated as treason. The very configuration of our national territory declares, "The Union one and inseparable, now and forever."

My fellow-men, I believe that we need just such exercises as those to which this historical service calls us. We need something to incite us to the study of the history of our country. Our national history is a page from God's own book, and is full of divine lessons. We need to know what our nation incarnates; we need to know what our institutions cost; we need to know how the builders of our nation suffered and worked. Our institutions cost time and blood and brain. Our Republic incarnates scholarship and patriotism and reformations and revolutions, and the wise providences of that God who is the eternal Master Builder of states. Are these things so, then we have something in our Republic to prize, something to be proud of, something to be loyal to, something to perpetuate, something to pray for, and something for which we should send to God our whole-hearted and enthusiastic Te Deum.

I am here to-night to tell you one of the stories which pertains to the evolution of our nation. There are other stories pertaining to this evolution, such as the story of the Pilgrims, the story of the Puritans, the story of the Hollanders, the story of the Scotch and their descendants, and the story of the Huguenots. To-night our story is to be the story of "Old Dominion, the Colony of Virginia."

This colony was the oldest of all the colonies. It was the first colony of the English on the new continent. It was unique; it was different from all the others; it was the last colony from which republicanism had a right to expect anything; but it turned out to be the colony that was foremost in the inauguration of the Republic. Without its lead and coöperation our Republic would never have had an existence. Virginia and Massachusetts, standing shoulder to shoulder, did the planning and the leading and the fighting which ushered in the American Revolution. They pushed the Revolution through to a successful conclusion, and afterward they gathered and organized the results of the Revolution so as to make them permanent.

I have said that the Virginia Colony was the last colony from which republicanism had a right to expect any aid. I base this remark upon the popular and ancient name which that colony bore —" Old Dominion."

Do you know why it was called " Old Dominion"? The answer is interesting. It received this name from the stand which it took and the part which it played during the days of the English Revolution and during the period of the English Commonwealth, inaugurated by Oliver Cromwell. As Virginia was largely Cavalier in those days, it was full of Royalists. It was intensely aristocratic. It was for the king and against the Parliament. When Cromwell beheaded Charles I., thousands of Cavalier Royalists poured into the colony of Virginia. The colony took action through its officials, civil and church, upon the execution of Charles I. It called his execution murder, and it denominated the Parliamentarians regicides. It was enacted that all in the colony who justified the king's death should be considered traitors, and treated as though they had handled the knife and had actually beheaded the king. Sir William Berkeley, a fiery Cavalier, was the governor of the colony at the time, and he led in this legislation. The sympathies of the colony went out to Charles II., the son of the executed king, and he was declared the legal successor of his father. Under the direction of Berkeley, Colonel Richard Lee, a rich planter and a Cavalier, went to visit Charles II. in his exile in France and to offer him Virginia as a kingdom. Lee besought him to cross the Atlantic and to set up his rule in the colony as king. This was the first dominion which Charles II. had offered him. It was his oldest dominion. Charles never forgot this. When he was crowned in England, on the day of his coronation he robed himself in Virginia silk to show his gratitude to Virginia. This lifted Virginia in the estimation of the British empire. When coins were minted under the reign of Charles II. they had stamped on them that the kingdom henceforth consisted of England, Scotland, Ireland, and Virginia. One of these coins may be seen to-day in the Massachusetts Historical Society's collection. This was considered a great honor for the little colony to rank it with such great countries as England and Scotland; and so the colony was ever after spoken of as "Old Dominion." Charles had dominion here when he had dominion nowhere else.

What hope for a republic, we ask, can come from a colony such as this? Yet the Revolutionary leaders of Virginia, who formed an illustrious group and who gave America its illustrious and Revolutionary sayings,—the sayings that awoke the slumbering spirit of liberty far and near,—were men nearly all of whom were descendants of these bitter Royalists and Cromwell-hating Cavaliers. It was a descendant of this very Richard Lee who went to France to bring Charles II. to Virginia to rule as king, viz., Richard Henry Lee, who originated the Committee of Correspondence which brought the thirteen colonies together to strike unitedly for freedom, and who was the author of the "Address to the Colonies," and who, in the Continental Congress, moved America's Declaration of Independence in these words, which he offered as a motion: "*Resolved*, That these united colonies are and ought to be free and independent States, and that all political connection between them and the state of Great Britain is and ought to be totally dissolved." This motion, made by Richard Henry Lee, a Virginian, was seconded by John Adams, a leader from Massachusetts, and having been debated for three full days, it was finally passed. Thus Richard Henry Lee was a leader and a great man in the new times of Virginia, just as his ancestor, Richard Lee, was a leader and a pushing man in the old times of Virginia.

The first point which I wish to make is this: Old Dominion served America and told in its higher and present making by the things which she fought out of existence and eternally buried and by the progress which she made upon her own self. She struck down and buried the ideals and the principles and the prejudices and the proposals of Richard Lee of the time of the Cromwellian Commonwealth, and she made way for and adopted the advanced ideals and the republican principles of Richard Henry Lee of the Revolutionary era.

The history of the Virginia Colony has not as yet been fully and worthily written. No American history has been adequately written except the history of New England. New England, whose ideal has been *education*, has through its oldest and best-equipped universities produced the scholars of America and has given the country its national poets, and these have rewarded her by writing her history and putting it into verse and song. There is no discount on the history of New England; I am not derogating it; I am only saying that she is fortunate in having the pioneer historians of America. The other colonies will some day have their historians, and then we shall have a new era in American history-writing. Virginia's day is coming; her history is full of remarkable scenes; they only need to be well told or cast into the form of romance or allowed to flow from the pen of the poet in jeweled words. Give them a Longfellow and a Lowell and a Holmes and a Hawthorne to take them from their homely and traditional form and recast them and put into them the charm of wit and fancy and give them beauty of expression, and they will go thrilling through this nation with a power that will kindle anew the old spirit of liberty and bring into existence a strong, fresh love of country.

The colony of Virginia antedated the colony of Plymouth Rock some thirteen years. It sailed from London in three vessels on December 19, 1606. The names of the three vessels were the *Discovery*, the *Good Speed*, and the *Susan Content*. All London was moved at the sight of these three little ships sailing down the Thames. Prayers were offered in the churches for their welfare, and their praises were sung by the poets. Here are two verses from a glowing lyric of Drayton:

> " You brave, heroic minds,
>   Worthy your country's name,
>   That honor still pursue;
>   Whilst loitering hinds
>   Lurk here at home with shame,
>   Go and subdue.

> " And cheerfully at sea
>   Success you still entice
>   To get the pearls and gold,
>   And ours to hold
>   Virginia,
>   Earth's only paradise."

The voyagers reached a spot on the James River where they landed May 13, 1607. They called the spot Jamestown, after the then reigning king, James I. There were just one hundred and two in this noted company. In the sailing-lists we find them classed as "gentlemen, carpenters, laborers, gold-refiners, jewelers, and one perfumer." Unfortunately more than one half the company were "gentlemen"; and the term "gentlemen" signified persons unused to manual labor. "Gentlemen, jewelers, gold-refiners, and one perfumer" were not the stuff to fight the great American wilderness. Why did they come to Virginia? Some had it warmly at heart to convert the Indians to Christianity; some looked to the extension of the British empire; but the great majority expected easily to pick up pearls and gold. They expected to dig gold, wash gold, refine gold, and ship gold.

These Jamestown people had a hard time of it. In the first place, their leaders were worthless and indolent; and in the second place, the majority of them who came for gold were sadly disappointed and paralyzed with despair. Besides this they had chosen a swamp for a building-place, and they soon lost their health. The first years at Jamestown were years filled with mutiny, internal strife, treason, epidemic, exposure, fever, starvation, massacre, disastrous fire, famine, and death. There was only one masterful man among them, and that was Captain John Smith, whose presence and effort kept the colony from absolute extinction. This man was only three years, all told, in America; but he made for himself an undying name. He returned to England.

The experience of Jamestown was more terrible than the experience of Plymouth, and came nearer being a failure. . Was there a reason for this? Yes. Were not the two colonies precisely alike? No; they both came from England, that is true; but the Jamestown Colony lacked this, viz., the presence and the patience and the pacifying influence and the elevating power of a heroic Christian womanhood. The Pilgrims of the *Mayflower* brought their wives and children with them; they had the home in their colony. Woman makes the home, and the home makes the church and the state. If Plymouth Rock had been minus the home, the future of New England would have been changed. The men who came over in the *Discovery*, the *Good Speed*, and the *Susan Content* left the women and the children in England. There was not a single woman in the whole colony; and that is the reason they acted as savages and quarreled and were decimated. What could we expect from a hundred and two old bachelors—a community of bachelors? It is as much as society can do to get along with one here and there in the community. A colony of bachelors never carried any cause on earth to a successful conclusion, and never will. God pronounced a bachelor in the midst of the glories of Paradise as unequipped for life. As it was, this colony of bachelors was saved by the hand of a woman.

Just here comes in the beautiful story of Pocahontas, who saved the life of Captain John Smith. Her father, King Powhatan, doomed him to death, but she gave him back to the colony that he might save it. Has Plymouth Rock the story of Priscilla Alden? Jamestown has the story of the Indian princess Pocahontas. She was beauty in bronze. Clad in doeskin trimmed with feathers, and with her feet sandaled with beaded moccasins and as beautiful as Trilby's, she came to the colony and went, an angel of God and a vision of love. Again and again, with her Indian maidens, she brought corn to the whites when they were starving; and again and again she warned the colony and saved it from massacre. Pocahontas became a Christian, and was publicly baptized by the Rev. Mr. Whitaker, the "apostle of Virginia." She married John Rolfe, with whom she went to England, where she was received by the royal court and greatly honored. Just as she was about to embark for home she fell ill and died, and was buried in the parish church of Gravesend, England. She left one son, who married a worthy Englishwoman and who became great in the colony. Like the Alden family in Massachusetts, the Pocahontas family in Virginia formed a sort of

American aristocracy. John Randolph, the famous orator of Virginia, was one of her descendants. Of her Captain John Smith wrote to Queen Anne: " Her services to Virginia were as great as those to myself, for she was the instrument under God of preserving the whole colony from destruction."

I relate the story of Pocahontas at this point, for it comes in here legitimately. I am now speaking of the power of woman in relation to the history of Virginia. She was the first woman in the colony, and her presence meant the very life of the colony. But she was not the only woman that exercised a power in Virginia. There were certain widows there whose names have become famous in history. It is marvelous how the widows gracefully figure in this history. In the battle of love the very greatest men of Virginia were finally captivated and captured by widows. I never heard or read anything like it. Jefferson, who wrote the American Declaration, was compelled to make another declaration—a declaration of the surrender of his personal independence,—and that by a dashing widow with a fortune. Madison, the father of the American Constitution, met Widow Todd, and she immediately set him at work writing another constitution besides the Constitution for the nation, viz., a constitution for home rule. George Washington captured Cornwallis; but when he came face to face with Widow Custis, she captured him. This last incident has led one of our pulpiteers to exclaim in a powerful sermon on woman: "Great is the power of woman! George Washington governed America, but Martha governed George." There is a moral here, and it is for hard-hearted bachelors; it is this: beware of Virginia widows; like Ruth of old, they glean everything that is in the field.

But my point is this: the Virginia Colony never succeeded until woman, with her tact and love and holy life, came upon the scene. Twelve years after the three ships, carrying only men, had landed at Jamestown, another ship landed there carrying only women. In the year 1619 those in England who were interested in the colony, recognizing its deficiency, induced one hundred of the handsomest daughters of the land to sail for Jamestown with the express purpose of entering wedlock and setting up homes in the colony. The scheme worked well, and in twenty-four hours after these beautiful daughters landed the parson of the colony had made a snug little fortune. The letters written home by these new-made brides brought another vessel over from England with sixty additional fair maids.

After the establishment of homes in the colony the colony took on a new life. Dissensions ceased, adventure gave way to solid, persistent work, the plantations gave large harvests, and the white angel of health hovered over the whole community.

There are two questions which I imagine thoughtful men ask me just here, and I will endeavor briefly to answer them.

The first is this: How did the colony of Virginia differ in its life and government from the colonies of New England?

That question is a useful question. We learn by contrasting things; there is a contrast right here, and a marked contrast. In the New England colonies the people lived in towns, and this determined their government. The township is still the unit of government in New England. In Virginia the county was the unit of government. There were no towns of any account in Virginia. Up to the Revolutionary War even its capital was only a small village. In New England each township had its own meeting, and there all were equal and had an equal voice. This Professor John Fiske claims was the germ of our Republic. He traces American liberties and American equality and American popular institutions to the town-meeting. Virginia did not have town-meetings, for it had no towns; so Virginia did not contribute to the American nationality popular institutions, as New England did. All of our popular institutions came from New England; but Virginia gave the American nationality *men and measures* instead of popular institutions. This will appear as we proceed. That is the contribution of Virginia to America—*men and measures*. Men to man institutions and lead, and measures for institutions to work out into a glorious consummation. If Virginia had no towns, what had it in their place? It had large plantations. Those of you who carry in your minds the map of Virginia will remember how it is blessed with rivers. Four large, beautiful, navigable rivers flow parallel—the James River, the York River, the Rappahannock River, and the Potomac. The great Virginia plantations fronted on these large rivers, and this allowed the ships of England to come to the plantations for the produce. As trade was direct with England, Virginia did not feel the need of towns. This also kept Virginia bound to England as Massachusetts and Connecticut were not. As the plantations were large, three or four were enough to make a county. As the county was the unit of government, the civil power was kept in the hands of the few who owned the plantations. In New England the people ruled; in Virginia the few ruled. The few were responsible; the few had to do all the thinking; the few had to do all governmental work and rule. While this concentrated, it developed also; that is, it developed the few and made them parliamentarians, diplomats, and skilled statesmen, able to plan and to draft and to lead. This was what the Virginian patriots did in the Revolutionary and pre-Revolutionary times, and this was what America needed. It was a Virginian who went into Massachusetts and took command, and he did that because in Massachusetts, with all its popular education and all its popular politics, there was not a man that could do what George Washington did. It was a Massachusetts man, Mr. Adams, who made the motion in Congress that put George Washington at the head of the New England army. Government by the few is not what we would choose to-day, but government by the few in Old Dominion made the men who drafted the Declaration of Independence and the Constitution of the United States and who led the continental army to the victory which gave us the American nation. *Men and measures*, that was the contribution of Old Dominion to the Republic.

The second question which you ask is: How did Virginia differ from New England in education and religion?

We are still learning by contrast. The idol of New England was education; it had its free public schools everywhere. Virginia did not take to education; it did not wish schools for its black slaves nor for its white servants. General education had very little place in this colony before the Revolution; you could count its free schools on your fingers. The few who were educated went to its one college, William and Mary, or they crossed the ocean and attended the universities of England.

As for religion, the church of New England was the Independent Church; the church of Virginia was the Church of England. There was no free discussion in the Church of England like the free discussion in the Independent Church; but there were in it the truth of the Bible and holy doctrine and inspiring prayers; there were in it that which brought God into life and that which created a conscience toward God and man. We must not forget that the Church of England carried in it the Puritans, and nurtured them until they blossomed and fruited. It also carried in it the Wesleys, until they blossomed and fruited. John Wesley and Charles Wesley both labored in the Church of England in the colony of Georgia. For Americans it was a good church to leave in order to become Puritans and Methodists.

Let us do justice here. The Virginia Colony brought that church with it. The Rev. Mr. Hunt was one of the one hundred and two who landed at Jamestown. The first structure put up was the canvas church. The services were regularly kept up; everybody was required to attend church or pay a fine of so many pounds of tobacco. Tobacco was the currency of that day. Ministers were paid their salaries in tobacco; whether they would or no they were compelled to be religious tobacconists. The markets were quoted in pounds of tobacco. My point is this: there were here and there in the Church of England as devout men and women as were found in the Puritan church. The individual got spiritual good from it; but the church as administered was administered in the interest of the English throne, and was therefore a hindrance to the march of American freedom. It was a state church; and it is logic that a state church must take its creed and its conduct from the state that owns it and pays its expenses. This is the history of the Church of England in Virginia during the Revolutionary times; it was for England and not for America. Madison says, " If the Church of England had been the established church in all of the colonies, the American Republic would have been an impossibility." In these early days it was exclusive. It bitterly persecuted. All who came into the colony were required to support it and swear allegiance to it. The Baptists were driven out of the colony, and so were the Presbyterians and so were the Congregationalists. Fines were imposed by its dictation, and so were tortures and imprisonments. It prescribed such things as ducking and boring the tongue with an awl. I do not think so much of that; for in those days such things were in the air. This intolerance actually was progress, if you put it side by side with the religious hate which scattered the ashes of Wycliffe on the Severn and which disinterred the body of Cromwell and insulted the dust of the hero who made England great. Did the Episcopalians persecute the Puritans in Virginia? The Puritans persecuted the Episcopalians in Massachusetts. There is nothing wrong with religion on this account; no, the wrong is in the application and administration of religion. The Episcopal Church of America in the process of time freed itself from a wrong administration and divorced itself from the state. It gave a welcome to republican principles; it ceased being English and became American. When it did that it was raised from the dead and became a power for liberty. There is a long distance from the church of the Rev. Mr. Hunt of Jamestown to the church of the Rev. Phillips Brooks of Boston; and the distance is every step of it progress. That progress carried in it our national development from a monarchy to a republic.

Virginia had one other thing which differentiated it from the colonies of New England, and that was the system of slavery. Within twelve months of the time the *Mayflower* landed at Plymouth Rock, a Dutch man-of-war entered the James River and landed there an ill-fated cargo of twenty negro slaves. That was a crime, which ended in our Civil War. Those two ships were two rival forces; they carried in them principles which were in deadly antagonism. The Civil War was simply the climax of the long battle between the two ships and their different thoughts and different principles and different civilizations. You know the result. It accorded with the overrule of a just and righteous God in the affairs of men. The *Mayflower* won and the slave-ship went down. That also was progress for Virginia.

I should like to speak here, if time permitted, of the great rebellion which took place in Virginia led by Nathaniel Bacon, but I cannot. That rebellion took place in 1676, just one hundred years before the Revolution, and embodied in it to all intents and purposes the very same principles as the Revolution. Had it succeeded our independence would have come a century earlier. Thus in that far-off day Virginia was training her sons to keep step with the coming continental army, and was also sighting her guns to bear upon tyranny.

I have said that Virginia's contribution to America was *men and measures*. I must hasten to speak of some of these. And here I must exercise selection; I must center our thoughts around the Revolution.

The first man with whom I begin is Patrick Henry. He was the leader of leaders. Speaking figuratively, he was the man who fired the first Revolutionary gun. He was the first to be called a traitor; he was the orator of the Revolution; he learned the principles of liberty from his Presbyterian ancestors, and taught them to the men of the Church of England. He gradually grew toward that famous saying of his which became the watchword of the Revolution, and which regiments carried on their banners and flags, and men in the ranks carried in letters that burned on their uniforms, viz., " Give me liberty or give me death." The framing of these words was impromptu, but the spirit back of them and in them, which gave them their power, was the growth of a lifetime. He had made his famous speech against the clergy of the Church of England and won the case before the jury. He had made his famous speech against the infamous Stamp Act and had seen its repeal. Now he was ready for the famous saying itself. His speech in which he uttered the famous saying was made in the old St. John's Church, which still stands on Virginia soil. Feeling that the time for decision had come, this " man of the people," as he was called, arose and took the floor and addressed the convention. This was the close of his address: "Virginians, there is no retreat but in submission and slavery. Our chains are forged; their clinking may be heard on the plains of Boston. The war is inevitable, and let it come. The war has actually begun; the next gale that sweeps from the North will bring to our ears the clash of resounding arms. Our brethren are already in the field. What is it that gentlemen wish? What would they have? Is life so dear or peace so sweet as to be purchased at the price of chains and slavery? Forbid it, almighty God. I know not what course others may take; but as for me, give me liberty or give me death." As Patrick Henry uttered these words with both arms raised and his eyes on fire, it is said that a great thrill ran through the whole assembly. The people were ready to start from their seats and shout, "TO ARMS!"

The next man to be mentioned is Thomas Jefferson, the "apostle of democracy." He first got his republican inspiration from Patrick Henry. He was a young student at William and Mary College when Patrick Henry made his great speech against the Stamp Act. Patrick Henry put fire into his voice, Jefferson put fire into his pen. One sentence, which he wrote months before the War of the Revolution, began thus: "There is not in the British empire a man who more cordially loves a union with Great Britain than I do; but, by the God that made me, I will cease to exist before I yield to a connection on such terms as the British Parliament proposes; and in this I think I speak the sentiments of America." It was Jefferson who said: "America was conquered and her settlements made and firmly established at the expense of *individuals*, and not by the British crown; therefore *the British Parliament* have no right to exercise authority over us." That was clear and irrefutable reasoning. Jefferson sums up his own life for the cause of freedom in these words in his diary: "I sometimes ask myself whether my country is the better for my having lived at all. I have been the instrument of doing the following things: procuring the disestablishment of the state church, putting an end to the entail system, which tended to aristocracy, securing the prohibition of the fresh importation of slaves, and drafting the Declaration of Independence." Fifty years after signing the Declaration of Independence he died, on the 4th of July. John Adams died the same day.

Next comes the greatest man of all, George Washington, the "father of our country." He was the Virginian of the Virginians, just as he was the American of the Americans. He carried the Revolution in himself and the Republic in himself and the great American future in himself. He was in everything, from alpha to omega, and everything was in him. From the battle of Dorchester Heights, when he took Boston from the British, to the battle of Yorktown, where he ended the Revolutionary War by the capture of Cornwallis, he was in everything. Thus the Revolutionary War, which began in Massachusetts, ended in Virginia, and ended right near the spot where Patrick Henry uttered his famous words. And it was a Virginian, too, who fired the first cannon in the last battle, General Nelson. General Nelson was a citizen of Yorktown. When Cornwallis entered the town he made General Nelson's mansion his headquarters. When the time came for the battle of Yorktown to begin, the gunners hesitated to fire on the home of one of their own men; so Nelson himself stepped forward and aimed a cannon at his own mansion, and touched the fuse and sent a thunderbolt of war crashing through his old homestead. That act was magic; it fired the whole army with a fighting patriotism.

When the Revolutionary War was ended and the treaty of peace signed, all was not over. America was not yet a republic. The critical time had only been reached. What was done afterward was as great as what had been done before. The victories of peace were yet to be won. There were still dangers, great dangers. The colonies were in danger of falling apart and of entering into battle with one another. The war debt made trouble. There was financial distress. The Articles of Confederation which bound the new States together were too indefinite and too feeble. There was a lack of power to raise taxes. Everything was chaos. In resolving things to order the Virginians took the lead. Madison the Virginian, trained, according to Bancroft, under the Presbyterian Witherspoon, president of Princeton College, was the father of the Constitution which gave the nation unity and power, and Washington was the president of the famous Constitutional Convention. It was this convention that gathered up the results of the Revolutionary War and built them into our great Republic.

To sum up, this is what Virginia did for the American Republic by way of *men and measures*. She gave the country such men as these: Patrick Henry, the orator of the Revolution; Thomas Jefferson, the pen of the Revolution; Daniel Morgan, the thunderbolt of the Revolution; John Marshall, the chief justice of the Revolution; and

George Washington, who carried the Revolution to success. She gave the country such measures as these: the resolutions of 1765, denouncing the Stamp Act as a violation of American rights; the origination in 1773 of the Committees of Correspondence, which united the colonies in the defense of their rights; the call in 1774 for a general Colonial Congress, which inaugurated resistance against British tyranny; the instructions to the Virginian delegates to propose to Congress the American Declaration of Independence, which Jefferson wrote and which Washington made a reality. After this she gave to the country the Constitution of which Madison was the father and under which George Washington was the first President.

A Virginian raised the first public voice against the tyranny of the mother-land; a Virginian first moved our national independence in the Continental Congress; a Virginian wrote the Declaration of Independence; a Virginian was commander-in-chief of the continental army all through the Revolutionary War; a Virginian brought that war to a successful close; a Virginian was the father of the American Constitution; a Virginian was the president of the Constitutional Convention; a Virginian was the first President of the United States; a Virginian first shaped our foreign policy; a Virginian first saw beyond the colonial into the national future of our country, and first discerned in the opening and new times that future which is now our *manifest destiny*.

It is easy for me to draw this address to a conclusion and to point its moral. The conclusion of my address is this: *If we are to be true sons of our renowned fathers, we must do as they did; we must give our country* GRAND MEN AND GRAND MEASURES.

We have seen to-night the type of men that make a magnificent nation. They are apocalyptic men; men who see in the future sublime visions for their country; men of large prevision; men who are not colonial nor local, but national; men of sacrifice; men of persistence; men of progress; men who are not afraid to improve on their ancestors; men of eloquence; men of powerful pens; men of executive ability; men like George Washington, who had not only the genius of intellect and the genius of war and the genius of statesmanship, but who had also and preëminently the genius of character; men who are genuine through and through; true men and God-fearing men.

> "God give us men! A time like this demands
> Clean minds, pure hearts, true faith, and ready hands.
> Men who possess opinions and a will;
> Men whom desire for office does not kill;
> Men whom the spoils of office cannot buy;
> Men who have honor; men who will not lie;
> Tall men; sun-crowned men; men who live above the fog
> In public duty and in private thinking;
> Men who can stand before a demagogue
> And denounce his treacherous flatteries without winking.

> For while base tricksters, with their worn-out creeds,
> Their large professions, and their little deeds,
> Wrangle in selfish strife, lo! Freedom weeps,
> Wrong rules the land, and waiting Justice sleeps."

If we give ourselves to our country in the form of such men, we will be certain to give our country the grand and needed *measures* which its destiny demands; for grand men always carry in themselves grand measures. We are still in our formative period. The clothes of the boy will not answer for the clothes of the man. Growth brings new problems. We need measures that will handle vast numbers and that will give to the individual his rights, while at the same time conserving the rights of the many; we need measures that will deal with minorities and majorities, and be fair to both; we need measures that will absorb our foreign elements and conform them into a right and lofty political type; we need measures that will secure to the country an honest monetary system and that will not fail to put a hundred cents into every dollar. We talk of the old colonial and Revolutionary times as times that were big. Times are always big to earnest men; our times are big to us if we are earnest; they are crowded with problems that can only be solved by men like Washington and Jefferson. There is the money problem, and the labor problem, and the tariff problem, and the emigration problem, and the education problem, and the problem of our foreign policy. Then there is the great problem of our relation to broad humanity. The oppressed in all the nations of the globe are looking toward America for light, for ruling principles, for certain guidance, and for a helping, uplifting hand. We have a mission to all the nations of the earth as well as a mission to our citizens at home. Our experience gives us that mission; our progress gives us that mission; our holy ambition to reach the highest civilization gives us that mission. It is our mission to lead humanity on all continents, and it is our mission to lead just because civilly we are ahead of humanity.

To take a concrete case: there is the suffering Armenian race trampled ruthlessly into annihilation by the merciless heel of the God-forsaken Turk. Oh, what shrieks of anguish pierce the air of the Orient this very hour! What unnamable atrocities are inflicted upon pure-minded Christian women and innocent little children! what profane and unholy mutilation of noble men—men made in the image of the one living and true God! Behold how virtue is mocked! Great God! how can these human monsters go into Thine ineffable presence besotted, blood-stained, dehumanized, and crime-covered? How can they face Thy judgment-throne to receive their final damnation? Has the American Republic no interest in all this? has it no duty? has it no mission? One thing I know, and that is this: *silence is not its duty.* It has a voice in this world, and it is its mission to make its voice heard. Let the Senate speak; let the House speak; let the navy speak; and in God's name and in humanity's name command that rapine and self-inflicted famine and cold-blooded murder shall cease at once and cease forever. Oh, for a Patrick Henry to propose a measure for the present emergency, or a Jefferson or a Washington! Oh, for a Marshall and a Lee and a Mason to call together a committee of conference from all the civilized nations of the world to set up permanently an international court of justice to try just such cases as this; to see that all men in power—men who are responsible to no one but themselves and their lusts—shall be held responsible to justice somewhere. No man on God's earth should be allowed to live a life irresponsible to justice. Why should there be courts of justice all over the world for subjects, and not courts of justice for rulers? So long as this is the case the system for the administration of justice among men is far from complete. With such an international court of justice in existence, the sultan of Turkey could this very hour be indicted for murder in the first degree, and tried; and if found guilty could be decently executed.

We have to-day in our possession as a nation the key of the old French Bastille, which in former days dealt out horrible death to innocent men and tender women, just as the sultan of Turkey is doing to-day. When the Bastille was leveled to the ground Lafayette sent the key to George Washington. It hangs on the walls of Mount Vernon, where our Washington peacefully sleeps. I have held that key in these two hands, and have praised God that the days of the Bastille were over forever.

Oh, for a measure, a wise measure, a strong measure, a righteous measure, an irresistible measure, *an American measure*, a measure with the ringing voice of Patrick Henry in it, a measure with the legislative lore of a Marshall in it, a measure with the sure victory of George Washington in it, which will hang the gory crown of the sultan of Turkey on the walls of Mount Vernon by yonder key of the fallen Bastille!

Measures—these are what our Republic needs; measures which will grow and protect and bring to perfection a fine Americanism. There is nothing grander than a fine Americanism. A fine Americanism is the equation of the highest civilization, of the broadest humanity, of the purest and simplest religion, of the largest liberty, of the grandest personal and political principles, of the richest and most progressive Christian life, and of a magnificent manhood and a holy womanhood.

II.

THE PILGRIM FOREFATHERS.

II.

THE PILGRIM FOREFATHERS.*

OUR chief duty in life is to look ahead. The golden age is in the future. It is among the attainments which as yet are unreached, but which are within sight of faith. The standing command of God through Paul to humanity is, "Forgetting the things which are behind, press forward toward those things which are before, and seize the prize of your high calling." Yet we have a duty which we owe the past: to search the past, appreciate it, exalt its virtues, praise its conquests, garner its fruitage, incorporate its wealth of thought and experience, and transmit its good to posterity, and in this way give it an earthly immortality. *A right use of the past is a moral uplift.* It is a necessary equipment for the tasks of the present and a preparation for pushing on into the future.

I have often been impressed by the large place which God has given history in the great Book of the world. In the Bible historical book follows

* Delivered in Lafayette Avenue Presbyterian Church, Brooklyn, at a Forefathers'-day service.

historical book. The Old Testament opens with no less than eighteen books of history. They are interspersed with codes of law, it is true, but their chief characteristic is history. Then comes a book of sacred songs, but of the songs in this book many of them are historical from beginning to end. After the Book of Psalms comes the Book of Proverbs. Then a poetical book or two. Then sixteen books of prophecy. But what is prophecy but the forecast of history? It is history in the form of vision. The New Testament opens with five books of history, the four gospels and the Book of the Acts: the history of Jesus Christ, and the history of His apostles. Then follow a few epistles, and the volume closes with the Apocalypse. But what is the Apocalypse? Simply the history of the future. In the Bible history is piled on history. The Bible is God's voice crying to man, Study history! And God's voice should be heard. God is in history. Truth is in history. The exposé of error is in history. The exhibition of the possibilities and the potentialities of man is in history. The exhibit of the rewards of faith and of virtue and of courage is in history.

Appropriate to this Forefathers' service, we should not fail to notice how God puts in the forefront of the experience of the nation of Israel the most striking pages of human history, and how attractively He writes up these pages of history. The nation makes many grand pages of history in after time—pages which bear the names of David and Solomon and Elijah and Isaiah and Daniel; but none of these surpass the pages which open the national volume of the Hebrews: the stories of Abraham and of Isaac; the courtship of Jacob; the romance of Joseph's exaltation, a literal transcript of real life; the biography of Moses; the plagues of Egypt; the miracle of the Red Sea; the fall of Jericho. I tell you that in all of these we have romance piled upon romance, and power added to power. There is the exhibit of God here; there is the wonderful fulfilment of promise; there is marvelous growth from unlikely seed; and there is the magnificent triumph of right over wrong. Back to this history of the opening of their race the Hebrews constantly reverted. Fathers repeated its stirring things to their children. The prophets and leaders of the nation used it to reclaim the people and to incite to faith and enterprise; the poets ran it into sweet verse, and minstrels sang it to the stroke of the harp. Abraham and Moses and Jacob and Joseph never ceased to be powers and leaders in the land.

When I read the early history of the Hebrews I instinctively say, Blessed is that nation that has grand men for its ancestors, whose first page of history teems with interest, and whose opening chapters are filled with God, and with human heroism, the product of union with God. Such a history will send a holy and inspiring thrill through the body politic age after age. Such ancestors will stand as eternal sentinels, guarding the liberties of the nation and the principles of the nation and the faith of the nation. Such men will rebuke and command the nation and forever lead the nation.

In its possession of noble ancestry the American Republic is like the commonwealth of Israël. Israel had Abraham, who left his native land to found a nation for God's holy purposes. America has the Pilgrim fathers, who left their native land for precisely the same purpose. They took possession of this continent for us, and they left us as a heritage a history which embodies the very principles that have worked themselves out into this vast Republic, with its boasted institutions. They left us a free church and a free state and a system of free schools. They left us this golden principle, incarnated in working form: *All men are equal before the law.* Our nation in its greatness to-day is nothing more than the oak which has sprung from the acorn which they planted. And what we see is only a prophecy of what shall be. There are prayers of the Pilgrims still before the throne of God awaiting an answer; and God feels their strong pulsations beating in harmony with His purposes for America, and God keeps them constantly in sight, that they may be ultimately realized when the right day comes. When that day comes they shall be translated from divine decrees into human realities. The Pilgrim fathers are not through with America, and America is not through with the Pilgrim fathers. God grant that we may never part from them. God grant that our nation may never have any future into which Plymouth Rock cannot be built unhewn.

I wish at this time merely to recount in a plain way the story of the Pilgrim fathers, and then to draw some lessons.

The Pilgrims landed at Plymouth Rock December 21, 1620. Their story is more than a quarter of a millennium old. In telling their story let us begin away back. Let us begin with Henry VIII. of England. Henry VIII. threw off his allegiance to the Roman pontiff, and constituted himself pontiff, the head of the church in his own land. His motives were bad, but his step was overruled by the Lord, and made the starting-point of a great good to England and the world. He gave a staggering blow to a great system of iniquity. Bloody Mary took the English church back into allegiance to Rome, but, after Mary, Elizabeth broke again the yoke of Rome, and made the Church of England free. She brought with her a reformation, but it was a reformation which needed to be reformed. She was a religious tyrant. She made herself supreme in her church, and passed laws that all should conform to her church. She established censorship over human thought, and lorded it over the human conscience. All who differed either in worship or in doctrine she subjected to severe persecution. By sheer brute force she determined to create religious uniformity.

Just here the Pilgrims come in. They could not conform, and they would not conform. Their inability existed in their will. Their principles conflicted with both the doctrines and the practices of the established church. What were these principles? These: (1) Christ Jesus alone is the head of the church, and it is a usurpation for any man or woman to claim to be head, or dictate to the church, or to prescribe its creed and worship. (2) The Bible is the sole rule of faith and practice. All the appointments in the church must have a divine warrant before they can be tolerated or be allowed. It is not enough to say, There is nothing in the Word of God against such and such an ordinance in the church; every ordinance must be able to show, as a warrant, a "Thus saith the Lord." (3) The church is an independent organization, ruled by the people, under God. This principle was directly contrary to the constitution of the established church. In it a few bishops were the governing power. But out of the equality of all before the Lord, and the right of all to a voice in the church, grew the great principles of the rights of conscience and of individual liberty, the foundation-stones of our American institutions.

Believing thus, the Pilgrims withdrew from the fellowship of the established church. They organized churches of their own, where they preached the truth as they understood it. The result of this was persecution by the reigning powers in the church and by the civil government of England. At least three martyrs were executed for their principles. Henry Barrows, John Greenwood, and John Penry were put to death in 1593. The murder of these men led to the embarkment of many individuals, and even of whole congregations, to Holland, where religious liberty was offered to all men.

The story narrows itself just here. One congregation claims our attention from this point on. This church was formed in 1606 in Scrooby, Nottinghamshire, England. It was organized by mutual covenant in what was called the Scrooby Manor, a house with royal associations. The Scrooby Manor was the cradle of Pilgrim liberty. The church organized in this house was the *Mayflower* church, and it carried in it the future of America. To this church Richard Clifton at first preached; but he gave way to a young minister who came to them, the famous John Robinson, a graduate of Cambridge. In that church were men destined to be famous in the Plymouth Colony, America. Here was William Brewster, the elder, and the leader of finance. Here were his children, Patience and Fear and Love and Wrestling. Here was William Bradford, the future historian of the church and governor of Plymouth Colony. This church in Scrooby Manor escaped persecution longer than the other churches, but at length its time came, and this drove it from England to Holland. In Holland it went first to Amsterdam, and thence to Leyden, where it remained some eleven or twelve years.

Now for the most important step, the embarkation for America. Why did this little church determine to quit Holland? This question brings again into view the principles of the Pilgrims and the swaying motives of their lives. They had several reasons: (1) They found that they had no room for growth, no place or opportunity to develop themselves to their satisfaction, and give visibility and practicability to their principles. The original stock of emigrants was growing old, and they were afraid that their whole enterprise would fade out of sight. (2) They were anxious about their children. To use their own words, " they were in danger of becoming degenerated and corrupted;" for the Sabbath was not reverenced at Leyden as they would wish. (3) Their greatest reason was this: *they had a burning desire to spread the gospel in remote parts of the world.*

Actuated by these principles, they sailed from Delfthaven in the ship *Speedwell*, and, reaching England after various vicissitudes, sailed for America in the *Mayflower* from the port of Plymouth. There were one hundred and two souls on board, and among them were John Carver, the first governor, and Miles Standish, the soldier, small of stature, but large of heart.

Other events were taking place at the time they sailed. In England, Cromwell had just come of age and was moving unconsciously on to a career of influence which was destined to rock England and leave its stamp upon the whole world. John Milton was then but a boy, but drinking in the love of liberty which made him a liberty-loving man. Francis Bacon was a man of sixty. Shakespeare was working out his great dramas. On the Continent the Thirty Years' War was just breaking out, which was destined to embroil all Europe. Such was the time when the Pilgrims sailed.

Who can tell the tedium and the wear of that rough passage? Sixty-four long days passed before (November 9, 1620) they sighted land. The land which they saw was Cape Cod. This was not what they intended to strike; they had hoped to strike a spot near the mouth of the Hudson River. After excursions and wanderings and perplexities, the Pilgrims landed finally on the famous rock which they called Plymouth in honor of the port from which they had sailed in England. But before landing they drew up and signed the famous *Mayflower* compact, and elected John Carver governor.

The covenant carries in it the declaration of the Pilgrims' faith. It gives us an insight into their deepest purposes. It has the right ring in it, and shows a clear perception of the nature and obligations of civil government. Thus it opens: " In the name of God, amen. We whose names are underwritten, having undertaken for the glory of God and the advancement of the Christian faith, do solemnly and mutually, in the presence of God and of one another, covenant and combine ourselves together into a civic body politic." God should have the first place in civil government, and He has in the compact of the *Mayflower*.

The suffering of this little company of exiles upon the bleak and rocky shore of the Atlantic beggars description. Sickness and hunger and cold and perils from savages were among the things which wasted them. Still they held on; and when the *Mayflower* turned its prow Englandward once more, not a man went back. Half of the colony died during the first year; still the rest kept up their faith and looked for a golden future. They had to wait long for a harvest, but they accepted their scanty food, and always felt that they had reason for thankfulness to God. The historian tells us that Brewster, the ruling elder, lived for many months together without bread, and frequently on fish alone. With nothing but oysters and clams before him, he, with his family, would give thanks to God that they were permitted to enjoy the abundance of the sea and the treasures hid in the sands. But the harvests came by and by, and a better future opened. Then began the building of the church and the building of the school-house and the building of homes. Then began a life which opened and broadened until Plymouth Colony found incorporation in the confederation of the colonies, and the confederation of the colonies transformed itself into the Republic.

You will notice that in telling this story I have kept upon a single line of history: *the line of the Pilgrims.* There is another line of history, viz.: the line of the Puritans. On that line I purposely have not run.

This suggests the question, What is the difference between the Pilgrims and the Puritans? From what I have presented you see that the Pilgrims were *separatists.* They left the Church of England; they separated themselves from it entirely. They had their own churches. They were exiles for religion. The Puritans, on the contrary, who thought very much as the Pilgrims did, still continued in connection with the Church of England. They said, "We will work inside of the church and purify it." The Pilgrims landed on Plymouth Rock. The Puritans came later, and settled on Massachusetts Bay and elsewhere. The Pilgrims did not persecute. The Puritans did. It was the Puritans who burned the witches and executed the Quakers and quarreled with the Baptists. In England they even helped in the persecution of the Pilgrims, the separatists. The established church often used them as spies among the Pilgrims. The Pilgrims were broader minded. They befriended Roger Williams when the Puritans drove him out. Governor Bradford of the Plymouth Colony even visited Roger Williams in Providence, R. I., and gave him help. In Holland the Pilgrims had come into contact with religious liberty, and had imbibed the spirit of that liberty. They had grown into broad toleration. For Holland was the refuge not only of exiles from England, but also from France and from Scotland. The Pilgrims met with these refugees of other faiths, and learned to love them. It was this education in Holland that made them the true liberals when the federation which issued in our Republic was first formed. It was the Pilgrim spirit that dominated this federation and sent down to us that which is distinctively American.

Having the story of the Pilgrims thus before us, the question meets us, What is our duty in reference to the Pilgrims? There is only one answer, and that is this: We should reproduce them and perpetuate their principles and their ideal institutions. To do this two things are necessary.

1. If we would reproduce the Pilgrims and perpetuate their ideal institutions, we must have the Pilgrims' loyalty to the Bible. Where did they get their principles? From the Word of God. It was the truth that made them free men, and God's Word is truth. It was in the Bible that

they found their ideal church. It was in the Bible that they got their manner of life. It was in the Bible that they got all their principles. It was to the Bible that they went for those deadly parallelisms which they brought against everything that was false.

They looked on the Bible as an all-sufficient book, and they were right. There is no sphere in life in which it does not give ample instruction. What about Miles Standish and his courtship? Some one asks, "Does it teach anything on that line?" Yes. I verily believe that Miles Standish, when he sent the young and eloquent John Alden to court and woo the maiden Priscilla for him, thought he was thoroughly biblical, and he was biblical in a measure. He had a Bible precedent. Do you not remember how Isaac got his wife? Abraham felt that the young Isaac was too bashful to do his own courting, so he sent the old and trusted household servant, Eliezer, to do his wooing for him. No doubt that is where Miles Standish got his idea. But why did he fail? Because he did not follow the Bible closely enough. He did not notice that when Abraham chose a representative to do the courting for his son he chose a very, very old man, and not a handsome young man. Had young John Alden been chosen to do Isaac's courting, I am morally certain that Isaac would have lost Rebecca just as Miles lost Priscilla. There is a moral in the story of Miles Standish, and that is, if you want some things well done you must do them yourself. It was in the Bible that they got their ideas of civil government and civil liberty, and this I especially wish to emphasize. As Milton says, "The Bible doth more clearly teach the solid rules of civil government than all the eloquence of Greece or Rome."

There is no book like this Book to inspire liberty. It has inspired all the liberty that has found incarnation in our national life. It struck Plymouth Rock, and immediately that rock became our American Horeb to send forth a perpetual stream of blessing. It was the Bible that inspired the heroes of '76. We all admire the utterance of Patrick Henry, which electrified the colonies, made the Revolutionary War a certainty, and helped in the inauguration of the American Republic. His words thrill through the nation unto this day: "Give me liberty or give me death." But that sentiment was not original with Patrick Henry. It was a Bible sentiment. Solomon uttered it in substance. Two millenniums before Patrick Henry's day, looking upon the oppressed in the world, and walking among the downtrodden of humanity, and realizing their terrible degradation, he said, "I praise the dead who are already dead, and who have escaped human woe, more than ye living, who are thus miserably alive," i.e., "Give me liberty or give me death." Bible-loving men have always been liberty-loving men. The Lollards in England, the adherents of Luther in Germany, the followers of Knox in Scotland, the Huguenots of France, the friends of Zwingli in Switzerland, Cromwell and his Ironsides, the Waldenses and the Albigenses of the Alps—all these were lovers of the Bible, and all these were heroes in liberty's cause. The Pilgrims breathed into the American atmosphere the principles of liberty, and these have gloriously marched through our history ever since: first into the Declaration of Independence, then into our national Constitution, and then and finally into the Emancipation Proclamation, the crowning glory of the nation. Only as we are true to the Book of the Pilgrims can we carry on the Pilgrims' cause. The Queen of England, when asked once what was the secret of England's greatness, pointed to the open Bible. That which made England has made America. This certainly is the truth which those who designed the monument to the Pilgrim forefathers meant to teach posterity.

On the brow of the hill overlooking the bay where the *Mayflower* was moored, and where the waters continue to beat in volleying thunders or in musical laughter upon its sand, they have reared a colossal statue of national significance. On the four corners of the pedestal repose four figures representing law, morality, freedom, and education. There these should rest by right. But above these stands erect the gigantic figure of Faith. Thirty-six feet she rises from the foot, which rests upon a slate from Plymouth Rock. With one hand she grasps an open Bible, and with the other in graceful gesture she points the nation up to God. The only book she opens to the eyes of the nation is the Bible. And so it should be. The Holy Word holds the only true light which has led our advances into any national virtue.

2. My final thought is this: If we would reproduce and perpetuate the principles and ideal institutions of the Pilgrim fathers, we must possess the Pilgrims' character and the Pilgrims' manhood. Manhood and character! These are the things above all things which the world admires, and these are powers. The Pilgrims were men—men moral in fiber, granite in nature. They were manhood's noblest types. Manhood! Nobility of life! Nobility of thought! Manhood—manhood fashioned into a character which is luminous and harmonious and self-adjusted and perpetual! What is there on earth beyond this? There is something grand in it. There is something more than grand in it; God is in it; Christ is in it. A Christian manhood is a radiant thing; it is full of majesty and sanctity; we never think of it but we desire it. From the Pilgrim fathers I learn this lesson: for the furtherance of the cause of God we must have manhood; we must have men as well as principles; we must have character as well

as creed. There are multitudes of grand principles and grand creeds in the world, but they meet with little or no success, and the reason is that they are not married to men. They are crippled and thrown into disrepute by the weak personality of their professed advocates. You cannot make heavenly and holy principles effective apart from effective men. Even the Bible itself needs men behind it in order to produce reformations and inaugurate revolutions. It is not the Bible alone that reforms and revolutionizes; it is the Bible plus Zwingli; the Bible plus Luther; the Bible plus John Knox; the Bible plus John Calvin; the Bible plus Augustine; the Bible plus the Pilgrims. Men are to principles what the cannon is to the cannon-ball. Men with no larger caliber than a toy pistol cannot hurl against the fortress of the foe principles which are the size of cannon-balls. For the victory of the truth we want men—men with a large caliber of faith and a large caliber of liberality and a large caliber of hope and a large caliber of enthusiasm.

One of England's greatest statesmen was asked by a friend if he thought a certain measure would pass through the Parliament. His quick reply was, "It will not." His friend began to dispute his decision, and to forecast, and to reason with him as to the righteousness of the cause. The statesman replied, "I acknowledge that the cause possesses all that you claim for it, and I believe that it ought to succeed; but nevertheless it will not, and the reason is that it has not the right kind of men as its advocates; they have not the character and the consistency that hold and sway the respect and judgment of their fellow-men." My fellow-men, essential as principles are, principles are not everything. Principles and creeds of the very best type are lying all around us utterly powerless, and they are powerless because they are divorced from the right kind of personality and the right kind of character. We owe the Bible, we owe the church, we owe our nation, we owe the cause of liberty, we owe the Pilgrim fathers a personality full of love, and full of sincerity, and full of steadfastness and constancy, and full of self-subjugation, and full of the spirit of self-sacrifice, and full of faith and holy ambition. Let us band together for the payment of our debt.

III.

THE PURITANS.

III.

THE PURITANS.*

THE American Republic is a great way on in human history. Plymouth Rock is a milestone that speaks of centuries of imperfection and experiment left far behind, and that tells of the nearness of the world's greatest liberty. This is but saying that the American Republic is the latest result of the world's progress. It is the flower of which all the rest of time is the bud. This is the way all historians present the American Republic. They do not present it as an isolated thing, but as a related thing. And this only is true history; this only is the way to exhibit the play of principle and the operation of cause and effect in the world of human life. Only by such a presentation can we draw helpful conclusions and construct advanced plans for the future.

Do you know how Motley speaks of the American Republic? He says: "The American democracy

* Delivered in Lafayette Avenue Presbyterian Church, Brooklyn, on the Sabbath evening prior to Forefathers' day.

is the result of all that was great in bygone times. All led up to it. It embodies all. Mount Sinai is in it, Greece is in it, Egypt is in it, Rome is in it, England is in it; all the arts are in it, and all the reformations, and all the discoveries." Beginning at the beginning of time, he thus sums up the march of events which ends in the American Republic: "Speech, the alphabet, Mount Sinai, Egypt, Greece, Rome, Nazareth, the feudal system, the Magna Charta, gunpowder, the printing-press, the mariners' compass, America."

The method of Motley is the method of John Fiske. He follows this method in writing his book, "The Beginnings of New England." He traces the history of nation-making from the beginning of time down to the making of our nation. Three methods have been followed. There was first the Oriental method of nation-making, viz., conquest without incorporation. You see this method in power away back in the past, and in the valleys of the Nile and the Euphrates. This was the method of Babylonia and Assyria and Egypt. The second method was the Roman method, viz., conquest with incorporation, but without representation. The third method is the English method, viz., conquest with incorporation and representation. This method has been worked out into its highest form upon our American soil. This is the method which we are commissioned still to improve and to bring to an ideal perfection.

This much we have gained by our present trend of thought, viz.: we must know America's past in order fully to know and appreciate America's present; this is the only way to see the real, full, great America of to-day.

Thus it is with every nation. Thus it is with England. What is England? The present millions living there to-day? The present government ruling there to-day? No. These are not England in its entirety. No. Let any nation in Europe clash with England in war, and it will find that it strikes against the whole past of England. England buried in Westminster Abbey will rise and live again, and fight again, and nerve the arm and give courage to the heart of men to-day. That nation will have to fight old Cromwell with his Ironsides, and old Nelson with his fleet, and old Wellington with the army that won Waterloo. Past England lives in present England. Past America forms part of present America, and lives in present America. To use a concrete illustration, although Webster's body had been in its grave for almost a generation before the inauguration of our Civil War, yet Webster's spirit was in that war from Bull Run to Appomattox. Webster was the first American to teach America her own greatness and the power of the federal government; and Webster's arguments were behind every bayonet, and were carried home by every cannon-shot, in the war for the American Union.

If what I have said concerning the relation between the past and the present be true, two things follow as a duty which posterity should perform: first, posterity must study history; and second, posterity must honor the past with suitable memorials. Does any one say, "I have no taste for history; it is only the stale story of every day's doings"? Believe me, history may be made a delight as well as a benefit. The way history is written in this last decade of the nineteenth century makes it a delight. The golden threads of romance are so woven into the sober russet of every day's doings that if you hold it up in the true light it will glow and glitter as brilliantly as though the hand of an enchanter had wrought it out of golden tissue, and constructed it into a robe for holiday attire. Does any one say, "I do not see any value in memorials"? Believe me, you do not inherit this faith from your civil fathers. What means the Bunker Hill monument? What means the Washington obelisk in the capital of the United States? What means the Fourth of July, the great monumental day of the nation? What means Forefathers' day, which comes to us every year? Daniel Webster closed his oration at the dedication of the Bunker Hill monument with these words:

"That motionless shaft will be the most powerful of speakers. Its speech will be of civil and religious liberty. It will speak of patriotism and of courage. It will speak of the moral improvement and elevation of mankind. Decrepit age leaning against its base, and ingenuous youth gathering around it, will speak to one another of the glorious events with which it is connected, and will exclaim, 'Thank God, I am an American!'" The words of Webster have been verified. He whose love of country is not kindled by standing upon Bunker Hill is not worthy of his country and possesses but the minimum of patriotism. His only due is expatriation.

We have not made ourselves nationally; we have been made. We are an evolution, and gratitude is our becoming attitude. We did not dig up the first precious gold; we did not first unlock the secrets of philosophy; we were not the first to give tone to the moral sense; we did not first think the Republic into being. I can hear the drum-beat of the American Revolution as far back as the seventeenth century. We were not the first to think of the welfare of the masses or to assert the rights of the individual. We are not half so wise as we take ourselves to be. Back of our new machinery, and our new processes of industry, and our better homes, and our improved furniture, and our finer clothes, and our easier methods of locomotion, and our increased facilities of exchange of thought, are the old slow-crawling, worm-moving ages. We have received our inheritance as a bequeathment from the fathers, and it is our duty to make acknowledgment of our indebtedness and celebrate the reign of God in their lives. This we can do by observing a memorial day in honor of their fidelity.

A memorial day is a holy page from the book of God's providence, and on that page there glows the very same truth that glows upon the page of the Holy Bible. The study of the lives of the makers of our nation is not necessarily a secular study; it may be and it should be a religious study. Our fathers came here and built here largely, if not solely, in the interest of religion. This was so with the Huguenots, and the Hollanders, and the Episcopalians of Virginia, and the Quakers of Pennsylvania, and the Covenanters of the Carolinas, and the Pilgrims and Puritans of Massachusetts. This we will find as we study the separate history of these makers of America. Besides all this, we believe that the American Republic is the creation of God, and has a grand commission from Him to work out among the nations of the world. Now, the study of the Republic as a creation of God is a religious exercise.

One thing is before us this evening as we celebrate Forefathers' day, and that is the play of the

Puritan influence in the making of the American Republic.

On the evening of last Forefathers' day we studied together the history of the Pilgrim; now we are to study together the history of the Puritan. Then there is a difference between the Pilgrims and the Puritans? Certainly. If we were living in Boston and failed to make a distinction we should never be forgiven.

Let us here and now set before our mind the distinction between them. Henry VIII., King of England, threw off his allegiance to the Roman pontiff and constituted himself head of the church in his own land. His motives were bad, but God overruled the step which he took and made it a starting-point of great good to England and to all the world. The reason he broke with the pontiff was, the pontiff refused to divorce him from the queen, his lawful wife. Separated from papacy it was not possible for England to remain Catholic. The consequence was the establishment of the Church of England.

But when the English church was established it was found that all in this church were not of one mind. There were advanced thinkers who wanted more liberty and who hated oppression in a prelate just as much as they hated oppression in a pope. Where did these dissatisfied men come from? Where did they get their advanced ideas?

The answer of that question is a history in itself. They were the spiritual descendants of Wycliffe and of the Lollards. Wycliffe and the Lollards got their ideas and principles from the Holy Scriptures. Wycliffe translated the Bible for the people, and thus set the cause of liberty in England in motion. Henry VIII. lived in the time of Martin Luther, and wrote against him. He did not want England to become Protestant, but he could not help it. The accumulated power of Wycliffe's Bible was irresistible and gave rise to the Puritans whom the king found in his church. From this you see that there were forerunners of the Puritans long before the time of Luther. There were scattered voices all through Europe, like the early-awakening birds of the morning preluding the full choir of the noontide day. There was a growing cry rolling across Europe, and that cry, which rang from Wycliffe to Savonarola, from John Huss and Jerome of Prague to Zwingli and Erasmus—that cry, which swept from the Alpine glaciers to the fiords of Norway, and which broke from the lips of Luther like a peal of thunder—that cry was a cry demanding reform.

I cannot here detail the conduct of the Church of England. It became oppressive. The church would not listen to those who asked for reform. On the contrary, it subjected them to cruel persecution. But persecution has never put down any cause of God;

it has always strengthened it and has always drawn sympathy to it. This proved true here. In proportion as prelacy grew Puritanism grew. The claim of the prelates ran higher and higher through Parker, Whitgift, and Bancroft, until it culminated in Laud; but the resistance of the Puritans became stouter and stouter through Hooper, Cartwright, and Bradshaw, until it culminated in the Westminster divines.

After Henry VIII. came Edward VI., and after him Bloody Mary. Queen Mary took the Church of England back into allegiance to Rome. Under her persecutions many of the Puritans fled to Switzerland—a land where the people were as free as the singing waterfalls, the land of William Tell and of the reformer Zwingli, the land where Calvin made his home and taught his system. Here they met with Calvin and drank Calvinism from the fountain. Every Alpine canton was a republican community. So here these exiles of God drank in the spirit of liberty.

Mary was followed by her sister Elizabeth, England's famous queen, and in her reign the Puritans who had fled to Switzerland returned. She again broke the yoke of Rome; she established the Church of England by law. In her efforts to make the Church of England all in all, she declared that all her subjects should think alike, and worship alike, and conform to the ritual of the English church. She determined by sheer brute force to create religious uniformity. The thing was an absurdity. Until God unmakes us, and then makes us over again, religious uniformity will remain an eternal impossibility.

Just here the Pilgrims come in. They rebelled out and out against the policy of Queen Elizabeth, and separated themselves from the Church of England, and formed churches of their own. Of course they were persecuted. This led to the emigration of a company of them to Holland, from whence, in the course of time, they sailed to America, landing on the famous Plymouth Rock December 21, 1620, and forming the famous Plymouth Colony.

The Pilgrims were separatists. The Puritans were not. They were only nonconformists, and as nonconformists they remained in the Church of England in hopes that in due time they might reform that church and mold it to their ideal. The Puritans were still in England while the Pilgrims were in America building up their new colony. They remained there until the year 1628. This was during the reign of Charles I. The usurpations of this king made them restless, and, hearing of the success of the colony of Pilgrims in America, they determined to emigrate. In very many cases they were led by their ministers, and the plans for emigration were often formed by these. It was during this year that Salem was settled by John Endicott and his company. Now began what is known in American history as "the Puritan exodus." This lasted for eleven years, from 1629 to 1640, i.e., during the time that Charles I. arbitrarily governed England without a Parliament; 1640 was the year in which the Long Parliament began which ushered in the wonderful times of Cromwell. Cromwell's time gave the Puritans of England something to do in their own land, and hence emigration ceased. Their mission then was to rally around Cromwell and Pym and Hampden and Milton, and assert the rights of the people against the tyranny of the crown.

It was during the period of the exodus that John Winthrop, the first governor of Massachusetts, came to America. It was then that Boston and Cambridge and Watertown and Roxbury and Dorchester were settled. All were separate communities. It was during this period that Roger Williams settled in Rhode Island, and that Davenport came with his company from England and settled in New Haven, and that Thomas Hooker, wanting more liberty, migrated from the Charles River with a hundred of his congregation, and went to Hartford. It was in Hartford, Conn., under Hooker's inspiration, that the first American constitution which issued in a distinct government was framed. Thomas Hooker deserves more than any other man to be called an American father. The government of the United States of to-day is in lineal descent more nearly related to that constitution of Connecticut than to the constitution of any of the other thirteen colonies. It was during this period that Harvard College was founded, and also Yale, and that the free public schools were planted. Away back here began also the oppressive enactments of England with respect to trade. As England's laws oppressing the people of the colonies could not execute themselves, away back here began the spirit of rebellion against England which culminated in the American Declaration of Independence.

When the Puritan exodus ceased there were in New England twenty-six thousand Puritans. The Pilgrims of Plymouth Rock were the small minority; but that mattered little, for now in America all the Puritans equally with the Pilgrims were separatists. They all adopted the independent form of church government; they were all here for the advancement of religion; they were all striving to work the Bible out in every-day life. The Pilgrims largely believed in the separation of church and state; the Puritans believed in a theocracy which made both church and state identical. Hence the condition of suffrage with the Puritans was church-membership. Thus it was at first, but by and by suffrage was enlarged so as to take in those who were baptized, though not church-members. This was called the "half-way covenant." Finally all religious tests were abolished.

For one hundred and fifty years after the Puritan exodus, i.e., from 1640 to 1790, New England received very few by means of immigration. Its increase came from its own families; it enjoyed a remarkable seclusion. There were only three exceptions to this. In 1652, after his victory at Dunbar and Worcester, Cromwell sent two hundred and seventy Scotch prisoners to Boston as a punishment. They grandly bore the punishment; they rather liked it, I imagine, for their descendants are there to this day. In 1685, after the revocation of the Edict of Nantes, one hundred and fifty families of the Huguenots came to Massachusetts; their names are perpetuated in Bowdoin College and Faneuil Hall. In 1719 several Presbyterian families from the north of Ireland settled in New Hampshire; their descendants are still in that State. Londonderry, N. H., marks their settlement. These were the three exceptions, and they were very small. When the hour of the Revolution struck, there was no county in old England itself that had a purer English blood than New England. The homogeneity of population accounts for the oneness of belief and action in New England in the matter of the American Revolution. The people of New England were one people, and they struck like a trip-hammer when they struck. It was this unity and homogeneity which made them the power they were in the formation of the American Republic, and which helped New England to stamp itself upon the whole country for the country's good.

It was only after the American Revolution that New-Englanders began to move into the western part of our land and there form new States; but this they did so effectively that there is a Portland to-day on the Pacific as well as a Portland on the Atlantic. They now number one fourth of the entire population of our sixty millions, and are a beneficial force in every State in the Union.

While the Puritans were diligent in building up New England, let no one suppose that they were indifferent to what was going forward in the motherland; they were one with the progressives there. It has been said that the English Revolution virtually began in Boston, where Sir Edmund Andros, King James's representative, was arrested and put in prison. New England was the first to hail the enthronement of William, Prince of Orange. During the Cromwellian conflict Cromwell's strongest friends were in New England. The pen of New England, fertilized by freedom, became marvelously prolific. Cromwell, Hampden, Sidney, Milton, Owen, were scholars of teachers mostly on this side of the Atlantic. Professor Masson, of Edinburgh University, in his biography of Milton names seventeen New England men whom he describes as potent in England during the days of the Commonwealth. Numbers went back to England in person to join Cromwell's Ironsides. Twelve of the first twenty graduates of Harvard prior to 1646 were among the New-Englanders who were with Cromwell on the fields of Marston Moor and Naseby.

New England served the liberal-minded of old England by opening to them sheltering arms in the hour of their peril. We have a striking instance on this line in the welcome given to two of the men who sat as judges and pronounced the sentence of death on King Charles I. Their names were Edward Whalley and William Goffe. Charles II., determined to destroy his father's murderers, as he called them, ordered their arrest and transportation to England; but the New-Englanders protected them, and baffled the king's detectives, and saved them from the fury of Charles. This romantic story is told of Goffe, showing his appreciation of the protection given him. At Hadley the savages, during King Philip's War, made an attack upon the villagers. The inhabitants were at church keeping a fast when the yells of the Indians resounded. Seizing their guns, the men rushed out to meet the foe, but seeing the village green swarming with the horrid savages, for a moment their courage gave way and a panic was imminent. All at once a stranger of reverent mien and stately form, and with white flowing beard falling on his bosom, appeared among them and took command with an air of authority which none could gainsay. He bade them charge on the screeching rabble, and after a sharp, short skirmish the tawny foe was put to flight. When the pursuers came together again after the rout their deliverer was not to be found. In their wonder, as they knew not whence he came or whither he went, many were heard to say that an angel had been sent from heaven for their deliverance. It was the fugitive, William Goffe, a major-general of Cromwell's army, who from his hiding-place had seen the savages stealing down the hillside, and who came forth for one more victory ere death came to take him from his wilderness retreat. The Puritans harbored this political refugee, and this refugee saved the lives of the Puritans.

In giving this brief history of the Puritans in the favorable form in which I give it, I am not ignorant of the antipathy which prevails in a large area against the Puritans. The term "puritanical" is a term that carries in it to-day a slur and a sneer; but I am one who believes that the slur and the sneer are a slander. The Puritans have left too grand a work behind them to be written down; the great Republic is still too much Puritan in its make-up to allow gross slanders to live.

True history is more and more taking the place of caricature in dealing with these fathers. It is sometimes said, "The Puritans stand for all that is austere and intolerant and somber and crooked and ungainly and unattractive and bitter and dogmatic and sour." It is said also that the Puritan protesting against the pope is himself in his peaked hat a worse pope than the Italian who wears the triple crown. He is called a fanatic, but let no one be frightened by that word; fanaticism is simply a mighty grip upon a mighty idea. It was the fanaticism of Columbus that discovered America; it was the fanaticism of Luther that gave the world the Reformation. You cannot sneer the Puritan down. Macaulay says: "No one sneered at the Puritan who had met him in the halls of debate, or crossed swords with him on the battle-fields." The Puritans are often laughed at as those who delighted to sing psalms through their noses. This is a fling at Cromwell's Ironsides. Well, Cromwell's Ironsides used to go to battle singing psalms through their noses, but they sang through their noses to some purpose. If other battalions can sing through their noses with a like effect, I advise their singing. There never was a troop of men on earth whose footfalls carried such courage and power as Cromwell's Ironsides. The story of their battles is the romance of history; it has a power to thrill which even the heroism of the nineteenth century cannot exceed. The sparks flew from their swords like the flashes from a surcharged cloud; their ringing saber-strokes still echo in history.

The Puritan's lack of the esthetic has been criticized. In this he has been called narrow, and he was narrow. He was not in full communion with God here. God delights in the esthetic; His mind teems with beauty; and wherever in creation He has an opportunity He scatters beauty broadcast. " He lines the tiny seashell with lines of beauty, and tints the scales of the fish, and tones the hidden fibers of the trees, and flashes beauty on breast and crest of flying birds, and causes it to break in the tumbling avalanche into myriads of feathery crystals, and builds the skies into a splendor which neither words nor colors can paint." But the Puritan's lack here can be explained; there was a cause. Beauty itself, painting, music, sculpture, all the fine arts, belonged in the Puritans' day to the oppressors of the Puritans. Those things had been so long a time in Egypt that to the Puritans they were Egyptian; they were redolent of oppression; so the Puritans simply put them in quarantine until the plague was out of their garments, and then they would be allowed to come back again. They are coming back.

But what have we to say concerning their treatment of the witches and of Roger Williams? We have this to say: that even in the harsh measures, as they dealt with these, *they were the progressives of their age*, and were the most merciful people of that century.

With regard to the witches, you can count all that were burned upon your fingers, while throughout the nations of Europe they were burned by the thousands and tens of thousands. With regard to Roger Williams, he is able to take care of himself. There is altogether too much made of his affair. He was not hurt much, if hurt at all. I have only this to say of Roger Williams: if he came into our day with his broad, open-communion views, he would have as tough a time among his own children, the close-communion Baptists, as he ever had among the Puritans. It is a picture—it is nothing short of a lively scene—to think of Roger Williams in the Baptist Church of America to-day. His battle-ax would make splinters of every human barrier which barricades the Lord's table as found in that sect.

In our criticism we forget to put the Puritans back in the seventeenth century. This only is justice. They must be judged by the day in which they lived. They were progressive men in that day, and if they were living they would be progressive men in our day. John Endicott and John Winthrop and Cotton Mather, were they living to-day, would be civil-service reformers,

Prohibitionists, and full-fledged women's rights men.

We have reached an age when there is light enough to see the Puritan in his true character, as a royal man of God and a noble leader of men. If the word "mugwump" had not been tossed about in these latter days until it has become defaced and soiled, I would say he was a magnificent "mugwump." The word "mugwump" belongs to him. It is found in John Eliot's translation of the Bible for the Indians. It means a great chief. Eliot uses it in setting forth Joshua, Gideon, and Joab. These Bible heroes were "mugwumps"; this is where modern politicians get the word.

Let us look at the characteristics of the Puritan! He was a man of God; this was his starting-point. God was with him in everything he did; this was his constant consciousness. Listen to an extract from one of the Puritan New England writers in confirmation of this: "Strike the Lord's cymbals! blow the silver trumpet! set the battle in array! For the Lord is with us. He is not an idle spectator, but an actor in all action to bring down His and our enemies. He orders every shaft that flies, and leads each bullet to its resting-place, to the wound it makes." This consciousness of God's presence made the Puritan self-sufficient in God, and gave him his persistency and courage.

He was a man of one book, and that book was

the Bible. The Century Company have not made a mistake in their design of the statue of the Puritan. They represent him as a rugged man with flowing cloak and peaked hat, and with a large copy of the Bible under his arm. In reading his Bible he delighted in the Apocalypse with its wild and stirring grandeur, but he was especially a student of the Old Testament. Moses constructing a nation and giving laws was his favorite; and he often opened the Book of Joshua to listen to Joshua as he whets his sword on the tables of stone, and cuts his way through the nations of the Canaanites. The Puritan was the Old Testament hero reproduced.

He was a man of principles. "Righteousness" was the great word in his life, and the great white throne was to him the most real of all realities. That built ethics into his nature and made him swift to render obedience to the voice of conscience. He was a lover of knowledge, and this led him to found schools and build colleges. So long as the Puritans' enthusiasm for education lives, just so long will Harvard and Yale be multiplied in our Republic. He was a man of religion, and because of that he has sent down to us the spirit which has built the churches that bless the land. The Old South Church of Boston comes direct from his hand. He was a man of large hopes, so he inaugurated large enterprises. He was a daring optimist; his creed was, "Every good thing that is possible shall some day become real." That is a grand creed for any age. He believed that obedience to conscience, as the voice of God, should be the rule of conduct for the state as well as for the individual man; hence he sought to make the state a theocracy.

The motto of Daniel O'Connell was his motto, viz.: "Nothing is politically right that is morally wrong." He was a growing, progressive man; hence the outcome of his religious life was this: coexistence, toleration, forbearance, mutual respect among the different churches of Christ, the one Lord and Master. Take him for all in all, and I choose the Puritan. He is my choice after a thorough sifting of the age in which he lived. I choose him a hundred times over in preference to the Cavalier, who was his rival and his despiser. Chivalry refined manners; Puritanism created manliness and fortified the soul in virtue. Chivalry feared dishonor; Puritanism feared to do evil. Chivalry adorned life; Puritanism enriched life with conscience and duty and God. Chivalry taught a man to die for a lady's glove, a stolen kiss, a fancied slight; Puritanism taught a man to die for human rights, for justice, for freedom, for truth. I choose the man who represents Puritanism, and him my whole being honors and blesses.

His character is the one character and his power is the one power I wish to perpetuate in the life and in the progress of my nation. How can I best perpetuate his character and his power? By giving myself up to the cultivation of his spirit, and by taking a front rank in my age as he took a front rank in his age; by making a man out of myself and giving a God-filled manhood to my country. It is as Humboldt says: "Government, religion, property, books, are nothing but the scaffolding to build man. Earth holds up to her Maker no fruit like the finished man." The citizen gives to his country no gift like the gift of a Christian manhood. I must give my country an ideal reincarnated Puritan. If I give my country that, then with that I shall give it God, the one living and true God; the Bible, His law for nations; an enlightened and living conscience, i.e., the power and willingness to respond to God's law; institutions instinct with righteousness and truth. These things will make the Republic great; they will make its institutions perpetual, and they will make its army invincible. There are no regiments like Cromwell's Ironsides, where bayonets can think and pray, and where the highest spiritual qualities have been drilled into the ranks. Men of ideas, of holy passions, of genius, of enthusiasm, of faith in God, of righteousness, of spiritual personalities, of high ideals, these are the strength and the defense of any nation. Such are the men our Republic is searching for among her citizens; the Republic wants nineteenth-century Puritans—Puritans refined and idealized.

IV.

THE HOLLANDERS.

IV.

THE HOLLANDERS.*

PAUL, the chief of the apostles, upon an important occasion, in depicting the glories of the Hebrew nation, climaxed his description with these words: "*Whose are the fathers.*" He felt just as we feel when we give ourselves to the celebration of Forefathers' day. He pointed to Abraham, the father of the faithful, who pioneered for the coming generations and found them a territory; and to Solomon, the wise, who filled the territory with cities and wonderfully increased the wealth of the land; and to Moses, the lawgiver, who gave the nation a magnificent code; and to Elijah, the reformer, who brought the nation back into true allegiance to God; and to David, the poet, who put soul-stirring patriotism into the national songs; and to Isaiah, the prophet, who saw thrilling visions for the kingdom and who proclaimed the coming of

* Delivered in Lafayette Avenue Presbyterian Church, Brooklyn, at a Forefathers'-day service.

the golden age. He pointed to these and said, "*Ours are the fathers.*" He catalogued "the fathers" as among the chief blessings of the nation. He said in effect, "Men, grand men, men of enterprise, men of holy optimism, men of faith, men in oneness with God—these are God's best gifts to a nation, and these in their grandeur and goodness are worthy to be catalogued with Mount Sinai and with Calvary, for they carry in their personalities and in their feelings and in their principles and in their characters *all*—all that is contained in the law and the gospel, and all that Sinai and Calvary stand for."

Fellow-Americans, we have come together tonight to say the one to the other, "*Ours are the fathers,*" and to recall together the words and the conflicts and the cardinal doctrines of the men who made America what we find it. We have our history; we have American men and women; we have our authors, our poets, our historians, our scholars, our generals, our publicists, our philosophers, our divines, our journalists, our jurists, our scientists, and all of these have personalities crowned with a world-wide fame. The question is, Whence came we? As a nation we are young in years. Whence this tremendous growth and this great national power? What is the story of the evolution of this great Republic? I answer, the story of the fathers is the story of the evolution of our commonwealth.

I answer, the greatness of the fathers is the explanation of our rapid growth and the secret of our political power. You cannot explain this age and leave out of sight the earlier age; you must bring forward the things that synchronize and the things that precede our age. Take the fifty years prior to the settlement of those American colonies which were the most mighty and the most permanent—the Jamestown Colony, the colony of New York Bay, Plymouth Colony, the Massachusetts Bay Colony; take the fifty years prior to the day the first English ship, the *Good Speed*, sailed up the Potomac, prior to the day the *Half-moon* stopped at Manhattan Island and explored the Hudson, prior to the day the *Mayflower* landed at Plymouth Rock, and then add the fifty years after, the years of the first struggles of the new and daring colonies, which take us to the close of Cromwell's Commonwealth, and to the hour when Peter Stuyvesant surrendered New Amsterdam to the forces of New England, and you can explain the American Republic. The growth upon this continent was rapid, because there was back of it the growth of the old continent.

The American colonies sprang up in the midst of one of the most marvelous centuries of all time. It was the century which carried in it both the Elizabethan period and the Cromwellian period. It carried in it the golden age of the famous Dutch republic, the United States of the Netherlands. No century has ever seen more than this century which I have bounded saw. It saw the close of Titian's life, and of Michelangelo's. It saw the completion of the dome of St. Peter's. Tintoretto was in it, with the audacity of his genius and the lightning of his pencil. It saw the youth of Leibnitz and of Newton. It saw the entire life of Descartes, and the middle manhood of Spinoza. It watched Grotius from his birth to his burial in the Holland city of Delft. In it the telescope came and recreated the very heavens for man. In it the microscope was perfected and revealed to man God's perfect work in the realm of the infinitely small. It taught that the speck of dust is with God an organized mountain. The thermometer, and the barometer, and the air-pump, and the circulation of blood, and the nature and use of electricity were among its discoveries. In it the Dutch and the English East India Companies were established. It saw the magnificent reign of Elizabeth, the great English Rebellion, the beheading of Charles I., the Huguenot struggle in France, the revolt of the Netherlands, and their final establishment of the Protestant republic. In it the Bible received a new life and a wider mission. It had just been translated into English in time to gild with its light of Hebrew glory and Christian faith the rude life of our savage shores. Its liberating truths broke forth over the nations like light from the heights celestial. Men learned afresh the vast promises of God waiting to be realized, and these promises filled them with irrepressible ambitions. They learned the dignity of the individual man, and began to think for self and to assert their personal rights. This self-assertiveness and this holy ambition, which came from God, and this expectation of something better in the future, this, *this*, THIS, explains the bound onward and the new enterprise which resulted in the American Republic. Crowded into this century were Bacon and Shakespeare in England, Cervantes in Spain, William of Orange in the Netherlands, and Galileo in Italy. (Galileo was condemned just five years before Harvard College was founded.) Into this century must be crowded the names of Richard Hooker and Walter Raleigh and Kepler and Rubens and Vandyke and Claude Lorrain and Pascal and Milton and Cromwell. It was a century in which the world received, as it were, a new God to serve and obey and to fellowship with; a new view of the powers of nature, with a new hold thereof; a new faith in man, his worth and his power; and a new world to be the stage on which to act out new visions and new hopes. It was a century energized by new emergent opinions, new forces, new movements, new achievements, new ideas, new opportunities.

Looking at this century, in the midst of which the American colonies were planted on this new continent, the evolution of the American Republic with its prescient greatness and its opening future is no wonder. It exists as a matter of course. There were, under God, a hundred social and moral forces all crying, "Let there be an American Republic," and there was an American Republic. We have a vast genealogy; our roots run back centuries; our annals are interlinked with the noblest of time. We are the result of a hundred wonderful historical developments wrought out in almost a hundred lands of the Old World. Our Republic is like a fine picture skilfully woven into a costly piece of tapestry composed of many beautiful threads, each single thread of which is a marvelous work in itself and sufficient for a profitable individual study.

In the addresses of this Forefathers'-day course, we are taking up and examining the threads of this tapestry, one at a time. The one thread before us to-night is the rich yellow and golden thread of old Holland. In our last address we listened to the Jubilate as it sounded out from the chimes of Westminster; in this address we are to listen to the Jubilate as it sounds out from the chimes of Antwerp. There is no discount on the chimes of Antwerp; they are not one whit behind the chimes of Westminster. It is something inspiring to hear an anthem rung into the air by the bells in the tower of the Antwerp cathedral. A shower of bell-notes falls from the vast spire. There are all kinds of notes; there are the deep notes of the great bells, which make the anthem roll through the atmosphere with the intonations of thunder; then there is the ringing of the little bells, pealing forth the same notes in a higher key. These notes are fine and small and sweet, small as a bird's warble. They fill the air with crisp tinklings, which are as distinct as the sonorous notes of the great bells. All have their individuality, and all help in making the anthem one which enraptures and enchains. I take the chimes of Antwerp to be a symbol of that glorious Dutch republic which gave the world the anthem of liberty during the days when our American fathers prepared for and built our civil institutions. The doctrines of liberty were proclaimed in the legislative halls and battle-fields of Holland by the deep-toned, rich voices of statesmen and soldiers; and at the same time the same doctrines of liberty were proclaimed by the higher-keyed, musical voices of Holland's boys and girls, when, in the free public schools of the land, they sang the patriotic songs of the republic.

In taking up the story of our Dutch progenitors, I notice in the very start that there are new claims being made to-day on behalf of the Dutch.

American history is being rewritten; new research is being made to find the origin of our civil institutions. This is as it should be. History must be written and rewritten a score of times before we can reach the truth. We need the iconoclast and the scientific critic. We need the redactor. History is often written under prejudice, or under repression, or for a partizan purpose. There is such a thing as Anglomania. Now, Anglomania, if it had the opportunity, would warp all American history so as to secure the constant laudation of the English over the just claims of all other nations. I would not trust the man who turns up his trousers and carries an umbrella in New York on a clear day, for the sole reason that the Atlantic cable reports it is raining in London, to write American history, no matter what brain power he might have. You know how historians have been treated in the past. Louis XIV. withdrew a pension from an historian of his day, because he made some adverse remark about taxation. Richelieu charged a certain French chronicler with treason and treated him as a traitor, because he told some distasteful truth about a king who had been dead for centuries. Certainly history written during such times needs to be rewritten. It is the God-given mission of the modern iconoclast to knock all such history into shivers. Besides this, how often are hindrances put in the way of the historian, and that by those from whom we would least expect hindrances! Let me give you an example pertaining to our English friends who have so loudly claimed to be the direct and indirect authors of our American civilization. In 1841 John Romeyn Broadhead was sent to Europe by the State of New York to procure copies of documents relating to our colonial history from the public offices of England, France, and Holland. He was well received and assisted in France and Holland; but how in England? Lord Palmerston replied to his application that "if he would designate the particular paper he wished to see, it would be officially examined, and if no objection were found he could have a copy of it at the customary rates." Thus obstacles were put in his way for a year. It was only when a new ministry came into power that he was able to secure access to documents known to be stored away, but not sufficiently known to be numbered. The fees charged were exorbitant. In the interest of history and the science of history, free access to all public documents should have been allowed him. Now, remember, Mr. Broadhead was not a private individual; he was the representative of the Empire State of America. Davies, the historian of Holland, went to the same source for historic light, but he was absolutely denied in his own land any access to historical documents. He was compelled to issue his work in a limited form. These are instances in history-making relating to that nation which, for the most part, has furnished the men who have written American history—the men who have left out of American history almost in toto the influence of the Dutch in and on our national life. Honest and thinking men are rising up and are putting an interrogation-point against all such history; and do you wonder? I hold that the iconoclast has a work just here in American history written under English influence and by English descendants.

Our history should be rewritten, because we are constantly reaching and bringing to light new historical material. Let me give you a striking case. At the time I was born it was not even known where the New England Pilgrims originally came from. The writings of Bradford, the first governor of the Plymouth Colony, had been carried to England in 1776 by the British, and we were all in the dark. These writings have been recovered in my day, and hence our present knowledge.

At least two things have worked against the Dutch in America and have kept them from their historic due. The first is this: the caricature of the Dutch by Washington Irving. The magic pen of Washington Irving, that prince and father of American literature, made the Dutch the victims of a caricature which captivated the fancy of the world. The history of the fictitious Diedrich

Knickerbocker is but a humorous romance. It is worse; it is a bold travesty, and that according to Irving's own admission. It is a gross caricature. It lauds only Dutch courage for drink and Dutch valor in the use of the pipe. The only halo which it weaves for the brow of our Dutch fathers is the halo woven out of the cloudy wreath of tobacco smoke. Besotted with beer, nicotinized with tobacco, ill-natured, clownish, fit objects of ridicule—such are the Dutch fathers of the humorous Diedrich Knickerbocker; and yet, many persons know only this travesty. This travesty has stood in the way of true and real history.

The second thing which has worked against the Dutch in American history is this: the precedence which has been given to the Puritanism and heroism of New England. The English and their Yankee descendants have monopolized all that is good in American history. Their appropriation has been wholesale. The English have a genius for appropriation and assimilation. They have put their hands on the ends of the earth—Canada, Australia, East India; they have grasped all of these. In 1664 they appropriated New Amsterdam, and took it from the Dutch, and called it New York. This taking from others is an old trait of theirs. Go back as far as the Elizabethan period; a recent writer shows that even back there, in the sphere of literature, they took from others and exhibited marvelous assimilative faculties. Shakespeare borrowed from every quarter not alone single scenes, but whole plots and plays. Hooker, in his "Ecclesiastical Polity," follows out the train of thought worked out by Buchanan, the Scotchman. Milton, at a later date, takes from the Dutch poet, Vondel, the scheme for his "Paradise Lost" and "Samson Agonistes," with many of his happiest expressions. In no case is any acknowledgment made to the foreign authors thus devoured and used. Modern investigation alone has brought out the fact of these English appropriations.

We all know the Yankee's proclivities for tall talk and self-appropriation and self-help. He excels even his English father. The well-known dialogue between the old Englander and the New-Englander sets this forth. It is Yankee through and through. The New-Englander had just told of a wonderful swimming feat which he once performed; he swam twenty miles at a stretch. The old Englander laughed at that feat as a mere trifle, and then told his story. His story was this: When he left Liverpool on the steamship, he looked behind and saw a man in the water swimming after the ship with the evident intention of following the ship across the ocean. Certain enough; on the second day out, there was the man swimming leisurely along. He was there on the third day, and the fourth, and the fifth, and on the tenth day he came up Boston harbor even with the ship. Nothing abashed, the New-Englander asked the old Englander if he would take his oath to that, and when he had taken the oath, he thanked him, and with the old-time spirit of English appropriation he said, "Stranger, I am a'mighty glad to have such a credible witness as you to that swimming feat, for that fellow you saw and have told us about was me."

An illustration in point of what I am setting forth is seen in the claims of the English historian, Edward A. Freeman. In his lectures on "The English People in their Three Homes"—in their home in old England, i.e., on the European continent, the Netherlands, from which the English originally came; in their home in middle England, i.e., the British Isles; and in their new home, i.e., New England of America—he deliberately argues that New England is simply the fruitage of old England and middle England. Here are some sentences from these lectures as he delivered them to American audiences: "Wherever the English folk dwell there is England." "Your Constitution is really our constitution put into a formal written shape and then modified." "Your President is beyond all doubt the English king modified." George Washington George III. modified! God forbid! It seems to me that Mr. Freeman has a tremendous eye for seeing resemblances. He simply burlesques the word "modified," which he so often uses. Let him try American modification in England and see what a revolution it will create. Away goes the House of Lords. Away goes the distinction between the child born in the palace and the child born in the hovel. Away goes the unwritten constitution. Away goes the prime minister. Away goes the titled nobility. Away goes the throne. The American Republic is in no sense the English monarchy. The American Revolution did something far other than "modify." It cut us forever and completely loose from the old, and gave us institutions which were entirely new and grandly un-English.

The time has come in the writing of American history when we must give credit to others besides the English, and when we must, for the sake of fairness and for the sake of historic fact, break up the English historical monopoly. It is time to say that there were *Dutch Puritans*. American history has been too largely written from the English standpoint. Let us divide honors all around and give all of our forefathers their share. This will change the order of things and will in many cases compel us to revise our judgments, but if this be fair it is also right and needed. The praise of the Pilgrims and Puritans has crystallized into public opinion. Poets and novelists have woven into their story brilliant fictions, and these captivate;

they have almost the authority of history. The English Pilgrims and Puritans have had the good fortune to have the highest genius and eloquence and philosophic acumen, and have devoted themselves to the exaltation of their mission and their deeds and their creations. The English Pilgrims and Puritans have absorbed public attention; they have gotten into the public schools of the nation, and thus into the hearts and brains of the American boys and girls. The time has come when in fairness the Dutch Puritans must get there too. I do not mean to rob our English forefathers, but I do mean to be fair to our Dutch forefathers. I have already spoken the praises of the Pilgrim and the Puritan, and I will not withdraw what I have spoken; but this is a Dutch night and the praises of the Dutch must be spoken. I will not go back on the New England farmer's shot fired at Concord and Lexington, which echoed around the world. It was a grand shot, and thus I characterize it when I walk over these battle-fields. I will not go back on that shot, but this I must claim and this I do claim, viz.: that shot was the heroism of the old Dutch republic reproducing itself in the new civil life of American freemen.

How did the Hollanders help in the building up of America and American institutions? That is the question to-night. I have time to present only two points.

1. *By hewing and shaping and filling and inspiring the English Pilgrims and Puritans, who are boasted factors in American life.*

England was not the first to lead Europe. It was the Dutch republic that first led Europe; it first taught what true liberty was. The entire war of Holland with Spain was a Puritan war. Three quarters of a century this war raged. In this war Holland permitted thousands of English soldiers to fight. English soldiers came into her army monarchists, and left it republicans, and went home to spread republican ideas. For two centuries and a quarter the territory which the hardy Hollanders took from the Haarlem Lake and the Zuyder Zee stood first in civilization. It commanded the markets of the world, and the oceans of the world, and the commerce of the world, and the manufactures of the world, and the gold of the world; it was the great intellectual and institutional storehouse of the world. These are undisputed historical facts.

But our object now is to look especially at what Holland did for England, and especially that part of England which sent us the Pilgrims and the Puritans. It was the first to give the English-speaking people the Bible in their own tongue. The first complete English Bible in print was the work of Miles Coverdale, who was employed to make the translation by Jacob van Meteren, of Antwerp. The translation was from the Dutch and Latin, and was printed in Antwerp and sent across the channel by Van Meteren, to use his own words, "for the advancement of the religion of Christ in England." There was no country so saturated with Bible ideas as was Holland, and this fact accounts for the political energy of the Dutch. Under the persecution of Philip II. and the Duke of Alva one hundred thousand Hollanders crossed the channel and made their home in the eastern and southern counties of England. What a power this must have been in England! These one hundred thousand came from a land of public schools and universities. Each man brought his Bible, which he could read for himself and for his neighbor. They were not paupers seeking alms; they were industrious, self-supporting men, scholars, bankers, manufacturers, merchants; all of them were freemen, refugees for freedom's sake and for conscience' sake. They were men, grand men and brave men, men constructed out of the very prodigality of nature; they were massive in intellect and in soul. Never in all the history of the world was there such another missionary movement on such a magnificent scale. They taught England commerce, education, agriculture, banking, the trades, morals, republican politics, and, above all, the true religion. Their daily life was a sermon on Christian virtue and temperance and chastity. It was out of these counties into which the Dutch came that the University of Cambridge arose, that educational center of broad thought and Puritanism which gave America the first scholars and leaders of New England. Under the labors of these scholars of Holland the university was almost reborn. It was out of these counties that the English Commonwealth sprang, and that Cromwell sprang, and that Cromwell's army was mustered. Above all, it was out of these counties, impressed by Dutch ideas and principles and filled with Dutch blood by intermarriage, that the great English exodus to America came, the Puritan exodus which made New England what it has been. This is one of the ways Holland has been a builder of America.

I need not tell you that it was from these counties that John Robinson and his congregation of Scrooby went to Holland. These were the American Pilgrims. These Pilgrims dwelt in Holland for twelve years, and became citizens of the United States of the Netherlands, and sent their children to the public schools of the republic, and used the secret ballot, and learned the doctrine of the rights of the individual man, and then came, filled with Hollandic and republican ideas, straight from the shores of Holland to Plymouth Rock. It was Holland with its republicanism that hewed and shaped and gave us those granite blocks which were swung into and solidified into the foundations of our nation, viz., the English Pilgrims and the

English Puritans. Said I not the truth when I said that the farmer's shot at Lexington and Concord was the heroic spirit of the Dutch republic finding a resurrection in the new civic life of New England heroes?

2. *The Hollanders helped in the building of the American Republic by the colony of the New Netherlands which they established upon our shores, and by the influence which it exerted in sister colonies.*

What influence did Holland exert in other colonies, do you ask?

There was the colony of Pennsylvania. It exerted a tremendous influence in the Republic. William Penn, the founder of that colony, was the son of a Dutch mother as well as of an English father. He preached in Holland and brought hundreds of his converts to his colony. He drafted the Pennsylvania code according to the laws of his mother's republic.

There was the colony of Connecticut. Hollanders exerted a tremendous influence there. The Connecticut Colony has been rightly called the miniature American Republic. Our fathers patterned the national institutions more after Connecticut than after any other existent colony. But who modeled Connecticut? Thomas Hooker, an English refugee, direct from Holland.

There was Rhode Island. Holland exerted a tremendous influence in Rhode Island. Roger

Williams was a Welshman full of Hollandic ideas. He was the man who taught Milton, the poet, the Dutch language. He was a Baptist. Now the English Baptists were the converts of the Holland Mennonites or Anabaptists, who believed in the separation of church and state; this was the republican principle upon which Roger Williams built Rhode Island.

But the work of Holland in America was more direct than anything we have yet noticed. She built up what is now the Empire State of the Union, the State of New York. She founded it by her own sons and daughters; she molded it; she gave it the very institutions which have continued to this day. On Manhattan Island she built the first free church and the first free school of America. She gave New York half a century of the Dutch republic simon-pure. Manhattan Island was as much a part of the Dutch republic as was Holland itself. Manhattan Island was hers not by conquest, as Plymouth Rock with its surrounding region was the Pilgrims'; it was hers by an out-and-out purchase. Holland purchased Manhattan Island from the Indians for the sum of twenty-four dollars. A sharp Dutch bargain, you say? No; it was all that it was worth. Put that money at interest and let it compound, and the money will be equal to the market value of Manhattan Island to-day. I have seen the figures. Money and real estate must run close together, else we would have financial confusion.

Two things the Dutch Colony which once reigned where we worship to-night preserved in their integrity. These were freedom of worship, i.e., religious toleration, and the political principle that where there is taxation there must be representation, i.e., the consent of the governed. These two principles Peter Stuyvesant, the governor, once undertook to ignore. The people in the first instance appealed to the home republic, and the governor was rebuked and this proclamation was issued: "All men own their own consciences." The people in the second instance drew up a public and representative remonstrance, in which they declared that government should be administered according to the law of God, should respect individual rights, and should receive its power from the consent of the governed. This was in 1653. This was the first declaration of independence ever issued on the American continent. It was Bunker Hill, New York, one hundred and twenty-two years in advance of Bunker Hill, Boston.

Thus our debt to Holland opens before us. Our Constitution is written, not unwritten, as in England; this we got from Holland. We have the system of the public record of deeds and mortgages; this we got from Holland. We have the free-school system; this we got from Holland.

We have the doctrine that government gets its authority from the consent of the governed; this we got from Holland. The separation of church and state is an American idea; this we got from Holland. Our motto is, "United we stand, divided we fall;" this we got from Holland; that was a motto fo the Dutch republic—"Unity makes might." We have among us the freedom of the press; this we got from Holland. We have the secret written ballot; this we got from Holland. We have reform in the laws concerning the rights of married women; this we got from Holland. Above all, we have the principle that "all men are created equal"; this we got from Holland.

We shall not read history rightly if we only look at Holland of to-day and judge Holland by the present; the past was different from the present. The changes of two hundred and fifty years are such that it is necessary for us to use language that seems extravagant if we would do the republic of Holland justice. Our civil fathers knew it. It was a dominant power in the day of the three historic ships, the *Good Speed*, the *Half-moon*, and the *Mayflower*. It existed all through our colonial history, and it was a power our fathers felt when they wrote our Declaration of Independence and when they framed our national Constitution. It was the training-school of our nation's founders.

The Dutch republic is now dead; it was crushed

by Napoleon, who tramped the earth with the iron heel of a cruel despot; but before it died it safely handed the torch of liberty to the new Republic across the sea. The United States of America are in principle and in national life the United States of Holland amplified, refined, perpetuated.

In closing my address to-night, I call upon you to stand by the civil institutions bequeathed to us by our civil fathers. Let me particularize just one —one which has been a mighty blessing to the Republic. I refer to our public school; and I refer to it because to-day it is made the subject of special hostile attack. There are men in America who are striving to smite it into the dust. They are seeking to undermine it and to crowd it out by un-American substitutes. My fellow-men, the public school in itself is a little germinant American Republic keeping up true democratic equality. It is the nation's institution, and not the institution of a church with a bias on the side of self, teaching sectarianism and planting the seed of dissension and future schism in the very cradle. It is the nation's institution, and not the institution of a class segregating our boys and girls according to the amount of money in the pocket-books of their fathers, and begetting a class feeling in our communities. The American Republic owns the boys and girls born under its flag, and its public school is its one institution to fit them for citizenship. It fuses all classes and creeds, and makes the child in his ideas and feelings and sympathies and purposes, and in every fiber of his being, an American. Here the children are taught to sing the songs of the Republic, and are taught what our institutions cost, and are indoctrinated in the principles of Americanism. It is the great unifier of the different nationalities pouring in upon our shores. It is our defense against all hierarchies, civil and ecclesiastical, and against all deadly isms imported from foreign shores. It puts the American flag into the hands of our children, to be carried by them all through life. The man who strikes down this distinctively American institution, which has occupied the soil ever since the Hollanders planted it in New Amsterdam, should be treated as we treat the man who fires on the stars and stripes.

I call upon you to-night to honor the civil fathers of America. Hold on to their intense trust in God and to their reverent spirit toward God. Honor God's church as they honored it. Kneel at the prayer altar which they erected to God. Read God's Word as they read it. Let Turner's painting, "The Old Dutch Grandmother Reading her Bible," be translated into life in every American home. Make the lives of the children the glory of the fathers. Keep America intact as God's loom for the interweaving of all people into a republic of God. Renew the Declaration of Independence. Amend the Constitution; make it true to God; refill it with the spirit of the fathers; fit it to the times; make it proclaim the present truth. Keep America true to herself, and thus keep her true to the world. The world needs America, the latest beautiful civil flower of the past.

A noted traveler who has circled the world says: "At the bottom of the wail of every struggling people you find American aspirations. In Switzerland I heard the news of the death of Garfield, and all the Alps seemed quivering in sympathy with our national bereavement. In Ceylon I heard of the death of Longfellow, and all the tropical forests seemed trembling in pain at our grief. In the Inland Sea of Japan I heard of the death of Emerson, and all the sacred groves seemed uttering their sympathy with our loss. Wherever on earth I stood, I put my ear upon the heart of nations, and I have listened not to what the people are ready to say in public in the face of tyranny, but to what the people are saying at their firesides and in their secret thoughts; and this is what I have always heard: the echo of the prayer of our martyred Lincoln, that 'the government of the people, for the people, by the people, may not perish from the earth.'"

The world to-day needs America, as America once needed Holland.

V.

THE SCOTCH.

V.

THE SCOTCH.*

The commemoration of the deeds of our civil fathers is a perpetual duty. There come to us exhilaration and inspiration and vitality of holy purpose from living with the heroes of God who have glorified the past by their loyalty to the right. Macaulay says, " No people who fail to take pride in the deeds of their ancestors will ever do anything in which their posterity can take pride." Especially is this true when their ancestors have stood in the front ranks of human progress and, like our ancestors, have fought and won the battles of the ages.

Honoring ancestors should prove a large trade in the American commonwealth, and that because we are rich in ancestors. We can truthfully claim kinship to every line of human nobility that has done anything grand by way of sacrifice in the uplift of the world in these last centuries. The

* Delivered in Baltimore, Md., before the Presbyterian Union of that city.

best of a score of the leading races of the earth focalize right here. And this is to our national advantage. A great people is stronger and more fertile from the variety of its component parts and from the friendly play of the electric currents which have their origin in the diversity that is held in friendship.

I look upon our country as God's great loom for the interweaving of the peoples of the earth. The noble men and noble women from the different races of the Old World are the threads of silk and of silver and of gold, and the fabric woven is the American Republic, beautiful with its holy freedom, its constitutional rights, and its magnificent and elevating institutions, both civil and religious. The fabric of our national civilization, which is distinctively American, is complex, and the credit for its beauty and strength and value should be as manifold as its contributing constituents are multifold. There should be honest recognition and praise given all around. Let the Pilgrim be praised where the Pilgrim should be praised; let the Puritan be praised where the Puritan should be praised; let the Hollander be praised where the Hollander should be praised; and let the Scotch and their descendants be praised where the Scotch and their descendants should be praised. Let the highest type of manhood built into the construction of our civic personality be admired, no matter from what race it has come. The only restriction I would lay down is this: choose only the best manhood to honor, because the type of manhood which you honor is the type of manhood which you will inevitably seek to perpetuate. Admire only the best and choicest threads in the fabric. Up to this point in our national history we have not been impartial in our admiration of our ancestors. New England has created a monopoly here. The large-talking Yankee, true to his pedigree, has talked himself into a largeness out of all proportion with the facts. Hitherto he has written the history of the country, and he has so put himself into history that there has been little room there for others. He has not done justice to the Hollander; he has not done justice to the Huguenot; he has not done justice to the Scot. All of these were first-class believers in human liberty and not one whit behind either Pilgrim or Puritan in the sacrifices which they made for our Republic. The eyes of the public are being opened, and the result is there is an honest and a popular demand that American history be rewritten from alpha to omega, and that the uncredited heroes be enthroned in the midst of their lawful rewards, and that every omitted chapter be inserted in full. My fellow-men, American history has yet to be written. The Yankee has yet to hold fellowship on the historic page with the men of other races from whom he received his best ideas and who led him up to the alpine heights of republicanism in the colonial days. He must yet lift his hat with respect to both the Dutchman and the Scotchman. It is our duty to reach a full and an impartial view of our American nationality.

To-night we are to speak of the Scotch and their descendants as makers of America. They were the first on American soil openly to advocate American independence. We wish to do for them what the famous poet and novelist, Sir Walter Scott, has done for the physical beauties of the landscape of Scotia, viz., make them known. Scott has not added one particle of beauty to a single sprig of heather; he has not put a single additional touch of color upon a single bluebell; he has not created one added glint of light on his beloved lakes; he has not changed a particle of the country concerning which he so beautifully wrote. He has simply looked at Mid-Lothian, Lomond, and the Trosachs with his own eyes, has seen for himself the beauty and grandeur of nature's handiwork in Scotia, and has told in prose and poetry just what he has seen. What Scott has done for the physical country we must do for the noble actions of the Scotch, viz., take them in and tell them out.

Where shall I begin? With John Knox. And why begin with John Knox? Because the Scotch-

Americans are the sons of his faith, just as, spiritually, Knox himself is the son of John Calvin. The political truth which the Scotch-Americans held and for which they fought in revolutionary times and in prerevolutionary times was not a mushroom growth of a single night; it was the oak of centuries. It was the result of the unwavering fidelity which for two full centuries held sacred the political tenets of John Knox, the apostle of liberty, who said to the haughty queen, " If princes exceed their bounds they may be resisted by force." In that magnificent sentiment, uttered with a magnificent fearlessness, I hear the far-off drum-beat of the American Revolution. Froude, the greatest of modern English historians, declares of this bold utterance of John Knox, "It is the creed of republics in its first hard form." This utterance of John Knox became ingrained in the very being of all true Scotchmen, and they believed it and asserted it and lived it. In our own age a son of Scottish faith has said, " Government of the people, by the people, for the people, shall never perish from the earth." This saying, received with universal applause, has been lifted into a classic by the American people of the nineteenth century. But what is this saying? Only the utterance of John Knox grown large.

I have referred to John Knox as a spiritual son of John Calvin. He went straight from Calvin's home in Geneva to Scotland when, at the call of his countrymen, he entered Scotland to inaugurate the glorious reformation which he carried to success. His theology was Calvinistic, and so has been the theology of his descendants. This gives me an opportunity to speak a passing word for Calvinism. I do not ask you to-day to read Calvin's "Institutes" or to study Calvin's commentaries, but I do ask you to read Calvin as he has written himself into history and then take the measure of Calvin. In history John Calvin wrote Swiss Protestantism, and French Huguenotism, and English Puritanism, and Scotch sturdiness of faith, and New England Pilgrimism. He put into human life a sense of reverence, and of liberty founded on reverence, and these will last in the world long after his "Institutes" and commentaries have become worm-eaten and have crumbled into dust. Now the point I wish to emphasize is this: Calvin has blessed America through John Knox. Listen to the voice of the great historians here. Buckle says, "Wherever it has gone in France, Switzerland, Britain, America, the Calvinistic faith has shown itself the unfailing friend of constitutional liberty." D'Aubigné says, "Calvin was the founder of the greatest of republics: the oppressed who went to America were the sons of his faith." Motley says, "Holland, England, America, owe their liberties to the Calvinists." Bancroft says, "He that will not honor the memory and respect the influence of Calvin knows but little of the origin of American independence. . . . The light of his genius shattered the mask of darkness which superstition had held for centuries before the brow of religion." These are the voices of the authorities in history, and we can see how facts accord with their testimony to Calvinism. Calvinism exalts as its cardinal doctrine the absolute sovereignty of God. Let a man believe with all his heart the absolute sovereignty of God, let him believe that his first and last allegiance is to God as sovereign, and he will know no such thing as fear of the face of man, king or potentate or peasant. He will feel that in every battle for truth and liberty "one man with God is a majority," and that victory is sure.

That was the fate of John Knox when he came from the presence of John Calvin and worked out the reformation of Scotland. He began his work with the cry, "O God, give me Scotland or I die!" and God gave him Scotland and he lives. What was the reformation which he wrought? It consisted in this: He exterminated from Scotland the Roman Catholic hierarchy, that representative of monarchy, that natural enemy of republicanism, and he exterminated it root and branch. In its place he gave Scotland Presbyterianism pure and simple. He was the founder of the famous Scotch kirk. Lecky, the historian, says, "The Scotch kirk was by its constitution essentially republican. It was in this respect the very antipodes of the Anglican church and of the Gallican branch of the Catholic Church, both of which did all they could to consecrate despotism and strengthen its authority." Carlyle says, "A man's religion is the chief fact with regard to him." Knox gave Scotchmen their religion. He taught them to learn from the Bible their rights as Christians and as citizens. He taught them that in the New Testament there is no sacerdotal class save that which includes all of the people: "Ye are a royal priesthood!" He taught them from the Bible the principle of representation and the right of choice. That certainly is Americanism as we have it to-day. He put the Bible into the hands of the people and taught the right of private interpretation. He introduced schools for the people and gave them education. He established a system of schools. Thus he laid the foundation of future Scotland and built up the institutions which were destined to mold the character of the men about to cross the ocean and become the makers of America. This one thing is to be kept prominently in mind: John Knox worked largely for the church, and through the church, and by the church. All of his institutions centered in the kirk. In short, John Knox made and built up the church, and the church made and built up the people. Carlyle says,

"Knox gave Scotland a resurrection from the dead. Scotch literature and thought and industry,—James Watt, David Hume, Walter Scott, Robert Burns (he who wrote 'A man's a man for a' that')—I find the Reformation acting in the heart's core of every one of these persons. Without the Reformation they would not have been." But Carlyle was a Scotchman. A man who was not a Scotchman says, " In proportion to their small numbers they are the most distinguished little people since the days of the Athenians, and the most educated people of the modern races. All the industrial arts are at home in Glasgow, and all the fine arts in Edinburgh, and as for literature, it is everywhere."

The natural sequence of John Knox in Scotland is just what we see on the page of Scottish history: (1) The Solemn League and Covenant, literally signed with the blood of the best sons of Scotland, the Covenanters. The Covenanters were most potent in their influence during the period of the colonization of New England and when the institutions of the colonies were taking shape. (2) The Sanquhar Declaration, signed by Richard Cameron and Donald Cargill, and the great revolution. (3) The notable movement which resulted, in our own day, in the Free Church of Scotland, which has given us the names of Chalmers and Candlish and Guthrie. All of these historic movements show the features of John Knox, in that they exalt and declare the equality of man, liberty in religion, the value of the open Bible, the need of a sanctified Sabbath, the power of a pure church, and the rights of free speech, free press, free schools.

The question before us now is, How did these men whom Knox made reach America? How did they come to cast in their lot with those who became the makers of America? At this point the history of the Scotch-Americans resembles somewhat the history of the New England Pilgrims. The two histories are parallel. The New England Pilgrims came to America by way of Holland; the Scotch-Americans came to America by way of the province of Ulster, Ireland. Only a small portion of the Scotch in the colonial times came to the colonies directly from Scotland.

Just here comes in the story of Ulster. In the early days of prelatic James I. the rebellion of two of the great nobles of the province in the north of Ireland furnished the king an excuse to confiscate their vast domains. To hold these domains and to populate them with men who could hold their own successfully against the rest of Catholic Ireland, James determined to found a colony of picked subjects. He offered special inducements to the Scotch to make Ulster their home. The inducements were such and the charter promised so favorable that large numbers responded. Of these James took his pick. This colony received its charter April

16, 1605. The Scotch in their new home of Ulster were joined by many of God's noblemen, who were one with them in religious thinking and in a holy life, who came from the English Puritans and from the French Huguenots. This mixture modified and improved in some regard the Puritan Scotch stock. To-day this people are known by the name of Scotch-Irish. The name is a misnomer. It would lead us to believe that the Scotch of the colony of Ulster intermarried with the Irish, and that this people, therefore, is a people of mixed blood. But this is not the case. The name Scotch-Irish, which has its origin in purely geographical reasons, is ethnologically incorrect. The Ulster people to this day are Scotch through and through and out and out. There is no intermarriage; there is no union of the Scotch and the Irish races. The name Scotch-Irish is not used in the Emerald Isle, and in the interest of historical correctness I argue that it should not be used anywhere. In the Emerald Isle, by Irish and Scotch alike, these people are called Ulstermen, and that is their name.

I do not need to tell you what a country these colonists of 1605 made out of Ulster and the surrounding territory. They took with them all that John Knox gave them, and the result was prosperity on all lines. But the colonists were not allowed to pursue the even tenor of their way. They were oppressed, just as the American colonists were, by prelatic, Episcopalian England. First, England, by the passage of oppressive measures, took from Ulster its woolen trade. This was like a stroke of paralysis. It caused the first great exodus of the Scotch colonists to America. A second and a larger exodus was caused by the scandalous advancement of the rents of the farms and by a taxation on the improvements caused by the industry of the people. The first outrage made an attack on commerce and manufacture; the second outrage was an attack on the agriculture of the colony. For fifty long years, from 1720 to 1770, the people, abused and then ejected from their farms and homesteads, which they and their fathers had made what they were, poured in streams of twelve thousand a year into America. So great was the inpour that when we come to the times of the American Revolution the Scotch formed almost, if not altogether, one third of the entire population of the American colonies.

And where did they go in America? They formed no colonies of their own. Where did they go?

Some of them went to New England and settled in Boston and in Worcester, and some threaded their way up into Maine and New Hampshire and Vermont. Twenty thousand settled along the Atlantic coast from the Charles River up to the

Kennebec. Froude holds that in Boston it was they who gave the name to Bunker Hill. There are Scotch Covenanter churches to-day in Maine and Vermont and Massachusetts, and there are Presbyterian churches in New Hampshire. In 1754 the Presbyterian congregation of Londonderry, N. H., numbered over seven hundred communicants. Although comparatively but a few of the vast Scotch exodus settled in New England, yet those who did have made their record and have told on American life. They took with them into New England the things John Knox gave them: the kirk, and the school, and the civil creed of equal rights, and the sanctified Sabbath, and the inherent dignity of man.

It was from the New England Scotch that George Washington got Henry Knox, a member of his cabinet, and the first Secretary of War in the American Republic. When the Revolution broke out it was the Scotch who fought the battle of Bennington. General Stark and his "Green Mountain boys" were Scotch. The Scotch of Maine gave to the country Matthew Thornton, one of the signers of the Declaration of Independence. In latter days the New England Scotch gave to journalism Horace Greeley, the father of modern journalism, and to science Professor Asa Gray, one of Harvard's leading professors.

But the greater part of the enormous Scotch

exodus poured into the Middle and the Southern colonies. They literally took possession of Pennsylvania. Philadelphia, with its Independence Hall, was their city, just as Boston, with its Faneuil Hall, was the city of the Puritans. They hold Philadelphia to this day. It was to Pennsylvania the Rev. Francis Makemie came, the first Presbyterian minister in America of whose history we have any knowledge. He was the man who was imprisoned in New York for preaching in his independent way, and he was the man who formed the first American presbytery. We find the Scotch also in New Jersey. A large company of them came to New Jersey, we are told, under the prompting of William Penn. As New Jersey was one of the leading battle-fields of the Revolution, the Scotch, who had become very strong there, were among Washington's chief supporters. New Jersey gave to the army the Rev. James Caldwell, the chaplain of the First Brigade, whose history is given in full in the "Life and Letters of Elias Boudinot." He was more than chaplain; he was at one time also the assistant commissary-general. Washington esteemed his service as invaluable. He was well-nigh ubiquitous. The British burned down his manse and murdered his wife before the eyes of his children, and they tried also to burn the children in the flames of the manse. His children were saved only by a hairbreadth escape. Lafayette took one of his motherless boys and adopted him and gave him the love and opportunity of his princely home. George Washington subscribed twenty-five guineas out of his own private funds for the support of the other children. Mr. Caldwell fell by the hand of an assassin. On one occasion it is told of him that, seeing one of the companies slacking their fire for want of wadding, he rushed into the Presbyterian church near by, and gathering an armful of Watts's hymn-books he distributed them along the line, with the order, "Now put Watts into them, boys." With a cheer the soldiers rammed the charges home and gave the British Watts with a will. It was the New Jersey Scotch who founded the famous Presbyterian university, Princeton College, the college that can outkick anything on the continent, and that up to date.

Having located at first on the western and southern borders of the old colonies, the Scotch naturally pressed their way west and south. While they founded no colonies, they did in the course of time found new States. They poured their thousands down into the Carolinas, North and South. They made the States of Kentucky and Tennessee and Alabama. They poured also into Virginia until they out-influenced there the haughty Cavalier. They took possession of the Mississippi valley and brought it into the Republic. Ohio, too, felt their influence. They became so strong in our own Empire State of New York that even our first governor, Governor Clinton, the man who has given his name to the principal avenue of Brooklyn, was a scion of that race.

I imagine some son of the Scot saying, just here, "How I wish my ancestors had massed themselves together as did the Puritans, and had formed a colony of their own! Then they could have struck with a trip-hammer on the anvil of time the elements making this nation. They could have made a name for themselves in American history like that of Massachusetts." This wish is a mistake. No matter about the name in history. The name is coming, for the facts of early days, which are being resurrected and glorified by modern historical research, will build up the Scotch name and set it in a noonday splendor before the universe. The Scotch elements were too strong and too good to be massed; they were of the kind fitted to be scattered as a leavening influence through the land and among the diverse peoples of the land. Thus scattered as they were, they worked more mightily for American liberty than they could have worked if they had been solidified into a single colony. Here allow me to illustrate and give concrete cases. Being Presbyterian in faith, they formed a general synod, which met once a year. Through this synod they worked powerfully for American liberty. They were the sons of John Knox, and, like Knox, they used the church in the cause of freedom. In the General Synod there were delegates from all the colonies, and they formed a union of thought and purpose and plan. Thus the Scotch demonstrated to America that what was possible in religious affairs was possible in civil affairs, viz., a union of all parts of the land, and a union by representation—a federal union.

The Scotch General Synod was a model of the coming Colonial Congress. It made it possible. It suggested it. For fifty years this synod was the most powerful and compact religious organization in the country. The men in the synod, like the Scotch from Ulster, were men of the very highest type. The ministers were men educated at Glasgow and Edinburgh and Dublin and Harvard universities. They discussed all questions that pertained to the interest of the country, and sent their delegates home to all the colonies to spread their advanced principles concerning their rights and duties.

See the results of this. Four years before the battle of Lexington the Presbyterians of North Carolina resisted the oppression of the British crown as unjust. The governor of the colony treated them as outlaws, and sent an army against them and shot them down, and took captive and hung thirty of them. This was the first blood of the Revolution. It is known in history as the War of the Regulators. Bancroft says of it, "The blood of the first rebels against British oppression was first shed among the settlers on the branches of the Cape Fear River." This was May 16, 1771.

See the results of this. One year before the Philadelphia Declaration of Independence the Presbyterians of Mecklenburg, N. C., met together and publicly issued their declaration of independence from the rule of Britain. Here is one sentence from that declaration: "We hereby absolve ourselves from all allegiance to the British crown; we hereby declare ourselves a free and independent people." The men who issued this Mecklenburg declaration were the men on the walls of whose homes hung the National Covenant of Scotland, which many of their ancestors had signed. Thus you see that the famous and historic covenant of Greyfriars Churchyard formed the rugged and solemn background of American liberties. "It can be said, without fear of challenge, that Scotch blood flows through every principle in the Declaration of Independence, which forms the foundation of American freedom."

Bancroft says, in writing of the Mecklenburg declaration, which antedated the Philadelphia Declaration one whole year, "The first public voice for dissolving all connection with Great Britain came not from the Puritans of New England, nor from the Dutch of New York, nor from the planters of Virginia, but from the Scotch Presbyterians."

Wallace Bruce, a man with a double Scotch name and a double Scotch nature, our honored consul to Scotland, puts Bancroft's eulogy into verse, and in these fitting words honors the event of Mecklenburg:

> " Manhattan and Plymouth and Jamestown
>   Can boast of their heritage true,
> But Mecklenburg's fame is immortal
>   When we number the stars in the blue;
> The Scotch-Irish Puritan Fathers
>   First drafted the words of the free,
> And the speech of Virginia's Henry
>   Is the crown of our liberty's plea."

In 1775 the General Presbyterian Synod, meeting in Philadelphia side by side with the Colonial Congress, issued a pastoral letter calling on the people to defend their rights against British usurpation. This letter was a mighty power with the people and with Congress. You see here the power of the Presbyterian Church and how aggressive it was. It was ready in advance for July 4, 1776, and so were all its people scattered through all the colonies. When that day came it was Thomas Jefferson, a scion of the Scotch race, according to the record of the Scotch-Irish Congress, who was the author of the Declaration of Independence. Professor McCloskie, of Princeton, says the Declaration of Independence, as we have it now, is in the handwriting of the son of Scotland; it was first printed by another Scotchman, and a third Scotchman, Captain Nixon, was the first to read it publicly to the people.

It is in place just at this point to speak of two men whose names will always be connected with the American Declaration of Independence and with the great Revolution. The first is the name of the man who first sounded the tocsin of war in that great sentence of his, "Give me liberty or give me death," and made the tocsin reverberate from mountain to mountain and from lake to lake until the thirteen colonies heard the echo and resolved to be freemen or die. I refer to Patrick Henry, of Virginia, whose mother was a Presbyterian. Of him Webster, speaking to Jefferson, says, "He was far before us all in maintaining the spirit of the Revolution."

The second is the name of that Presbyterian minister whose voice it was that brought the Congress finally and irrevocably to sign the great instrument, the Declaration. I refer to the venerable Dr. Witherspoon, President of Princeton College, who was at the time a member of the Continental Congress. We are told that the Congress was hesitating. The country was looking on. Three million hearts were violently throbbing in intense anxiety, waiting for the old bell on Independence

Hall to ring. "It was an hour that marked the grandest epoch in human history." What a scene was there! On the table in the presence of that able body of statesmen lay the charter of human freedom in clear-cut utterances, flinging defiance in the face of oppression. It was an hour in which strong men trembled. There was a painful silence. In the midst of that silence Dr. Witherspoon, a lineal descendant of John Knox, rose and uttered these thrilling words: "To hesitate at this moment is to consent to our own slavery. That notable instrument upon your table, which insures immortality to its author, should be subscribed this very morning by every pen in this house. He that will not respond to its accent and strain every nerve to carry into effect its provisions is unworthy the name of freeman. Whatever I have of property, of reputation, is staked on the issue of this contest, and although these gray hairs must soon descend into the sepulcher, I would infinitely rather that they descend hither by the hand of the executioner than desert at this crisis the sacred cause of my country." *That was the voice of John Knox in Independence Hall.* And that voice prevailed. The Declaration was signed, the liberty bell of Independence Hall rang out, and the foundation of the American government was securely laid. Fourteen of the sons of Scotland signed this Declaration.

From the signing of the Declaration of Independence American history grandly enlarges, and the sons of the Scotch race are seen in nearly every high place. Their generals led in the great battles of the Revolution: General Wayne at Stony Point, and General Campbell at Kings Mountain, and General Montgomery at Quebec. When the great American Constitution was framed their wisdom prevailed there. Madison is claimed by more than one member of the late Scotch-Irish Congress as a scion of this race. He is known as the father of the American Constitution. Lincoln also, the author of the Emancipation Proclamation, is claimed, and his lineage is traced back to the Scotch who settled in Kentucky. Seven governors out of the thirteen original States were Scotch. Then come their Presidents of the United States, Jefferson, Jackson, Monroe, James Knox Polk, Madison, Taylor, Buchanan, Lincoln, Johnson, Grant, Hayes, Arthur, Harrison, and Cleveland.

My friends, as I give the history of this magnificent Scotch race in its relation to American life, I am heartily glad that I have the good fortune to have the Scotch for my theme to-night, and not the Pilgrims, and not the Puritans, and not the Hollanders; for when the Scotch have claimed the first battle for our liberty; and the first blood shed; and the first declaration of independence publicly issued; and the privilege of naming Bunker Hill; and Davy Crockett, the most picturesque of

American characters, the wizard of the woods; and Patrick Henry, the resistless orator of the Revolution; and the peerless Poe, the illustrious poet; and Commodore Perry, the illustrious naval officer; and Jefferson, who wrote the Declaration of Independence; and Witherspoon, whose voice charmed America into accepting it; and Madison, the father of the American Constitution, which Gladstone pronounces the greatest instrument ever penned in a given time; and Abraham Lincoln, with his Emancipation Proclamation, America's greatest glory; and Ulysses S. Grant, the man who carried the Civil War to its grand and proper close; and Robert Fulton, the father of steamboat navigation, which has so wonderfully enlarged commerce; and the phenomenal Morse, who with his telegraph has linked all parts of the world in instantaneous touch, and helped on the brotherhood of man; and McCormick, the inventor of the American reaper, which has multiplied indefinitely the forces of American agriculture; and Andrew Jackson, the hero of the War of 1812; and Winfield Scott, the hero of the Mexican War—when the Scotch have claimed all these great men and all these noble things, *what is left for the other makers of America to claim and exult over?*

I wish to speak a brief word relative to some of the striking and racial characteristics of the Scotch—characteristics which have made them what they are.

I do not know that I can do better than simply name these traits and illustrate each by relating a pertinent anecdote. I notice first that the Scotch are:

1. *Preëminently truthful.*

They are truthful even to the point of bluntness. When I was a boy this story was told of Dr. Blank, a Scotch clergyman of Pittsburg, and it illustrates my point. The doctor had just a touch of vanity in his nature, and when a certain college gave him a D.D. his vanity was not in the least crushed. Indeed, it led him at once to plan a trip home, that his friends in the old country might feast their eyes on a doctor of divinity. Once in Scotland, he called upon his old pastor, who knew John's fondness for John. But he got no flattery from the old pastor. He was too truthful to flatter. He greeted the new-comer: "Well, well, John, I hear they have made you a doctor of divinity?" The new D.D. replied, "Yes, they persisted in giving me the title, although I was the last man in the world to deserve it." The old man, detecting the vanity in the tones of the voice, replied in his blunt way, "Yes, yes; that's just what I thought myself, John, when I heard it."

2. *The Scotch are men of principle, and largely given to protest.*

A Scotchman is a natural nonconformist. He loves to protest against things and institutions and customs. He must protest or die, but die is the very last thing that a Scotchman does on earth. That he may find an opportunity to protest he is always in search of some principle to take hold of and advocate; he finds a principle in everything. He will split hairs and then imagine that the points which he has made are every one of them principles, and he will die for them before he will give them up. He can even, if need be, convert prejudices into principles and thus transfigure them. Let me illustrate how the Scotchman reads principle into everything and in everything acts on principle.

Probably you have heard of the old saying that "a Scotchman never shuts the door after him." That was true in olden times. He knows that a door will shut; he knows what the latch is for; he knows what good breeding is; he knows that other people shut the door after them. He is not acting from ignorance; he leaves the door open on principle. He has argued the whole question out to his own satisfaction, and logically he feels that he could not conscientiously shut the door. If you wish you may shut it; he will not criticize you; that is a matter for your own conscience; but he cannot. Raillery cannot compel him, neither can force. He has argued the question out. He has canvassed the arguments in favor of shutting and the arguments in favor of leaving the door open, and he has balanced the two, and the balance is on the side of not shutting, and that makes it a principle with him. In favor of shutting the door there is:

1. A cold wind may blow into the room. But this is not probable, for those within would shut the door and protect themselves.

2. By shutting the door you will keep people on the outside from hearing the conversation carried on within. But people should not talk about things or say things they would not want others to hear or repeat.

These are the only arguments he can think of for shutting the door. There are more arguments in favor of leaving it open:

1. If the door slam in shutting it would be exceeding unpleasant, and would suggest the idea that you were in a passion.

2. If it did not slam it might make a creaking noise.

3. Suppose that it makes no noise at all, the impression is conveyed that you are going away not to return, while you have no such intention. You must not give false impressions.

4. There are chances that when you come back you will make a noise in opening the door, which is an interruption to the conversation. That is bad manners.

5. By not shutting the door you give the parties

remaining behind the option of shutting it or not, according as it may please their own fancy. This disposition to please is an amiable disposition and should be cultivated.

These are some of the reasons which determined the Scotchman of old not to shut the door, and he found a principle in every one of them. This looks like a burlesque, but, after all, it is infinitely better to be a man of principle than to be a man of no principle. A man who will put principle into a little thing like "not shutting the door," when he comes to deal with the eternal verities, when he comes to stand face to face with gigantic wrong and with political tyranny and with unholy oppression, is there for all he is worth; the whole man is there; and when a whole Scotchman is there, out into the open air is flung a Mecklenburg declaration of independence, and up in the highest court of the nation you have a Patrick Henry uttering an oration so full of conviction that it ushers in the American Revolution.

3. *The Scotchman has as a trait the element of persistence.*

Upon his drumhead he never beats a retreat. It is liberty or death. This story illustrates how a Scotchman will hold on and follow what he considers to be his one line of duty. It is told of a clergyman in the days when Knox was battling against the Roman hierarchy. His congregation brought a charge against him before the presbytery that he never could preach a sermon without breaking a lance with the pope—i.e., his sermons were all the same thing: pope in the exordium, pope in the body of the sermon, and pope in the peroration or conclusion. Thus it was fifty-two Sabbaths of the year. His preaching grew monotonous and the people grew weary. The presbytery said, "We will try him: we will give him a text to preach from, and we shall hear his sermon, and we shall see if your charge be true—that it is popery and pope no matter what text he takes." They gave him for a text these three proper names: "Adam, Seth, Enos." When the presbytery met there was a great congregation there, and the minister felt that they needed sound doctrine and timely warning. He saw a great opportunity. Solemnly he took his place in the pulpit and announced his text, "Adam, Seth, Enos," and this was his first sentence: "My dear brethren, these men lived in a day when there was no pope nor popery, and consequently they had not to contend against the following evils," and he enumerated in full and without waste of time all the evils of Romanism.

You smile at that man, but I tell you that we need just such a son of John Knox at this very moment in America. The Roman hierarchy is in our midst insidiously at work trying to weaken and to defeat the object of one of our noblest American institutions, the free public schools, manned, conducted, and supported by the state. It is these schools of ours, supported and conducted by the state, that unify the children of all classes and of all nationalities, and that take out of the cradle and out of childhood all sectarian prejudices and religious hatred and strife, and make all from the very start of life American through and through. This means a solid, intelligent American future. Rome has stepped upon the scene and has made a public demand that our public-school funds shall be divided; that is, that part of the taxes raised from the people shall be given to the Roman Church to be used for sectarian purposes. The Roman Church is pitted against the American state, and the issue is fairly on. We need a stalwart son of John Knox who knows the hierarchy through and through to tell Rome through Mr. Satolli that the American people mean to educate their own citizens, and that they are going to keep the schools of the Republic just as their fathers founded them. Sons of John Knox, tell that to Rome not only fifty-two Sabbaths every year, but tell that to Rome every day the whole year round.

I have been speaking to you of your duty of protest against the machinations of a corrupt church; let me now in closing say one word to you concerning your duty to the pure evangelical Christian church. My word grows out of this history of the freemen of Scotland as it touches American national life. John Knox, who gave Scotland its national power and character, was in loyal relation with the true church of Jesus Christ. Through the church of pure doctrine and equal representation, the church which honored the Sabbath and the open Bible and the rights of the individual man, he worked his great work; that is, through the church in which every one had the liberty of private judgment he molded public sentiment, and by the fearless and free discussion of the truth in this church he freed man's mind from superstition and welded his countrymen together to act as one man against the usurpations of oppression, civil and ecclesiastical. He has taught us that a pure, holy, untrammeled, independent church is a mighty safeguard of the liberties and rights of a people; that it means the suppression of all hurtful evil and vice and tyranny. It is the enlightener of the nation and its educator in the holy principles and moralities which perpetuate national liberty and life. In the light of his teachings let us learn our duty of loyalty just here. There is no way in which we can so bless our country as by giving it a pure, free-thoughted, Bible-loving church of Jesus Christ. Such a church is a power which will make citizens of brain and character and holy devotion to the rights of mankind. Such a church will be a power on any question when it asserts itself on the right side. It can send its protest through the land like a thunderbolt. It can lead. Church of John Knox rooted to-day in American soil, I greet you as such a power, and assure you that you have still a patriotic mission in this Republic which you have helped to build. You are equipped to-day for work as you have never before been equipped; enter that work with hope and consecration. Guard the liberties which you have purchased with your blood. Guard the institutions which incarnate the best thought and life of the American fathers.

You remember what Angelo said to one of his pupils, Donatello, who asked him to come and look at his figure of St. George on the outside of a church at Florence. "The great sculptor looked at it with admiration and surprise. Every limb was perfect, every outline complete, the face lighted with almost human intelligence, the brow uplifted, and the foot forward as if it would step into life. As Donatello waited for Angelo's decision the great sculptor looked at the statue, slowly lifted his hand, and said, 'Now march.'" That was the grandest possible encomium he could give to the figure of St. George in marble. That is God's word to the church of John Knox in America to-day: "I have given thee opportunity; I have given thee royal men; I have given thee freedom of thought; I have given thee knowledge;

I have given thee numbers; I have given thee My day and My Book; I have given thee the inspiring promises. *Now march.* Battle for Me; honor Me; keep My day holy; keep My truth uncorrupted; and, above all, guard and serve My nation, which I have refined by the fires of conflict and revolution. Lead America to higher and better things. Make it the refuge of the oppressed. Make it the land of Beulah—a land married unto the Lord."

VI.
THE HUGUENOTS.

VI.

THE HUGUENOTS.*

THE chief object of a service such as this is to enlighten and broaden and deepen American patriotism, to secure a proper valuation of our Republic with its popular institutions, and to exhibit the overrule and supremacy of God in human history. There is no better way of doing this than by setting forth and analyzing the forces which worked in the founding and upbuilding of our commonwealth. The hand of God was at work for long centuries, shaping events and raising up men and evolving great principles and incarnating the truth of civil and religious liberty, that in the fullness of time there might be the rise and establishment of the American Republic in the New World.

If there had been no God in history there would

* Delivered before the Presbyterian Ministerial Association, New York City.

have been no American Republic. God made *the Pilgrims* and guided the *Mayflower* and founded the Plymouth Rock Colony. God made *the Puritans* and gave being to the Massachusetts Bay settlement. God made *the Hollanders* and planted the New Netherlands at the mouth of the Hudson and laid the foundations of New Amsterdam. God made *the Scotch*, and the Scotch made the church of John Knox, and the church of John Knox made the province of Ulster, and the province of Ulster gave America one third of its colonial population which struck for independence. God made *the Huguenots*, who brought to America their Bible and their love of liberty and their heroic conscience, which could sacrifice every earthly good before it could prove false to God's cause and the Huguenots' own best self. All these were makers of America, but you cannot think of them divorced from God, because they were not divorced from God. These men were the national fathers of the Republic, and they were all God-made men. They sought God's guidance in their private life, their social life, their business life, their church life, their civil life. God went before them, and the invisible camps of God were all around their camps when they pushed their campaign for principle. Napoleon said, "God is always on the side of the heaviest battalions;" but American history shows that that is not true. If that were always true our civil fathers would have gone down before the guns of Britain.

When the clock of time struck 1776 the hour had come when God wanted the American Republic as a part of his world-plan. He did not bring it into existence as the ultimatum of civil progress, but only as the instrumentality for introducing greater things all around the globe. America under God exists for national progress, but America exists also for more than that: it exists for cosmopolitan progress. God is using it as His object-lesson to teach mankind the value of freedom of thought, the potentiality of popular education, and the absurdity of kingcraft and priestcraft. He is using it to create a rising tide of republicanism which shall roll in glory over every nation of the earth. The influence of the American Republic is at work to-day in Spain with the Castelars, and in Italy with the Cavours, and in England with the Gladstones. It turned the empire of Brazil into a republic without the shedding of a drop of blood. De Tocqueville predicted that "the growth of great cities would ruin America unless these cities were kept in order by a standing army." New York answers De Tocqueville. She sends him this message: "All the standing army which the greatest republican city of America needs is the people, armed with a free ballot and led by a courageous preacher of righteousness." Lord Beaconsfield was accustomed to lift up his jeweled finger and point across the Atlantic and affirm, "No American city of any commanding size is well governed under universal suffrage, or ever will be." Brooklyn at the present hour is an answer to the scorn of Beaconsfield's jeweled finger. Lord Macaulay wrote, "As for America, I appeal to the twentieth century. Either some Cæsar or Napoleon will seize the reins of government with a strong hand, or your Republic will be as fearfully plundered and laid waste by barbarians in the twentieth century as the Roman empire was in the fifth century, with this difference: that the Huns and Vandals who ravaged Rome came from without her borders, while your Huns and Vandals will be engendered within your own country and by your own institutions." The answer to Lord Macaulay is the American Republic on the eve of the twentieth century still holding its own, and stronger than ever, and on a perpetual lookout for all such Huns and Vandals. A Forefathers' service such as this gives us an opportunity of pointing to the glad fact that our nation is reversing the black prophecies of pessimists and realizing the predictions of the optimists of the ages. More than this, such a service enables us to place before our thought that which is the bed-rock upon which rest the cornerstone and the upholding pillars of our Republic; to find out also what the corner-stone is and what the pillars are. It gives us an opportunity to find out where the nineteenth century came from, and to discover the foes of republicanism, that we may be able to recognize them whenever they reappear in our midst. It brings to light the battles which had to be fought before we could be, and also the victories which were essential to our existence. The principles and the men that made us in the beginning are alone the type of principles and the type of men that can perpetuate us and keep us in triumph. As we canvass these to-night let us resolve to lock hands with them forever.

A service such as this exalts before us the value of the existence of patriotic orders in our broad land. Patriotic orders are always in order in a land where there is such a constant influx of new and foreign elements. They are of value to educate and to protect and to feed the patriotic spirit. If they exist in advance of foes they will prevent the rise of foes, and that is a grand work. If they exist alongside of designing foes they will checkmate them and save our reigning principles and institutions. Look out for the man who talks against patriotic orders; he is either seeking a cheap reputation for broad-mindedness or he is cloaking some deadly treason. What has genuine patriotism to fear from patriotic orders? The question is its own answer. Instead of putting your interrogation-point opposite patriotic orders, put your interrogation-point opposite the man who questions the right of such orders to exist.

To-night, speaking as a Christian minister, I am required to look at American history from a religious standpoint; to mark the play and power of large-thoughted religion in the conception and construction of our national life.

In the making of America the element of religion was by far the largest element at work, and no one could give American history in its completeness, from rostrum or platform or professor's chair or pulpit, and leave out the play and power of religion. What religion was it that had such a large play and power in our early history? I answer in a single word: Protestantism. *The Pilgrims* were Protestants, and so were *the Puritans*, and so were *the Quakers*, and so were *the Scotch*, who brought with them the church of John Knox, and so were the men of the Jamestown Colony, Virginia, and so were *the Huguenots*. When you have mentioned these, who are left as makers of America?

The American Republic is the exponent of Protestantism, the fullest and most all-around exponent on the globe. Americanism and Protestantism are synonyms. Do you object to this statement because by implication it bears hard on Romanism? Do you demand that Romanism shall be named in some way with Americanism, the on-

marching and triumphing political ism of the age?
Very well, I will name it and put my thought
in another form. Americanism is Romanism Cal-
vinized, Lutherized, Zwingliized. Americanism is
Rome minus the pope, minus the papal ablegate,
minus the cardinal, minus Mariolatry, minus the
dogma of infallibility, minus the parochial school,
minus the mass, minus the sword of persecution,
minus the hierarchy, minus the union of church
and state with the church supreme, minus the
censorship of the intellect, minus the priesthood.
Pare these excrescences off Romanism and I am
a Romanist. Pare these excrescences off Romanism
and your remainder will be something like Protestantism. Pare these excrescences off Romanism
and you will unfetter the consciences of men, take
away the censorship of the intellect, and inaugurate freedom of thought and speech and choice and
religious action. You will insure a free press, a
free platform, a free school, a free church, and a
free state. The clear verdict of history is this:
Romanism as a system, without these modifica-
tions, can make no claim to be one of the makers
of America. Only a stray Romanist here and there,
Romanists who were better than the system, who
acted without ex cathedra authority, lent a helping
hand. They represented themselves and not the
system. The system was at work on the other
side of the Atlantic and represented itself. This

the story of *the Huguenots* fully shows. It was the persecutions of Romanism that drove *the Huguenots* and the Dutch Puritans and kindred peoples from their native lands to this New World in search of liberty.

I will give right here a specimen from Huguenot history indicative of the spirit and conduct of Romanism back in the early ages when this continent was being peopled. Back in the year 1562 Admiral Coligni, a commanding Huguenot of France, seeing troublous times ahead for the people of his faith, thought to establish a refuge for them in the New World. For this purpose he sent a colony of Huguenots out to Florida. This angered Philip II. of Spain, who was the right hand of the pope of Rome. He could not bear the thought that the religion of John Calvin should have a single foothold on the American continent. He sent over Pedro Melendez to destroy them. This man, fired by Jesuit priests, gathered an army of twenty-five hundred, crossed the sea, and landed at St. Augustine, Fla. He issued this message on landing: "The Frenchman who is a Catholic I will spare, but every heretic shall die." Then began the work of death, and the Huguenot colony was wiped out of existence. The men, the defenseless women, the little children, the sick, were all cruelly massacred. That was a scene enacted on the soil that is part of the American Republic to-day.

Was Pedro Melendez one of the makers of our Republic?

One thing is certain, and that is, Romanism in America is not represented by *the Huguenots*, nor by *the Pilgrims*, nor by *the Hollanders*, nor by *the Scotch*. Its largest representation is found in the Irish. The Irish stand as the exponents of Rome. Now the Irish emigration is a late importation. The people of this race were not here early enough to be added to the list of the makers of the Republic. They have been here only long enough to be makers of modern New York—New York prior to November 6, 1894, New York which is now on the dissecting table of the Lexow Investigation Committee. I have the statistics to show that the Irish emigration to America belongs largely to the last half of this present century. Now I am not finding fault with this race for its tardiness in coming here, nor for its lateness in discovering that there is no Romanized state in all Europe equal to our Republic, though Rome has had centuries upon centuries to make such a state, and has had kings at its command. With all my heart I forgive the Irish for their lateness in coming, and for their comfort I would assure them that *the Hollanders* and *Pilgrims* and *Puritans* and the *followers of John Knox* filled their places admirably back yonder in the formative period of our national life. But I am not going to strike a single narrow note in this service to-night, so I say—I am American enough to say even to this people: If you want the freedom of our land; if you want to enjoy our citizenship; if you want to educate your children in our free public schools; if you want to help build up our institutions and defend our Declaration of Independence and Constitution; if you want to take our oath of naturalization, which cuts off every man who takes it from all allegiance, direct or implied, to every other civil power whatsoever, and which makes the American Republic exclusively supreme; if you want to become Americanized through and through, in and out, head and heart; and if you want to be an American henceforth in all your life—school life, home life, business life, social life, church life, civil life—then come. If you come in this spirit and for these purposes, then, in the name of the great American commonwealth, welcome. But remember this: the battles fought and won in the Old World declare that any other type of coming will be utterly vain and futile. The things of medieval times have taken their departure from this earth forever. The eagle is out of its shell. Our chariot of nationality is drawn by the noble steeds of individual liberty and popular education. You may ride with us if you wish, but you cannot drive. Uncle Sam does that.

But now for the special history of the evening,

viz., "The Story of the Huguenots." *The Huguenots* are two centuries older than the American Republic. Their cause began with the French Reformation, which antedated by several years the Reformation in Germany under Luther and the Reformation in Switzerland under Zwingli. Like these reformations, it began by the unchaining of the Bible and the putting of the Word of God into the hands of the people. Their cause arose under the reign of Francis I. of France, and continued through the reigns of Henry II., Francis II., Charles IX., Henry III. and IV., and Louis XIII., XIV., XV. and XVI. Louis XVI. was on the throne of France when the American Revolution began.

The French people are just a people in which a great reformation might be expected to succeed, and D'Aubigné asserts that their reformation was of indigenous origin. They are a people of aggressive spirit, susceptible to great suggestions, and quick in the apprehension of ideas. They are full of vivacity and of brightness and of irresistible impulse and enthusiasm. The Reformation began with Professor Lefèvre, who taught his pupil, William Farel, the doctrine of justification by faith and a love for the Bible. These two were timid until they were joined by John Calvin and Theodore Beza, when the cause received a great impetus. Calvin was the great French reformer, and Beza was the man who uttered that immortal saying to the king, "Sire, it is in truth the lot of the church of God, in whose name I speak, to endure blows and not to strike them; but also, may it please you to remember that it is an anvil that has worn out many hammers." *The Huguenots* were Calvinist in faith and had Calvin himself as their teacher. They were a people of the open Book. Their church polity was Presbyterian. They were great lovers of the Psalms, and upon all occasions sang the version translated and put into meter by Clement Merot. The Psalms were the Marseillaises to which they marched in all their battles. I do not need to say that their religious faith and their church polity were such as to awaken in *the Huguenots* the spirit of liberty and plant in their souls the germs of republicanism. That is the legitimate product of Calvinism, which exalts God and conscience as supreme; and the legitimate outgrowth of Presbyterianism, which is representative in its genius and which gives every man the liberty of choosing those who shall represent him and of holding them to account. It was an old-time saying—as old as *the Huguenots* themselves—"*The Huguenots* are all republicans." The hierarchy of Rome saw this, and so did the kings of France, who were under the control of Rome. Hence the bitter and bloody persecutions which were inaugurated against *the Huguenots* and which continued for two hundred years.

My fellow-men, Calvinism carries in it republics, just as the acorn carries in it fleets of sailing ships. All that Calvinism needs is just what the acorn needs, viz., soil to grow in. Give the acorn growth and the ships will come. Give Calvinism growth and the republics will come. Give Calvinism Geneva and you will have a republic; give it America and you will have a republic; yes, give it even France itself and give it time and you will have a republic. Away back in the seventeenth century *the Huguenots* converted the city of La Rochelle into a republic which for years lived in the hearts of Roman Catholic, monarchical France. Although in the course of time La Rochelle was leveled to the ground, France never forgot it. It left more or less of a longing for another republic larger and more endurable. That longing we have seen realized in our own day; it is realized in the present republic of France. M. Grévy, the first president of the new republic, in 1879, in publicly giving its history, turned to the surviving Huguenots and used these words: "The Huguenot church is the mother of modern democracy." That was a tribute to Calvinism. M. Grévy might have enlarged; he might have particularized; he might have pointed to the new system of public education which is the corner-stone of the French republic, and have given *the Huguenots* credit for that, for the public schools of France were instituted largely through the influence and labors of *the Huguenot* statesman, Guizot.

I cannot relate here in detail the persecutions to which *the Huguenots* were subjected during the two hundred years prior to the American Republic. If I entered into details I should have to give you ten thousand touching stories of woe, in which tender women and timid, tiny children, equally with brave-hearted men, rose to the dignity of moral heroes.

My fellow-men, there are centuries of suffering and struggle back of our liberties. They cost whole generations of self-denial and patience and fortitude and sore experience. A people cannot rise from serfage to best sovereignty in a day; the training of generations cannot be fire-cast at will.

The persecutions of the fathers whom we honor to-night began by a prohibition of the assembly of their General Synod, which was nothing less than the congress of a religious republic where the thinking men of *the Huguenots* were trained to free thought and equal rights and the principles of representation and the exercise of religious freedom. When these things are put into a man's religion they will soon find their way out into a man's politics. Civil liberty and religious liberty are inseparable. Hence the French Jesuits raised the cry, "Crush these things out of the religion of *the Huguenots!* Crush out *the Huguenots* themselves!"

No Huguenot synod was allowed to assemble for two hundred years. Before they could meet Napoleon III. had to fall and the present French republic had to be established. To-day that synod does meet, and it legislates for one million Huguenots.

The persecutions which followed the hostile cry of the Jesuits culminated in three marked historical events: the massacre of St. Bartholomew in the reign of Charles IX., 1572; the siege and demolition of the republic of La Rochelle under Cardinal Richelieu in the reign of Louis XIII., 1628; and the revocation of the Edict of Nantes in the reign of Louis XIV., 1685. I can speak now only of the first and last of these.

The massacre of St. Bartholomew was ordered by Charles IX., who was the tool of others. It was radical, cowardly, and cunning. It meant the extermination of *the Huguenot* cause, root and branch. It equaled the atrocities of Nero and Caligula. It was the slaughter of the unsuspecting and unarmed. The streets of Paris ran blood. Seventy thousand of the purest characters of the land were butchered in cold blood. Protestants everywhere were horrified. John Knox delivered this philippic to the French ambassador to Britain: " Go tell your master that God's vengeance will never depart from him nor from his house. His name shall remain an execration to posterity, and no heir of his shall enjoy the kingdom in peace." That sounds like a message from one of the old Hebrew prophets. But it was literally fulfilled. Charles died heirless and in an agony of remorse and despair, with the thought of the massacre tormenting him and setting his soul on fire with the fire of hell. This festival of blood was looked upon as a grand triumph by the head of the papacy. He issued a medal to celebrate it, and had all the bells of Rome ring a Jubilate. Was that the true spirit of Rome? If so, then I ask, has Rome changed? If so, in what respect? In nature or simply in manner? In purpose or merely in policy? Has it repudiated its old self? Where? When? How? History is terribly against it, and we have a right to demand the unquestionable evidence of a change. When that massacre was celebrated Rome had crowns at her feet. Now, to-day, there is not a single sovereign in her councils. The nations have changed; has Rome changed?

The revocation of the Edict of Nantes by Louis XIV. came later, and as a piece of diabolism it equaled the massacre. It was preceded by such acts as these: a decree that a Protestant boy of fourteen and a girl of twelve might lawfully renounce the faith of their parents; finally the age of conversion was fixed at seven. A child that could be coaxed to say Ave Maria was instantly claimed as a Catholic, and taken from its home and placed in the schools in the hands of the priests to be brought up as such. That was a direct strike at the family. That was the parochial school grown ripe. Preaching was forbidden; the singing of psalms was forbidden. Catholics owing Protestants were given three years' extension. Protestant seamstresses were forbidden to work for themselves, and thus left to the mercy of Catholic employers. Decrees were issued which took away the trades and the professions and the means of a livelihood from all Protestants. Then came the thunderbolt of revocation, which left no hope for a single Huguenot in all France. The churches were closed and leveled to the ground. The pastors were given just fifteen days to clear the country. Then followed the Inquisition, the breaking of human bodies on the wheel, imprisonment, servitude in the galleys, nameless and shameless indignities, banishment, and death by the thousands. I hear you cry, "Tell us no more of this; is there no divine Providence?" Yes, there is a divine Providence. Divine Providence is seen in this: this inhumanity was the seed that grew the French Revolution, which shed the blood of the Church of Rome in the domain of France as though it had been so much water. Catholic France paid for all this in the horrors of the French Revolution. She sowed the wind, she reaped the whirlwind.

The romance of Providence is seen on other lines,

which turned these very events against Rome and made them issue in the upbuilding of Protestantism, which they were intended to destroy. Huguenot fugitives by the thousands flocked to Protestant Holland and Protestant Prussia and Protestant England, and built up these Protestant powers, transferring to them the industries and trades and professions which hitherto had made France great. Follow these refugees in England, for example; you will find their descendants in the very foremost families of that great nation. Some of them married into the nobility. There is Huguenot blood coursing even in the veins of Victoria, the Queen of England. As her offspring married into the royal family of Germany, there is Huguenot blood in the emperor of that great kingdom. If you will follow little Brandenburg of Prussia, which opened its gates to *the Huguenot* exiles, and if you will mark what the exiles did for it, and then what part it played in bringing into existence the present German empire, the great Protestant force of the European continent, you will find a very romance of Providence, and will see how France, by issuing the decree of the revocation of the Edict of Nantes, was casting the guns that did such dread execution in her humiliation during the late Franco-Prussian War.

But I must get closer to the American Republic. This cruel treatment of *the Huguenots* in their native land has a direct relation to it. These antecedent events in the lands across the seas were nothing less than the penning of the first words of the American Declaration of Independence. They were the far-off drum-beat of the American Revolution. They were the making and the drilling of the coming American soldiers, patriots, and statesmen. Out of these crucial fires came the sires, and from the sires came the sons who were the men of Lexington and of Yorktown.

Do you inquire of me how *the Huguenots* served the American Republic and helped in its upbuilding? I answer, they did this in a twofold way:

First, *they served America abroad and by anticipation.*

Second, *they served America on American soil.*

In speaking of the service which *the Huguenots* rendered to the American Republic abroad and by anticipation I shall confine myself to one line, viz., the line of service which they rendered through and by means of England. The American Republic came directly and largely from England. Because England was Protestant we are Protestant. If our liberties came from Protestantism, then the power that worked to make England Protestant served us. The refugee Huguenots were that power. They served us abroad by serving England. They helped to make Protestant England, which made America Protestant.

Let me give you two incidents illustrative of the way the Huguenots served England.

The first incident is the conflict between James II. and William, Prince of Orange—William III. If James succeeds, England will be Catholic; if William succeeds, England will be Protestant. The fate of Protestantism is trembling in the balance. The little army that invades England under William III. wins the day, and that little army has as its backbone the Huguenot refugees. Michelet, the great historian, says, " Amid the chilling delays on the part of the British people the army of William remained firm, and it was the Calvinistic element in it, the Calvinistic Huguenots, that made it firm." There stood men who had lost their all on earth, who had no hearth but the ground. They were overshadowed now by the flag of Orange, which was the symbol of their principles, and they would have died over and over again rather than give way to James. Around that little army rallied the Protestant force of Britain, and the royal power slipped from the grip of Romanism. James fled to France. But the struggle was not over. Louis XIV. of France, who issued the revocation of the Edict of Nantes, received James. He was mortified to think that his own refugees were the soul of this defeat. He determined to retrieve it. He fitted up an army and put James at the head of it. This army invaded Britain. It landed in the north of Ireland. There another battle was fought, the battle of the Boyne, and James was again and finally defeated. Who won that battle, the famous battle of the Boyne, which carried in it so much of the future and gave to Protestantism the possession of the British throne? A Huguenot. It was the Huguenot Schronberg who commanded the Protestant forces that day, and although he fell in the battle, he left the kingdom in the hands of William III. Thus it pleased the God of battles to use the persecuted and dispersed and downtrodden *French refugees* to turn the helm of the mightiest matters of destiny and to share in the glory of His providence over nations and over the march of truth.

England is now ready to bring its Protestantism with its republican principles over to the New World. This it does. And it here has another battle with Romanism. It has to meet the same foe that it met by the river Boyne, viz., the foe who persecuted the Huguenots. Rome determined to have this New World, and so through Spain it took possession of South America, and through France it took possession of North America. As far back as the landing of the Pilgrim fathers at Plymouth Rock Cardinal Richelieu founded New France in North America. He made this law: "Everybody settling in New France must be a Catholic." None of the hated Huguenots were to be allowed to enter. This was done to checkmate Protestant England. The English and French met at Quebec and fought out the question, To whom shall America belong? In the great battle of Quebec Montcalm led the French, General Wolfe led the English. Montcalm fought for the old régime, Wolfe for the House of Commons; Montcalm fought for allegiance to king and priest, Wolfe for the habeas corpus and free inquiry; Montcalm fought for the past, Wolfe for the future; Montcalm fought for Louis XV., Wolfe for George Washington and Abraham Lincoln. Although both men were killed in that battle, Montcalm lost and Wolfe won. With the triumph of Wolfe commenced the history of the United States.

France should have won that battle; she should have held America for Rome. She had the advantage. She had Quebec as her Gibraltar and she had a chain of forts from Quebec through the heart of the country down through the Mississippi valley to the very city of New Orleans. She had also allies in many tribes of Indians whom she converted to Catholicism. She might have won that battle, and she would have won that battle, if —and the Huguenots were in that "if"—if she had only used the forces against England which she used in persecuting and driving out *the Huguenots* from the home land. One historian says that the persecution of *the Huguenots* in France called from America, the important center of conflict, the forces that would inevitably have torn from the American Protestants the fair heritage they now have. My fellow-men, we gained our heritage at no less a price than the martyrdom of *the Huguenots*. They served America by occupying and keeping away the forces of France which would have crushed America.

I am ready now to speak of the service which *the Huguenots* rendered the American Republic on American soil.

The difficulty in tracing *the Huguenots* in direct American history comes from this: Often they changed their names into the language of the countries to which they fled, and ever after were known by their translated names; and often they married and intermarried with the peoples of these countries. An example or two of the way they changed their names will show what I mean. M. Le Blanc, if he fled into Holland, changed his name into the Dutch and became known as Mr. Dewitt; or if he went into England he changed his name into Mr. White. M. Letellier became Mr. Tailor. M. Le Roy became Mr. King.

Coming over from Holland with Dutch names, and from England with English names, it is hard to distinguish *the Huguenots* from the Dutch or from the English. The interblending of races is always destructive of genealogy. In all of the makers of America which I have discussed up to this point in this course of Forefathers' addresses there have been veins of Huguenot blood. Since I wrote the Scotch Forefathers' address I have come across the annals of the province of Ulster, and have found that two or three thousand Huguenot refugees cast in their lot with the Scotch of Ulster and became part and parcel of that people, and thus came to America in the exodus from Ulster. We know that there were Huguenots in the exodus of Hollanders who founded the New Netherlands. Peter Minuit, the first governor of that colony where New York now stands, was probably one of them, as his name shows. The first child born in the New Netherlands was a Huguenot child. Peter Stuyvesant, who ruled old New York, was married to a Huguenot.

Take the colony which has always been supposed to be the purest of all—that is, the purest from an English standpoint—the Plymouth Colony, which came over in the *Mayflower*. There was Huguenot blood in that! The most beautiful woman who sailed in the *Mayflower* was a Huguenot—she who turned the head of Miles Standish and won the heart of John Alden, and who to-day, as she walks the pages of Longfellow, captivates every man in America. She is our model for wife and mother. She is the ideal of our young men for their sister, and their ideal also for some other body's sister. I mean Priscilla Mullens. She was the daughter of the Huguenot, William Molines, a passenger on the *Mayflower*, whose name was corrupted by the clumsy lips of the Nottinghamshire and Yorkshire yeomen from Molines into plain, homely Mullens. We always supposed that the beautiful Priscilla was an English Puritan maiden, and yet she has been a puzzle to us as an English Puritan girl. I never saw an English Puritan girl quite as chipper, nor one who played her cards as Priscilla played hers. English Puritan girls as a rule are sedate, and fairly stiff and cold with propriety when being courted. They always wait until they are asked out and out before they say "Yes." They do not even give themselves away by a single blush. A fellow-townsman, Horace Graves, in a bright and interesting article in the December number of the " New England Magazine," 1894, is our teacher here. I quote from his article, not verbatim, but from memory: "It has always been a source of wonder to us men that an English Puritan girl could have had the ready wit to give John Alden 'the tip' that released him from his ambiguous wooing and herself from the domination of Miles Standish, the widower, the fierce little captain who had killed and buried one good woman already. How blind we have been to the Gallic coquetry of Priscilla, which belonged to her national blood—a coquetry which could hold on to old Miles until she had secured young John! I tell you, young men and old men who so much admire Priscilla, she was a worthy progenitor of the American girl, who knows how to take care of herself."

While *the Huguenots* came to our land through intermarriage with other people, and with changed names and incognito, they came not in that way only; they came as Huguenots, with their own names and with their national blood unmixed. It was the pure Huguenots who founded such colonies as the colony of Oxford, Mass., the place where the city of Worcester now stands; and the colony of New Rochelle, off Long Island Sound; and the colony of New Paltz, Ulster County, N. Y., between the Catskills and the Shawangunk Mountains. Charles II. sent a colony to South Carolina, where afterward there came sixteen thousand Huguenots. William III. sent a colony to Virginia, which settled near the James River. Thousands of *the Huguenots* came to the city of New York. Long Island was first settled by them. Bedloe's Island, which holds the Bartholdi statue, the gift of the French Republic to the American Republic, was owned by and named after one of *the Huguenots*. They did not care to perpetuate their nationality here, and being of a social nature, they allowed themselves to be absorbed into the population of the Republic. But they made their mark, and made it indelibly.

For, as John Fiske says, "In determining the character of a community one hundred selected men and women are more potent than a thousand men and women taken at random."

Nowhere is their influence brought out better than in an article by Henry Cabot Lodge entitled "The Distribution of Ability in America." This article is modeled after an article which appeared in the "Nineteenth Century," called "The Distribution of Ability in England." Henry Cabot Lodge gets the facts upon which he bases his tabulation from Appleton's "Encyclopedia of Biography," a six-volume work. In this article you can see at a glance the men who fought the battles of the country, governed the country, produced the literature and art and science of the country, built up its industries, gave it its inventions, and made its history. He groups them by States and then he groups them by races. The race rate runs in this order, and it grades the races: the English, the Scotch-Irish, the German, *the Huguenots*, the Scotch pure and simple, and the Dutch. Lodge says, "I believe that, in proportion to their numbers, *the Huguenots* produced and gave to the American Republic more men of ability than any other race." He contrasts them with the Germans, whom they outstrip in the production of fine American personalities, and he explains the reason of the difference. The Germans settled in communities and separated themselves from the outside world. *The Huguenots* at once merged themselves into the body of the people and became thoroughly Americanized. From all this he draws this wholesome moral: "The people who succeed in our Republic are the people who become most grandly and quickly and thoroughly American." This should be so! Make it so! Keep it so!

When we come to the great Revolutionary struggle *the Huguenots* grandly hold their own and do their part. Faneuil Hall played a part in the American Revolution. It was called "the cradle of liberty." Its four walls have heard the advocacy of every great cause pertaining to the upbuilding of America. Faneuil Hall was the gift of a Huguenot and bears his name. I called it the proudest day of my life when I first spoke in Faneuil Hall with Phillips Brooks and the governor of Massachusetts, and from that platform looked at the pictured faces of Faneuil and Webster and Adams and Hancock and Phillips and a score of others like them. The thought that my voice was echoing where their voices once echoed, and that I pleaded a cause which they would have pleaded had they been here, almost overpowered me with reverence. I said to myself, "This is honor enough for a lifetime." I wish I had time to tell you the story of the gift of that hall and relate the grand patriotic uses to which it has been put. There is no quainter story in our annals, and no story that has greater national thrill. Just as the holy temple stood in Jerusalem, a witness for God, a monitor to the conscience of man, a talking embodiment of all that was grand in the Hebrew's past, so Faneuil Hall stands in our Republic, great with the greatness of the grand men who have consecrated its platform, and strong with the strength of the magnificent and triumphant causes which have been advocated within its walls, and living with the intense life which comes from the moral and intellectual and spiritual electricity which has been stored up in every brick and timber of its historic structure. Faneuil Hall stands in Boston, the old city of the American Revolution, a constant rebuke to all that is low and degrading in national life, and a constant inspiration to every brilliant conception in the American mind that makes for patriotism.

Among the forces that worked in creating our Republic was the Colonial Congress. It issued the Declaration of Independence, and it educated the people into the acceptance of that Declaration of this Congress. William Pitt in Parliament said, "I have read Thucydides and have studied and admired the master states of the world, but I must declare that for solidity, force, sagacity, and wisdom of conclusion under difficult circumstances, no nation or body of men stands in advance of the

General Congress of Philadelphia. All attempts to impose despotism upon such men will be vain. We shall be forced ultimately to retract. Let us retract while we can, not when we must." Of this body, thus eulogized by the foremost statesman of Europe, a Huguenot was the first president. Out of its seven presidents no less than three were Huguenots—Henry Laurens, John Jay, and Elias Boudinot.

Henry Laurens was born in Charleston, S. C. He was an American patriot from conviction. When solicited by his friends not to take part in the American conflict he replied, "I am determined to stand or fall with my country." Besides being president of Congress he was chosen minister to Holland to represent the colonies. On his way to Holland he was captured by the British and imprisoned in the Tower of London. While there he was offered his freedom if he would give up the American cause. To this he replied, with the old heroism, "I will never thus tarnish my name with infamy, nor disgrace my family." He was one of the four Americans who drew up and signed the treaty of peace in Paris which secured for the thirteen colonies their independence and placed them among the nations of the world. The distinguished four who secured this treaty were Franklin, Adams, Jay, and Laurens; and Jay and Laurens, the peers of Franklin and Adams, were Huguenots.

No name in American history has greater prominence and honor than the name of John Jay, the first chief justice of the nation, and president of the Continental Congress, and president of the American Bible Society, and president of the earliest society for the emancipation of the slaves, and signer of the treaty of peace which brought the Revolutionary War to a successful finale.

To the names of Laurens and Jay and Boudinot must be added those of Gabriel Mannigault, who advanced large loans to the colonial government and kept it from bankruptcy, and Francis Marion, who was a noted general in the Revolutionary army. Both of these were Huguenots. We must add also the name of Alexander Hamilton, who was a Huguenot on his mother's side. Of Hamilton John Fiske writes, " Of all the young men of that day, save, perhaps, William Pitt, the most precocious was Alexander Hamilton. So great was his genius for organization that in many essential respects the American government is moving today along the lines which he was the first to mark out. In the financial department he has been equaled by no other American statesman save Albert Gallatin." But who was Albert Gallatin, the peer of Hamilton? He was another Huguenot, and the Secretary of the Treasury during Washington's administration.

I could make this address an address of nothing

but noted Huguenot names, so many are the eminent Huguenots in our American life. Theirs are names such as these: the Bowdoins, who gave us Bowdoin College; the Gallaudet, who pioneered in the education of the deaf and dumb; Christopher Robert, the New York merchant who built the college bearing his name at Constantinople; the Bayards, the Marquands, the Higginses, the Vassars, the Durands, the Bethunes, the Vincents, the Ballous, the De Lanceys, the Edwardses; the martyred President Garfield; and hundreds of other names with an equal luster.

But I am speaking now of Revolutionary times and must confine myself to these. In the great cause of the American Revolution *the Huguenot* patriots were in it from alpha to omicron and from omicron to omega. They played a conspicuous part both at the beginning of it and at the middle of it and at the close of it. At the very beginning of the American Revolution it was Paul Revere, the son of a Huguenot refugee, who took that famous ride from Boston to Concord and waked up the farmers and townspeople, and warned them that the British were coming to seize the stores which they had gathered and locked away in view of possible war emergencies. The British came, the battle of Lexington, the first battle of the Revolutionary War, was fought, and the American farmers won. That midnight cry of Paul Revere, *the Huguenot*, awoke the American people to a conflict the result of which was the birth of this great Republic.

At the middle of the Revolution it was a force of Huguenots, with the Scotch from North Carolina, under Colonel William Campbell from Virginia, which won the strategic battle of Kings Mountain, the turning event of the Revolutionary contest in the South.

At the very close of the American Revolution it was the son of a Huguenot who drew up the stipulations for the surrender of Yorktown. Yorktown was the grand end. This Huguenot was John Laurens, the son of the first president of the Colonial Congress. As an officer in the American army he took one of the strong redoubts of Yorktown, while Rochambeau took a second and Alexander Hamilton took a third. With these redoubts taken there was nothing for the British general, Cornwallis, to do but to surrender. To young Laurens, a bright lawyer, Washington assigned the task of drawing up the articles of surrender, and these Cornwallis signed and was made a prisoner of war. The romance in this surrender was this: At the time young Laurens was drawing up these articles his father, Henry Laurens, was still a prisoner of war in the Tower of London. Young Laurens was making Cornwallis a prisoner, and by this he was not only serving his country, but he was serving in a most signal way his imprisoned father. For when the time came to exchange the prisoners of war Cornwallis was exchanged for Henry Laurens, and Henry Laurens, bidding farewell to the Tower of London, went direct to Paris, that there, with Franklin and Adams and Jay, he might sign the treaty of peace and thus make the American Republic a fact for all time.

Such were *the Huguenots:* a people with an open Bible; who fostered popular education; who fought absolutism in all forms, civil and ecclesiastical, wherever found; who loved a large-thoughted, republican church; and who were willing to pay a great price for a great thing; who paid their all for liberty. They were a great people because they companionated with a great God. Well may we pray the prayer taught us concerning them by that sweet daughter of the Huguenots, Mrs. Sigourney:

> " On all who bear
> Their name or lineage may their mantle rest:
> That firmness for the truth, that calm content
> With simple pleasures, that unswerving trust in
> Trial, adversity, and death, which cast
> Such healthful leaven 'mid the elements
> That peopled the New World."

As we leave the study of this evening we do so with this conviction: that it is men who make the nation. They constitute its wealth; they carry in them its strength; they determine its future. Men

—men of ideas, men of faith, men of hope, men of pure loves and of pure lives, men of sacrifice, men of conscience, men who love their country, men who walk day by day with their hand in God's—these are they who have made us strong as a Republic and who keep us strong. It is men who make the nation.

"Ouida," in one of her stories, entitled "A Dog of Flanders"—a story which for beauty and pathos and pureness is excelled nowhere—puts this thought in a fine way. She illustrates the thought by showing how Rubens made Antwerp, with its sweet-toned, ringing bells. She writes: "The greatness of the mighty master rests upon Antwerp, and wherever one turns in its narrow streets his glory lies therein and transfigures every mean thing. This city, which is the tomb of Rubens, still lives to us through him and him alone. Without Rubens what were Antwerp? A muddy, dusky, bustling mart which no man would ever care to look upon save the traders who do business upon its wharfs. With Rubens, to the whole world of man it is a sacred name, a sacred soil—a Bethlehem where a god of art saw light, a Golgotha where a god of art lies dead." Having said this, she turns to the world and says, "O nations! closely should you treasure your great men, for by them alone will the future know of you."

What America needs above all things to-day is

this: a new consecration to that manhood and that womanhood which in the beginning made this Republic. It needs and it should earnestly seek the reproduction of the civil fathers. It should seek for sons and daughters who will write their names with the pen of holy deeds side by side with the names of *the Virginians* and *the Pilgrims* and *the Puritans* and *the Hollanders* and *the descendants of John Knox* and *the Huguenots.*

VII.

THE QUAKERS; OR, IDEAL CIVILIZATION.

VII.

THE QUAKERS; OR, IDEAL CIVILIZATION.

WE are apt to think of the Quakers as a people of peculiarities; they are before our mind as men and women of broad-brimmed hats and poke-bonnets, drab coats and gray dresses—a curious people of slow movements; a demure people, who are the victims of their own virtues. They *are* a peculiar people, but behind every Quaker peculiarity there is a consistent reason. The Quakers are more than an embodiment of oddities; they are an embodiment of great principles and an incarnation of a grand life. Both their principles and life have entered into the bone and sinew of our Republic, and both are still necessary for the realization of ultimate America. The reproduction of their spirit and purpose by American citizens will make real, by and by, our " manifest destiny."

We wish to look at this destiny as it exists in germ form in the souls of our Quaker ancestors. There is nothing more interesting or inspiring or profitable than the experience of those great souls who have helped to lead the nations up the heights of civilization and into the advances of civic life; who have led the human race nearer to God and into genuine and abiding liberty. The Quakers had such souls. Such souls looked out of the clear and striking faces of George Fox and William Penn, Elizabeth Fry and Lucretia Mott. Around the lives of such heroes and heroines the history of the world has turned as on an axis. They have helped to direct the main currents of human thought in the right direction. You call them single souls, but they have multiplied themselves into myriad souls; they have become a people. There is no getting away from the true man and the true woman, from the single soul, if you would get at the origin and history of great movements. The tendency of scientific study in our time has perhaps led us to undervalue the influence of great souls. History has been believed to advance according to definite laws over which neither human genius nor human freedom has exerted any appreciable influence. Mr. Buckle explains national character as the result of circumstances, and he claims that history and biography are wholly different in their sphere; yet the fact remains that *persons* are the ruling centers in history. Take such personalities as Augustine and Luther and Fox and Penn out of history and the course of history ceases to be intelligible. Because this is so, we emphasize in this course of study the names of the great men who stand chief among the races and peoples who form the constituents of our Republic, and we exalt their principles, which form the bone and sinew of American manhood.

We are digging up the past for the instruction and encouragement of the present. In this we are acting according to the spirit of the times. This is an age when there is a craze for digging up the past and making it a study and a story. After eighteen hundred years Pompeii has been excavated; the skeleton of its soldier in his rusty corselet, dug from its ashes after well-nigh two thousand years of silent guard-keeping, is made an inspiration and an example to courage and fidelity. Long centuries of oblivion have rested over Egypt and Troy and Assyria and the famous city of Agamemnon; but now Professor Sayce and Mariette Bey read the stones of the Egyptian dynasties found in the walls of the uncovered temples; Layard and George Smith bring us tablets from the libraries of Nineveh; and Dr. Schliemann gives us the gold bracelet of Hecuba and the necklace of Clytemnestra. We are doing in history what these men are doing in archæology : we are making the past speak. We have dug up the Virginians and the Pilgrims and the Puritans and the Hollanders and the Scotch and the Huguenots, and now we propose to dig up the Quakers.

The Quakers, when seen at their best, stand in American history for ideal civilization; and this civilization is their contribution to the American Republic. As historic characters the Quakers are a marked and influential people in the midst of the most marked and influential types of mankind. They have put their stamp indelibly on national and international life. If we enter into the courts of justice we can see that they have been there: the substitution of affirmation in place of the oath is their work. The jails of humanity show the results of their reform: it was they who changed our prisons from sties to sanatoriums. The dream of that beautiful prison angel, Elizabeth Fry, is being worked out into reality in criminal law, and the remedial element in punishment is being pushed to the forefront in the administration of justice. They have put their mark even on the pages of our Holy Bible and have made it a book of greater power. They have taken some of its grandest prophecies and statements and commands and beatitudes, and by believing them, living them, translating them into reigning forces in the home and in the church and in the state, they have so made these their own that in reading the Book we instinctively associate their names with these Scriptures. You readily recall the Scriptures to which I refer: "And He shall judge between the nations, and shall decide concerning many peoples:

and they shall beat their swords into plowshares, and their spears into pruning-hooks: nation shall not lift up sword against nation, neither shall they learn war any more" (Isa. ii. 4). Whenever we read that we say, "That is the Quaker's prophecy," and it is. "Dearly beloved, avenge not yourselves, but rather give place unto wrath: for it is written, Vengeance is mine; I will repay, saith the Lord. Therefore if thine enemy hunger, feed him; if he thirst, give him drink: for in so doing thou shalt heap coals of fire on his head. Be not overcome of evil, but overcome evil with good" (Rom. xii. 19-21). When we read that we say, "That is the Quaker's gospel," and it is. "Holy men of God spake as they were moved by the Holy Ghost" (2 Pet. i. 21). When we read that we say, "That is the Quaker's rule of speaking when dealing with truth," and it is. "Blessed are the peacemakers: for they shall be called the children of God." When we read that we say, "That is the Quaker's beatitude," and it is. "That was the true Light, which lighteth every man that cometh into the world." When we read that we say, "That is the Quaker's text of texts; that is the Bible's statement of their great cardinal fact and doctrine, which they call the *inner light*," and it is. By the incarnation of these grand parts of the divine Book, the Quakers have made the Bible a new and a fresh power in human life.

The Quakers arose in an age of dogmas and

creeds and persecutions and reforms and religious revolutions and quarreling ecclesiastics. They took their place among the ranks of reformers and were the most advanced of all. Their reforms were the most sweeping of all. They were the liberals and radicals of that age; they were the reformers of the reformed; they undertook to reform Calvin and Luther and Knox. The Episcopalians and Puritans and Presbyterians protested against the Romanists, but the Quakers protested against the Episcopalians and Puritans and Presbyterians. In the language of Milton, to them "*presbyter* was only old *priest* writ large." The Quakers were the Episcopalians and Puritans and Presbyterians of the seventeenth century, sweetened and modified and made over with a new and a large admixture of love. They denied all ecclesiastical authority and threw aside all the prevailing ecclesiastical rites; they went to God directly for their instructions, and worshiped before God in stillness and silence without prescribed forms. As the complement of *a state without a king*, they offered mankind *a church without a bishop*. Their aim was to humanize Christianity and substitute a gospel of hope for a gospel of despair. Sweeping aside creeds and councils and rituals and synods, they held that God and the individual man, living in loving fellowship, were sufficient. They simplified things in a wholesale way and struck for an all-round liberty. This was Americanism before its day; this was Americanism out-Americanized.

They were a people of great moral purpose. Their ideals were their inspiration, and the realization of these ideals was their goal. They got their strength from ideals and convictions and visions of which the senses take no cognizance. James Freeman Clarke calls them the "English mystics." If they were mystics they were exceedingly practical mystics. They were one of the most independent people among all the races. They differed from all the sects around them in that they renounced the use of all force in the propagation of their principles. They inculcated and practised religious toleration. They have the honor of being one of the few divisions of Christendom against which the charges of cruelty and selfishness and love of power cannot be brought. Their gun was a protest, their bullet a principle, and their powder the inner light. They served the church and state by what they were. Their method of pushing their faith was *to be* what they believed and then assert themselves. They exalted the passive virtues. This was the method of Jesus Christ. All which Jesus ever did in this world was to assert Himself and suffer. When violence was used against them their principle of action was, *Never retaliate*. Their method of growth was by patience and perseverance and quiet suffering, and their method was effective.

For example, they carried their religion into the Massachusetts Colony and planted it right in the midst of the hard-headed Puritans. The Puritans persecuted them, whipped them, robbed them, hung them, but they kept right on asserting themselves and suffering until by their patience they wore out the cruelty of the Puritans and brought the Puritan scourge and scaffold into public disgrace. The public, won over to them by their beautiful spirit, rose and demanded the cessation of persecution. Thus they purchased and established for us by their sufferings the religious toleration which now exists in our Republic. They served America by patiently suffering. Their martyrdom was like the martyrdom of the church of the catacombs, of which history tells us in thrilling words. The church of the catacombs was the kingdom of God in sackcloth, working underground, along channels and galleries of rock, to overthrow and replace the armed empires above. The Quakers were content to be in the minority on every great question until by self-assertion and honest argument and right living they could win men enough to their side to make them the majority.

In the first days their ways and principles spelled *anarchy*, but by the slow education of centuries, and by the beneficial changes which they wrought, they now spell *righteousness, peace, love*.

You see, I am giving the bright and beautiful

side of the Quaker story: I am telling what they contributed by way of strength and glory; I am speaking of them as *the children of the light,* shining with the celestial beauty of a Christ-like spirit.

In telling the story of the Quakers, there is only one starting-point: we must start with George Fox. He is to Quakerism what Christ is to Christianity, its incarnation. In him we find the traits and principles and hopes and methods and life of Quakers at their best. He represents the heroic age of the Quakers. He gave Quakerism as a life and started it out on its thrilling career to march through England and Holland and America. This has been the order and growth of Quakerism: George Fox gave the world a Quaker life. Robert Barclay took the doctrines and principles and purposes out of which that Quaker life was constructed and built these into a terse, clear, logical Quaker system. It was necessary to build such a theological system for the purpose of defense under attack and misrepresentation, and as a fair treatment of the public. This formulated Quaker system Edward Burroughs took and carried out to the world and expounded and preached, and by the conversions which he made built it up into a Quaker society. Then came William Penn and took the life of Fox, and the system of Barclay, and the converts of Burroughs, and built all into a Quaker commonwealth, which gave Quakers the civil embodiment of their cherished ideals, and which gave America the powerful colony of Pennsylvania, a bulwark in the defense of freedom. After this came John Greenleaf Whittier, who took the commonwealth and the converts and the system and the life, and beautified all. With chiseled words and sculptured cadences he built Quakerism into a cathedral-like poem of liberty, full of reverence for God, and of appreciation of man, and of praise for the truth.

George Fox, who was the spiritual father of the Quakers, was born in 1624. This makes him a child of the seventeenth century. Did he rise to power in that century? Was he so endowed and did he so assert himself as to make for himself an immortal name among immortal men? If so, he was a man among men. That was a wonderful century and brought forth wonderful products. It was a century when every weakling was relegated to obscurity; for George Fox to make his mark in that century is all the evidence required to prove him a great man. This was the century of great religious wars; this was the century of great books and measures and men. If you except the Bible, the most democratic books ever published were published in this century. Cervantes published "Don Quixote," which set all the world laughing at sham aristocracies and mock heroisms; that book helped to turn away the human mind from the worship of the false and artificial. Shakespeare's dramas were published then; his works tended toward human equality; they made kings and queens only men and women like their subjects. Bacon's works were published then; these taught men to feel it not only their right, but their duty, to look with eyes undimmed by a church creed at all things which the Lord had created. Bacon's works made it possible for Newton to open the heavens, Watt the air, Lyell the earth, and Darwin animal life. "The Pilgrim's Progress" was published in that century; so was " Paradise Lost," so was Baxter's "Saint's Rest," and so was the Authorized Version of the Bible, which gave the Book to the common people. The Book is the ever-enduring Magna Charta of civil and religious liberty. This was the century of the Westminster divines, with their Catechism and Confession of Faith. This was the century of Cromwell's guns. Can George Fox rise in this century? Can he in this century found a sect which shall live and prevail and modify society, and add freedom to freedom, and inaugurate reforms which, when carried out, will realize the ideal civilization? Can he lead in the strike for independence in an age when the whole trend of things is toward independence? He does.

We get the story of the life of George Fox from his own journal. His whole life is here, from the cradle to the grave; not only are his outward acts here, his motives are here, his soul, his inner life.

From boyhood he was distinguished for great purity of thought and act, and for modesty and sweetness of disposition. He was large of body and large of soul. He was first awakened to life in earnest by the shams and inconsistencies of professed church-members. What he saw in them raised questions like these in his mind: If these are the legitimate product of religion, have men got the true religion? Do they understand the way to God? Have they the true rule of life? Are the churches what they ought to be? Is civilization the true representative of the mind of Christ? He sought the leaders of the churches and asked them for light, but from them he found no light. Then he separated himself from men and gave himself to the study of the Bible until he became filled and saturated with its teachings. After this he gave himself up to solitary contemplation and deep thought and silent waiting for the voice of God. Here he found light, for the voice of God spoke to him, and he became God-filled and God-guided— one of God's prophets. God will fill any man and guide any man if he will only do what George Fox did. God will re-give by the voice of His Spirit the truths of the Bible to any man who is saturated with the Bible as George Fox was, and who will prayerfully and patiently and silently wait for that voice. He has done this for men in every branch of the Christian church.

Thomas Carlyle helps us to estimate George Fox aright; he corrects Macaulay's estimate of him. Spurgeon says Macaulay was so warped by prejudice that his measurement of George Fox was altogether inaccurate. Carlyle's words are: "The most remarkable incident in modern history is not the Diet of Worms, still less the battle of Austerlitz, Waterloo, Peterloo, or any other battle, but George Fox making himself a suit of leather. This man, the first of the Quakers, was one of those in whom the divine idea is pleased to manifest itself and, across all the hills of ignorance, shine in awful and unspeakable beauty. He is a highly accredited prophet of God."

Two incidents in the life of George Fox let us into a large knowledge of the man; they are an epitome of the man; they interpret the man. The first incident took place in a church at Nottingham on a Sabbath morning in 1649. The services were conducted according to the directory of the Westminster Assembly; the minister was a Presbyterian. Suddenly a young man stepped forth into the aisle in view of all, and unexpectedly a strong voice rang out like a battle-cry. In an instant the blood leaped to every brain; every sleeper awoke, and a thousand eager faces strained forward toward the youth. He was a tall, gaunt man with piercing eyes and long hair and a face emaciated with fasting; but the glow of his countenance lighted up as he flatly contradicted the preacher. His words were: "No; it is not the Scriptures; it is the Holy Spirit." The preacher's text was, "We have also a more sure word of prophecy; whereunto ye do well that ye take heed, as unto a light that shineth in a dark place, until the day dawn, and the day-star arise in your hearts." He had just told the people that the more sure word of prophecy mentioned in the text was the Bible. George Fox believed that the more sure word was the word which the Spirit directly speaks to the individual waiting heart; so he contradicted the preacher: "No; it is not the Scriptures; it is the Holy Spirit, who gave the Scriptures, who leads into all truth. The Jews had the Scriptures, and yet they resisted the Holy Spirit and rejected Christ. They undertook to try the apostles by the Scriptures, but they erred in judgment, because they tried them without the Spirit. When the apostles tried cases, they issued their decisions in this form: 'It seems to the Holy Ghost and to us to order thus and so.' No; it is not the Scriptures; it is the Holy Spirit." For this protest George Fox was arrested and imprisoned.

The second incident took place in the city of Lichfield, in the center of England. "On a winter day in 1651 a tall, strongly built young man, singularly handsome, of grave and dignified appearance, was seen approaching the city of Lichfield. He wore a broad-brimmed hat and a long coat of leather.

When the tall spires of the great cathedral caught his eye, he stopped, dismissed the few companions who were with him, and stood for a moment alone, silently praying. Then he moved forward again, but slowly as if deliberating, until he reached a group of shepherds keeping watch over their flocks. By the side of the shepherds he paused once more. His actions were peculiar, but on his face was an expression which awed the shepherds so that they durst not ask him any questions. Taking off his shoes, he gave them to the shepherds and resumed his march toward the city. Having entered it, he walked barefoot through the main street and market-place, crying in a strong, sweet voice, ' *Woe to the bloody city! Woe to the bloody city!* ' That man was George Fox." He knew he was risking his liberty and perhaps his life by that act, but he knew also that he was obeying his conscience and his God. He was speaking to a wicked public by the language of signs. The language of signs is ever a living language and ever a telling language. You may criticize the man for this act and you may call it a violation of good taste, but this one thing remains to be said: *Lichfield was a success.* It developed George Fox; it gave him a recognition in the world and set an example for his followers which made them effective witnesses. You might as well criticize the Hebrew prophets for putting truth in dramatic form.

Take these two incidents out of the early life of George Fox and you unmake the man. You do more than that; you take from his early followers that aggressive spirit which made them propagandists and which inspired them to fearlessness in making their public protest against tyrants and tyrannies. The Quakers were not a negative people, they were a positive people. Without the discipline of these two incidents, George Fox would never have faced Oliver Cromwell, before whom all England trembled, and have talked to him as he did. Cromwell felt his power; after the interview he said, "Now I see there is a people risen that I cannot win either with gifts, honors, office, or places; but all others I can win." Without his example, Quaker missionaries would not have gone to Rome as they did, to face the Roman pontiff and charge home upon him his errors; nor would they have gone to Constantinople to face the sultan and tell him that God would judge him for his barbarous inhumanities. Without his example, Edward Burroughs would not have written to Charles II., declaring to him the words of the Lord with a boldness which would have done credit to Elijah before Ahab.

We are now face to face with the question, What were the doctrines for which George Fox witnessed in his intrepid way, and which he gave to his followers, and which made them a factor in civilization? We place the doctrine of the *inner light* first; all others flow from this. The doctrine of the universal *inner light* is this: Jesus Christ lighteth every man that cometh into the world. This Spirit of Christ in every man is sufficient to guide him. This Spirit of Christ in every man is not to be confounded with conscience; the distinction is clear between the human faculties and the divine Spirit. Conscience is an original faculty of human nature; the Spirit of Christ is an added faculty. Instead of being identical with conscience, His purpose is to enlighten conscience. William Penn says, "God in Christ has placed a principle in every man to inform him of his duty and to enable him to do it." The way the *inner light* is perceived and increased is by waiting in silence for it before God and by meditation. The more it is honored and rightly used the more and brighter it shines. The *inner light* tells on the whole man; it illumines and quickens the mental and spiritual faculties, and it beautifies and transfigures the form and face. It makes the face calm and clear and crystalline, a very transparency for a lighted soul. You can see what this doctrine carries in it. If God speaks to the soul, then the voice of God frees the soul from all bondage to the false opinions and prejudices and faiths of men. That is liberty indeed. If God speaks directly to every man, then every man has a distinct individuality and is an independent personality. It is out of the consciousness of this fact that democracy is born. This consciousness, when nurtured and grown, makes an American citizen of the highest type; it breaks every human shackle, it quickens and deepens the sense of personal responsibility, for it brings God into every life and makes Him the sole authority. My fellow-men, give my country a people whose supreme desire and object in life are to reach the mind of God in all things, and you give it a people in whose hands the interests of the Republic will be perfectly safe: "For where the Spirit of the Lord is, there is liberty."

The experience which George Fox had with the clergy of his day gave origin to the mode of worship which he left his followers. In the midst of his religious perplexities he sought light from the clergy, but found none. The clergy were useless to him, so he protested against hireling ministers and dispensed with their services. In his journal he says, "Being at Oxford and Cambridge does not make a man fit to be a minister of Jesus Christ." George Fox protected his people against two things —ministers and choirs. He substituted the *inner light* for the clergy, and he put his foot upon the choir and buried it out of sight. He arranged for the assembling of his followers on the Sabbath to wait for the Spirit and His message. If the Spirit gave no message, there was nothing said, and the time of the assembly was spent in golden silence. Both Charles Lamb and John G. Whittier speak the praise of these silent Sabbath services. Charles Lamb writes of the power of the stillness of the meeting: " I have seen the reeling sea-ruffian, who came with the avowed intention of disturbing the quiet, from the very spirit of the place receive in a moment a new heart, and presently sit down in peace among the Friends to let God talk to his heart." Whittier writes:

> " And so I find it well to come
> For deeper rest to this still room,
> For here the habit of the soul
> Feels less the outer world's control.
> The strength of mutual purpose pleads
> More earnestly our common needs;
> And from the silence multiplied
> By these still forms on either side,
> The world that time and sense have known
> Falls off and leaves us God alone."

George Fox had a profound sense of the length and breadth of the love which God had for mankind, and this made him the philanthropist he was. "All men are members of the family of the All-father and are brothers." In his journal he says, "I saw the infinite love of God." God's love to man inspired his love to man. To him brotherhood meant the opportunity of doing good to all men; hence he inaugurated help for the helpless, and led in prison reforms and charities, and in the organization of societies for the emancipation of all human brothers in slavery; hence he inaugurated movements looking to the abolition of the horrid and ungodly practice of brother man shooting down brother man; hence he protested against imprisonment for debt and against the infliction of capital punishment for minor crimes. From the brotherhood of man he evolved, under the teaching of the Spirit, the doctrine of human equality. He made woman the equal of man, and to establish her equality gave her her full half of the meeting-house. He argued, if men are equal, why should some be greeted with idolatrous titles, and receive obeisance from others, and be addressed in flattering pronouns? With him every brother man stood for just one, and that one was no better than his neighbor; hence he refused to doff his hat to any man, or address any man as "your Reverence," "your Holiness," "your Grace," "your Honor;" hence he called men by their Christian name, treating all alike. William Penn, following his example, addressed even King Charles II. as "Friend Charles." There was democracy in that. Hence he introduced the use of the pronouns "thee" and "thou" into conversation as a protest against caste. William Penn has built up a grammatical argument for the use of these pronouns. "Thee" and "thou" are singular pronouns; "you" is the plural pronoun. Why should any single man be addressed as though he were plural—as though he were a regiment in one? A plural pronoun used in the place of a singular pronoun is a species of flattery for the purpose of magnifying a man or a woman. Recognizing that man is the brother of man, George Fox labored to promote honesty and truthfulness between man and man. This led him to secure a fixity of price for goods in all the trades, a custom which is now established. This led to simplicity of speech in conversation. He argued for the abolition of the oath, for the reason that he would have every word uttered by man as true as an oath. That honesty and truthfulness might be made easy, he argued for an all-round simplicity of life, and protested against extravagance and waste and vanity and idle luxury and the senseless change of fashion. Such was George Fox and such were the doctrines and practices which he contributed to civilization. The man himself was one grand declaration of independence, and he was that fully one hundred years before Thomas Jefferson penned the American Declaration of Independence. He issued declaration of independence after declaration of independence, all more radical than Jefferson's. His plainness of dress was a declaration of independence from the despotism of fashion and from the extravagance of the privileged classes. His employment of the singular pronouns and of the Christian names of men was a declaration of independence from the spirit of caste. Fixity of price in traffic was a declaration of independence from the cupidity of the grasping trader. Arbitration as a method of settlement of all international disputes was a declaration of independence from the monstrous iniquity of war. The doctrine of the *inner light* was a declaration of independence from the dogmatism of sects and traditions, and from man-made and self-elected authorities. George Fox was a magnificent freeman, and he introduced into the world of thought and life that genius of liberty which was calculated to make every other man a freeman like himself.

How did these legacies which George Fox contributed to America reach America? He brought them himself. The man himself trod the very ground we to-day tread. He traveled through the American colonies for the express purpose of asserting himself and his gospel of liberty. After he had worked out his mission here he went back to England to find a grave, and there he died, saying, "*I am clear, I am clear.*" And was he not clear? What man ever left the world having done his duty more fearlessly, or having declared more completely all the counsel of God as he understood it, or having given the world grander ideals for the coming civilization?

But the principles of George Fox came to America not only in the person of George Fox himself;

they came also in the person of his many followers, who settled in all the colonies, but notably in Massachusetts and Rhode Island and Pennsylvania. In most of the colonies they had patiently to work their way into recognition. This was especially so in Massachusetts. The first thing which met the Quakers there was persecution, and that from the holy Puritans. This is one of the stains which rest on the memory of the Puritans. It is vain to try to excuse it, for it cannot be excused; it can only be admitted and apologized for. In former years I offered my service to the Puritans and made a special plea in their defense, but I now beg leave to withdraw from the case. I once uttered and published the following words: " But what have we to say concerning the Puritans' treatment of Quakers? We have this to say: that even in the harsh measures, as they dealt with these, *they were the progressives of their age*, and were the most merciful people of that century. The Quakers in that day were not the ideal people who walk the pages of our novels to-day, and with whom we instinctively fall in love. They were not Friend Olivia and Hannah Mettelane and Roger Pryor, the Quaker characters and heroes of Mrs. Amelia Barr's charming book. No; they were loud-voiced people, disturbers of the peace, denunciatory in their language, rudely behaved. Two of the women, Lydia Wardwell and Deborah

Wilson, walked the streets of Boston unclad, and tried to pass off that conduct as witnessing for God. The Puritans knew better than that, and put them behind the bars of the prison out of sight. Thomas Newhouse rushed into the Old South Church with two glass bottles in his hand, which he wildly dashed together and in pieces before the affrighted congregation, crying, 'Thus will the Lord break you all in pieces.' When the governor of the colony walked the street the Quakers used to turn and hoot at him to show their contempt for government. The Puritans would not have persecuted Quakers of the type of to-day; they would not have persecuted our poet, John G. Whittier. The Quakers have improved beyond the need of persecution. Mary Dyer was hung upon Boston Common in front of my old church, but Mrs. Dyer was hung because she wanted to be. She wanted to hang; it was her way of giving her testimony, and she refused to take no for an answer. They sent her out of the city scot-free, but she came back and acted worse than ever in order to compel the Puritans to hang her. Her hanging was a piece of pure gallantry upon the part of the Puritan gentlemen. There were four thousand Quakers imprisoned in England at one time, but only a handful were imprisoned in New England."

I have just been reading "The Pioneer Quakers" and "The Quaker Invasion of Massachusetts," two valuable books published by my friend, Richard P. Hallowell, of Boston, and I have found that the Puritans did persecute men just as pure and as sweet as John G. Whittier. They persecuted Nicholas Upshal. And they did publicly expose the sacred persons of women as right-minded as Friend Olivia and Hannah Mettelane, and without mercy cut their flesh to the bone with the cruel lash. The Puritans, who desecrated temples and destroyed the finest works of art, are not the people to condemn others for rudeness, are not the people to bore the tongues of Quakers with red-hot irons, and cut off their ears, and brand their flesh, and strip them naked and publicly scourge them, for the crime of rudeness. Mr. Hallowell shows that where the Quakers went to an extreme in giving emphasis to their protest, a reason for their extreme can be found in the effects of the cruel treatment which they antecedently received. In some cases the cruelties inflicted had unbalanced them mentally. The Quakers used no force; theirs was the strength of the martyr nature. On behalf of the Quakers I instance the letters which they wrote in their prisons, and the words which they spoke on the gallows, and the prayers which they offered for forgiveness of their murderers. I put these in the deadly parallel column with the Puritans' cruel laws and branding-irons and knotted whips and public gallows, and then leave the decision of the case to posterity.

There is this to be said for the Puritans: a popular reaction set in against persecution, and by this means Puritanism rectified itself. The reaction came from such outspoken men as the Puritan sea-captain whose story John G. Whittier forcefully relates in a poem pertaining to the dark colonial days. Cassandra Southwick, a Quaker maiden of Salem, being unable to pay a fine of ten pounds imposed upon her because she would not attend a Puritan church, was sentenced to be taken to the island of Barbadoes and sold into bondage. When the sheriff asked the captain of the ship to transport the prisoner, and put money in his pocket by acting as agent in the sale, the old sailor growled back his answer like the roar of the sea:

"Pile my ship with bars of silver, pack with coins of Spanish gold,
From keel-piece to deck-plank, the roomage of her hold.
By the living God who made me, I would rather in your bay
Sink ship and crew and cargo, than bear this child away."

It was ringing voices like that which put an interdict upon Puritan whips and irons and gallows.

The Quaker power in America reached its height in the coming of William Penn and in the establishment and life of the colony of Pennsylvania. William Penn was second only to George Fox as a Quaker influence. He came to America in the ship called *Welcome*, in 1682. The *Welcome* added another ship to the grand historic ships which proudly rode the sea of American life. One could write American history if he but told the story of the famous ships which brought the famous men of the past to our continent. What a fleet that was which sailed the American seas! The *Santa Maria*, the *Good Speed*, the *Half-moon*, the *Mayflower*, the *Swallow*, which brought the first Quakers, Ann Austin and Mary Fisher, and the *Welcome*, which brought William Penn.

The territory of Pennsylvania was given to William Penn by Charles II. in lieu of money owed his father by the crown. The land was his to do with as he wished, and he devoted it to working into life a Quaker commonwealth. There was no man better fitted to establish such a commonwealth than William Penn. He had paid a large price for the privilege of being a Quaker, and this made him a man to be trusted. He sacrificed the friendship of his home; his father said of him, "William has become a Quaker or some such melancholy thing." He had ability; he was educated at Oxford. He was democratic in spirit; his definition of a free government shows this. "Any government," he said, "is free where the people are a party to the laws enacted." He was a kindred spirit to John Bright, the Quaker statesman of Great Britain, who for a whole generation was a leading spirit in the great movements of his country, and who was always on the right side.

John Bright got his principles from William Penn. An analysis of his public life will show the Quaker principle of civil life to be this: political power is rightly exercised only when it is possessed by the consent of the governed, and is used for the welfare of the community according to the permissions of the moral law. This principle guided William Penn when he organized his colony. He gave it a constitution and laws full of the genius of humanity and full of equal justice. He allowed all reforms to be pushed within its territory. There was not one good Quaker thing which did not flourish in it. Here the Indians were treated as brothers and here they acted brotherly in return. The colony was a temperance colony; it was an anti-war colony; it was a colony noted for its religious toleration. For over one hundred years the Quakers controlled it. Its homes were full of sweetness and strength. The colony was one of the greatest powers in the American Revolution, and furnished such leaders as Logan and Mifflin and Dickinson, all of them Quakers. Benjamin West, the great painter, was born here in a Quaker home; he was one of the founders of the Royal Academy of Great Britain. The liberty of thought granted by this colony bore its products and brought the colony honor. It enabled it to grow into what it is to-day, the second State in the Union.

The colony gave the country the city of Philadelphia, the one city of the Republic which rivals

Boston in old colonial landmarks, just as in olden time it rivaled Boston in that leadership which inaugurated the American Revolution. It gave the country Independence Hall; it was the home of the Continental Congress. Here was framed and debated and publicly signed the Declaration of Independence itself, which made the American Revolution an historic fact. All this took place not on Puritan soil, but on Quaker soil, and all this took place where it did because there was more freedom of thought in Philadelphia than there was in Boston.

One thing we cannot fail to notice in this historical study, and that is the general acceptance by our Republic of the principles and practices of the Quakers as these relate to civil life. The acceptance of each of their humane measures is a victory for humanity as well as for their testimony. They have reaped triumphs all the way from the abolition of capital punishment for minor offenses to the abolition of African slavery. One victory more remains for them to win, and that is *the abolition of war and the substitution in its place of international arbitration.* That victory is already more than half won, for men everywhere in Christendom are beginning to argue on the right side. Their triumph will some day be complete, because their aim is right. It is the ultimatum of Christianity. It has on its side also the verdict of history. The progress of civilization does not ride in a powder-cart. Take England as an example: has its progress been the career of the powder-cart? Let Hugh Price Hughes, an Englishman, answer the question. He writes: "The most splendid portion of Great Britain, which is now known as the United States of America, was that great Christian commonwealth, to which the future of the world belongs, founded or built up by the army? Every one knows that, on the contrary, it was founded by the God-fearing Puritan fathers, who crossed the broad Atlantic not to erect an empire upon bloodshed, but to secure liberty of conscience, which the soldiery of the odious Stuart kings refused them at home. Our soldiers had nothing whatever to do with this the most splendid colony, except to deprive us of it. If it had not been for the despotic temper of the military party of England the American colonists would not have revolted and the United States would have been an integral part of the British empire to-day. The army of Britain will never be able to compensate us for the loss of America." That is precisely to our point; that is history; that is invincible logic.

But this is not all that is to be said relative to England. The best part of Canada is not the part which was conquered in war, which was taken by the army from France; that part is the least

Anglicized of all Canada and it is the most unstable part of the Canadian structure; it is the disturbing, perilous element. Nor is this all. England does not owe her colonies in South Africa to her army; they were won by the enterprise and energy of travelers and traders and missionaries. She does not owe her colonies in the Fiji Islands to her army and navy. Veteran missionaries deserve the credit there. They took neither gunpowder nor brandy with them; they took Bibles and the implements of industry; they took swords and spears beaten into plowshares and pruninghooks. The only place where British militarism was powerful was in India; but who can tell the hundreds of thousands of British lives and the hundreds of millions of British treasure that India has cost England? To-day the army plays a subordinate part in India. English tenure would cease to-morrow if it rested only or mainly on the sword. It rests on the justice of English rule and on the influence of the missionaries of the cross of Christ, the Prince of Peace.

The teaching which we find in English history adverse to the claims of war we find true in American history. The most of Americans, I verily believe, imagine that it was the Revolutionary War which made us a republic. Our most profound dangers only began when the Revolutionary War ceased. There was imminent danger lest the colonies should throw themselves against one another in the shock of war, and devour one another. It was the statesmanship of Franklin and Washington and Jefferson and the Adamses which made us a republic and which saved the colonies from themselves. Let any one read John Fiske's "Critical Period of American History" and he will be assured of the truth of this. What was the critical period of America's history? Fiske says it was the period which immediately followed the American Revolution. It was the triumphs won in the time of peace which made us most and made us permanently.

What we find true in England and in America we find true also in Italy. We all admire Garibaldi and praise him for what he did for Italy; but what is the story of Garibaldi? Garibaldi himself did not emancipate Italy with the sword; he was not the sole emancipator of Italy. His volunteers would have been speedily crushed by the Austrian army had not Mazzini, the Italian patriot and coworker, changed the thoughts and hearts of the people by his powerful appeals and red-hot logic. Besides this, Garibaldi's greatest victory was won without the shedding of a single drop of blood. I refer to his victory at Naples. He entered Naples unarmed and in an open carriage. When the artillerymen of the cruel despot were commanded to blow Garibaldi into the air, the great Italian rose silently and opened his red shirt to receive the deadly volley into his heart. The effect of that act was electric and irresistible. The artillerymen flung down their fuses and shouted, "Long live Garibaldi!" "Long live Italy!" That was the way Garibaldi's greatest victory was won and that was the way Naples was made free.

In the study of history I have come to the conclusion voiced by Emilio Castelar, the most eloquent and noble man of all Spain, the man who would give Spain to-day a republic worthy of the name if his country would only let him and if the military despotism were not in the way. Castelar says: "National freedom can be permanently won only by pacific means. Soldiers are as unfit to build the temple of freedom as the warrior David was to build the temple of God. Those who depend upon the sword shall perish by the sword."

In America we are far on toward the acceptance of arbitration as a substitute for war, and the great thinkers of the world are with us. Arbitration today has its laurels. The settlement of the *Alabama* claims—that is a laurel; the treaty between the United States and France, with its arbitration clause—that is a laurel; a like treaty with Switzerland—that is a laurel; the present hopeful negotiation with Great Britain for a treaty of the same import—that too is a laurel; the International Arbitration Conference, which met in our land this very year—that is a laurel. This conference issued a magnificent address to the world last June, demanding law for war in the settlement of all difficulties between nations. The clock of time is getting ready to strike the hour which the poet laureate foretells, when

"The war-drums will throb no longer, and the battle-flags be furled,
In the parliament of man, the federation of the world."

The part which the Quakers have taken in building the American Republic makes clear this twofold way in which patriots can effectively serve their country:

1. *By uttering an emphatic protest against all destructive evils.*

History can ask no grander illustration of the power of protest than Quaker life on American soil. Why is it that there is no African slavery to-day within our borders? It is because the Quakers as early as 1688 issued their *protest* against African slavery, and kept it issued until the nation was educated up to the Emancipation Proclamation. But mark this: they invested their all in their protest. They meant it, and they made the American people feel that they meant it. Their protest was strong with the moral strength of a splendid personality and a consistent life; its power was moral.

2. *By keeping before one's country uplifting and inspiring ideas.*

We call guns, swords, powder, forts, ironclads, and armies national powers; the Quakers have taught us that there are powers beyond these. The powers beyond these are right thoughts, high ideals, holy visions, righteous principles, burning aspirations. These make a strong manhood and a pure womanhood, and such manhood and womanhood make a strong and pure state. The men and women who have these thoughts, ideals, visions, principles, aspirations, go straight to God for them; they are exponents of God. The ideal civilization exists only in the plan of God.

This is the message of the Quaker fathers to the patriotic sons of America: If you would render your country the highest service and lead it forward to the millennial age, be an intellect to your country, think for it; be a conscience to your country, make moral decisions for it; and think and decide within the lines of God's holy law. If you would render your country the highest service, be the Lord's prophet to your country; dream dreams for it and see visions for it. It was Socrates and Plato and Aristotle, men of thought and of vision, who were the promoters and conservators of the national strength of Greece; and it was Samuel and Elijah and Isaiah, the prophets of the Lord, who were the chariots of Israel and the horsemen thereof. Be to the American Republic what these men were to the kingdoms of which they were citizens. Hold up ideals before the people as they did, and then, like them, you will attain a civilization embodying your ideals; then you can look up into the face of your God and address Him in the words which the sweet Quaker poet of America left with his fellow-citizens as an ideal and a vision:

> "Suffice it now. In time to be
> Shall holier altars rise to Thee;
> Thy church one broad humanity.
>
> "White flowers of love its walls shall climb,
> Soft bells of peace shall ring its chime;
> Its days shall all be holy time.
>
> "A sweeter song shall then be heard—
> The music of the world's accord
> Confessing Christ, the inward Word!
>
> "That song shall swell from shore to shore,
> One hope, one faith, one love restore,
> The seamless robe that Jesus wore."

VIII.

COLUMBUS: THE RESULTS OF HIS LIFE.

VIII.

COLUMBUS: THE RESULTS OF HIS LIFE.*

WE possess nothing more valuable than history. History broadens human life by bringing the life of the one man into touch with the lives of all men. History makes us familiar with the shining footprints of God, who walks eternal among the ages. History reveals the issue of moral principles when these are acted out in life and are carried to their logical ultimatum. History gathers for us the treasures of the past, and lays at our feet the experiences and the accumulations and the attainments and the ideals of those who have lived before us.

The advantage of living in the nineteenth century is this: we possess the riches of all the centuries. Is it not something to you that somebody cleared the American forests, exterminated the

* Delivered in Lafayette Avenue Presbyterian Church, Brooklyn, on the four hundredth anniversary of the discovery of America.

beasts of prey, opened the mines, improved the crops, built the cities, erected the schools and the churches, and made the civilization into which you were born? The doing of these things, so far as you are concerned, constitutes the difference between riches and poverty, ignorance and education, hardship and luxury, barbarism and civilization. There is a difference between 1492 and 1892. The difference is tremendous—tremendous here in America, tremendous the world over.

If this be so, why then should we trouble ourselves with the past? It is over and gone. We have 1892, and that is all we need. Why burrow in the past and mine in it? Why? Because this is the only way to make it ours and compel service from it. This is the only way to find our possibilities. We must let history tell us what other men have done, that we may know what we can do. The men of the past who walk the pages of history still live; their ambitions are contagious and they inspire us. Let no one despise the past. We have not outgrown the need of it; it has great men who are still in advance of us.

The Christ looks out at us from the past. We are not through with the Christ, the Man of Nazareth, who thought and spake and acted eighteen hundred years ago. There are others with whom we are not through and whom we have not as yet overtaken. There are lost arts which we have not recovered and there is a human genius of the past which is still in advance of modern genius. There are things in the past which have never since been reached. In stability of institutions China has not been surpassed. In skill of mechanics Egypt has not been reached. How were those great Egyptian structures which look us in the face reared? The splendor of Assyria and Babylonia has never been equaled. These old kingdoms have been dug up by the pick and spade of our day, and we are compelled to stand appalled before their ruined grandeur.

Nineteen centuries of Christendom have not added to the grace of the Greek column or to the strength of the Roman arch. No book of proverbs has gone beyond the wisdom of Solomon. The sense for beauty in the old Greeks, and the sense for organization in the old Romans, and the sense for righteousness in the old Jews, can still lead us. No one has plucked the laurels from the brow of Homer; no brush has stolen a single tint from the fame of Apelles; no chisel has chased a line of loveliness from Phidias. The principles of the Mosaic legislation, many of them, are still grand; and the works of Plato and Socrates and Aristotle are republished to-day, and are quoted as authorities by modern philosophers. Paul's logic and thought are as much abreast of the times now as they were the day he uttered them. While we have outgrown the past in ever so many ways, yet enough of the greatness of the past remains and towers above us to create within us a wholesome respect for the past. Where we cannot excel the past let us willingly allow it to wear its laurels; let us run out on lines on which we can excel. It is our privilege to excel where we can, and it is equally our privilege to use what we cannot excel. If the past has given us any great thing which we cannot equal, that is a reason for being thankful to the past.

While there are things belonging to the past which we cannot equal, still we are making progress. Shakespeare is not equaled, but yet there is progress in the coming of Wordsworth and Browning and Tennyson, and also in the coming of our transatlantic poets, Longfellow and Lowell and Whittier. By their coming we own Shakespeare none the less; they are a plus; they give us what Shakespeare does not give us, and they will fill a place and do a work which he cannot fill and do. Then, besides, there is a growth in this, viz.: men, as time has moved on, have become better able to understand Shakespeare; he is more of a power than ever before, because of the general and universal growth which enables men to use him more. What we say of Shakespeare we might also say of Paul. Paul has not been equaled, but Paul has produced Augustine and Luther and Spurgeon, and the world is better off with Paul plus these men. Besides this, because of the spread of Christianity there are more people using Paul. All this is growth.

There will never be another Columbus. There will never be an opportunity for any other man to do the one thing which he did. Still, there is growth and progress in the world. The right use of the continent which Columbus unveiled is progress. To-day we are really celebrating the progress made on the new continent during the past four hundred years. We are celebrating the period rather than the man.

This leads me to ask the question, And what of the man Columbus as a factor in the past? How shall we place him and rate him? To my mind Columbus derives all his importance from the fact that God used him and enabled him to do one thing which resulted in profit. So far as he himself was concerned, and so far as his plans went, he was a mere accident in relation to the grandeur of what we to-day find in this New World.

It is the Columbian era that is everything, and not Columbus. He had not the first conception of the plan which God was working out. God saw the American Republic; he did not. God saw human freedom; he did not. God saw a new world; he saw only what he supposed was an old world. He was only the chisel in the hand of the great God Sculptor. What does the chisel know of the figure of beauty locked up in the marble? Nothing. But it matters not that the chisel is ignorant if the sculptor only have the knowledge. If the sculptor have in his soul the glowing ideal, the Apollo, the Venus, the Moses, will as a necessity step out from the marble into the vision of the admiring world. It is God over man, ruling and planning and working out His glorious and perfect ideal for the human race, that carries the security and progress of the human race. This is the highest thing that I can say of Columbus: he was an instrument in the hand of God, whereby God chiseled out the future according to the pattern of an infinite ideal.

In the discovery of America God is everything; He was the only intelligent actor; He alone saw what relation the opening of America sustained to the civilization which was to follow. This being true, I argue that one of the lessons which America should learn from the study of its own history is this: God has a mission for America, God has a claim upon America, and America should joyfully and voluntarily work out its mission and should absolutely and whole-heartedly give itself up to God.

In giving ourselves to the study of the discovery of America, let us put in the forefront of our thinking this fact: the discovery of America was not the simple and instantaneous affair which it is tacitly assumed to be; it was a long process. It was not an event at all; it was an evolution.

There is a pre-Columbian history and there is a post-Columbian history, and both of these are as important as the history of the man Columbus himself. The former opened the way for Columbus and made him a possibility; the latter took up what he did, and developed it, and made it effective.

Without the after explorers, the Cabots, Americus Vespucius, Magellan, Cortes, De Soto, Balboa, La Salle, Champlain, and Hudson, the discovery of Columbus would have been like the discoveries which preceded it—it would have been a comparatively fruitless affair. It is equally true that Columbus needed those who preceded him in order to his making as well as those who followed him in order to his development. His inspiration as an explorer grew out of what preceded him.

Let us turn a few pages of the pre-Columbian history and see how the world was working up to his one great event, his first voyage—for this first voyage was really the only thing in Columbus's life that had any glory in it. Pre-Columbian history tells us that Columbus was not the first discoverer of America; he was only one discoverer among many; he was only the recoverer of America. At the time the bold Genoese planned his scheme of reaching the Indies by a westward route, documents were in existence, the Scandinavian sagas, giving particulars of several visits to the Northern American continent five hundred years before. From these writings we gather the following:

Iceland was settled by the Norsemen A.D. 874. From Iceland the Norsemen pushed up to Greenland. Eric the Red founded a settlement there in 986; this settlement he named after himself, Ericsfiord. One of Eric's companions was an Icelander named Bardson, who had a son, Biron, then absent in Norway. When Biron came back to Iceland he was told that his father had gone to Greenland. He at once determined to follow him. On this voyage contrary winds bore him away from Greenland and carried him to the coast of North America. As this land did not correspond with the description he had of Greenland, he refused to land. Turning his course northward, he continued until he reached Greenland. The distance from the southern point of Greenland to Labrador is only six hundred miles, but little more than the distance from Norway to England.

Biron was the first European to discover the shores of North America. This was nothing in itself, but it led to something further. Biron related his experience to Eric, and Leif, the son of Eric, fitted out an expedition to go and explore this land. He sailed in the year 1000 A.D., with a crew of twenty-five men. In four days they came to Labrador, after that to Nova Scotia; from here they sailed until they reached an island which they called Vineland, because of its abundance of grapes. This island was somewhere off the coast of Massachusetts or Rhode Island. Here they erected huts and gave the settlement the name of Leifsbuthir.

It is to Leif Ericson that Boston has erected a monument on Commonwealth Avenue, its leading avenue. Leif Ericson returned to Iceland, and the accounts which he gave of America caused another expedition to sail, 1004 A.D., under Thorwald. Thorwald landed on a promontory below Cape Cod, Massachusetts. Here he was attacked by the Indians. In the battle he received a wound which proved fatal. His last words were the request, " Let me be buried on yonder promontory, which I so admire." His followers carried out his request and then returned home. This was the first white man's grave on our continent.

The third expedition was a failure. It was under the third son of Eric, who sailed with his wife, Gudrida, the first white woman explorer to come to the shores of America. Its object was to bring back the body of Thorwald, buried on the New England promontory. This expedition sailed from Iceland, but when it reached Greenland Thorstein died. The next spring his widow brought the ship back to Iceland.

In the summer of the following year, 1006, a much more important expedition was fitted out. It was under the command of Thorfinn the Hopeful. Thorfinn, captivated by the charms of Gudrida, Thorstein's widow, married her and brought into his life her daring and courage. There were three ships and one hundred and forty men in this expedition, a larger expedition than that of Columbus. As this was an attempt to found a permanent colony, all sorts of necessaries were taken on board the ships, including live stock and domestic animals.

This expedition came down as far as Martha's Vineyard and anchored in Buzzard's Bay. While here one of the captains of the company, Thorhall by name, was despatched with a small ship to look for the settlement of Leif Ericson. This man had a most untoward fate. A westerly gale took him and drove him right across the Atlantic to the coast of Ireland, where he and his crew were all made slaves. Thorhall, although against his will, was the first to hold the honor of sailing right across the Atlantic Ocean from shore to shore. And, what is still more remarkable, this first voyage from the one continent to the other, in a temperate-zone latitude, was from west to east, from the New World to the Old World.

Meanwhile Thorfinn prosecuted his journey farther south and founded a colony. Here, in this American colony, Thorfinn and Gudrida were blessed by the birth of a son, the first native-born American of European parents. The new son received the name Snorre. He was taken to Iceland when the colony, after great hardships, returned home, and afterward he became a famous scholar and bishop. Among his lineal descendants is included Thorwaldsen, the famous sculptor. How strange to think that the great Norwegian sculptor's genealogy should come by the way of America! It is supposed that Snorre wrote the sagas from which we have derived this information about these voyages of the hardy Norsemen, the most daring mariners of ancient times.

Had the Icelandic explorers only possessed what Columbus possessed, viz., firearms to enable them to successfully defend themselves against the Indians, North America would have been the first to have been Europeanized. A race of men equal to any upon the globe would have been here. But, as it was, nothing came out of these explorations save that a few furs were taken to Iceland and a cargo or two of American timber.

The discovery by the Norsemen was not the only pre-Columbian discovery of America. Frederick Saunders, the librarian of the Astor Library, New York, has published the story of another pre-Columbian discovery. His story is the story of a Welsh colony which, under the leadership of Prince Modoc of Wales, settled in the twelfth century among the red men of the West. This colony continued to preserve its native speech and customs for five hundred years. This accounts for the puzzling wonder discovered in after times, viz., certain clans of Indians who spoke the Welsh vernacular. They received their speech from this Welsh colony.

There is still another story to be noticed. It is in effect this. In 1482, ten years before the voyage of Columbus, a Spanish pilot named Sanchez, while attempting a passage between Madeira and the Canaries, was driven from his course by a storm and landed on the shores of an island said to be Haiti. Subsequently this pilot came to Lisbon and found lodgment with Columbus, to whom he related the facts, and at whose house he subsequently died.

How much inspiration Columbus got from the Norsemen we cannot assert, but this we can assert: he sailed as far north as Iceland, where the Scandinavian sagas were which contained the stories of the Norsemen voyagers. The air of his age was full of the spirit of navigation, and he breathed that air. He had the writings of Marco Polo and John de Mandeville. Both of these men were audacious romancers and explorers. They had pushed to the very limits of the East, and their accounts of its gold and luxury set all Europe on fire with a desire to possess the treasures of the East. The art of printing had brought out of their hiding-places the old classics, and Columbus had these. Some of these spoke of an Atlantic land. Columbus had married the daughter of a distinguished explorer. While a girl she had made several hazardous voyages with her father and was an enthusiast herself. Through her Columbus came into possession of all the results of her father's experience, as she inherited his charts and journals.

But, above all, the famous letters of Toscanelli had been written. This scholar in his letters openly advocated the practicability of reaching Japan and China by sailing directly west. This was precisely what Columbus attempted to do; this is what he thought he had done, and he died thinking so. He died ignorant of the fact that it was a new world that he gave Castile and Leon.

We have now reached the story of Columbus himself. For eighteen years he cherished his vision; for eighteen years he believed in himself. This was the secret of his power. For eighteen years he knocked in vain at the doors of the courts of the reigning monarchs of Europe. At last he won the confidence of that queenly woman, Isabella. She became the power back of Columbus and the power that sustained him all through his Atlantic career. It was a woman's faith and a woman's smile of encouragement that were back of the effective discovery of America, and this woman came upon the scene at the critical moment, the moment of peril.

The little fleet of three vessels, the *Santa Maria*, the *Pinta*, and the *Nina*, sailed from Palos August 3, 1492. The three crews consisted of about one hundred men in all. How were these crews recruited? Men were not anxious to go on such a foolhardy journey; they peopled the ocean with all manner of horrid monsters. They had no faith in Columbus; they looked upon him as a man not rightly balanced in mind. It was therefore difficult to get a crew. Special inducements were offered: immunity from the pursuit of justice was offered; criminals were offered pardon if they would go; debtors were offered release from all obligations if they would go. The fleet was made up of runaway criminals and debtors. The character of the fleet accounts for the after mutinies and the after dangers of Columbus, who was at the mercy of such men. Nevertheless the expedition was a success.

Columbus successfully handled his crew. I do not need to relate the sufferings of the voyage, nor tell of the hopes and the fears. To me the thrilling part of the story is the end—reaching land just when hope was about to become despair. The first thing that cheered the crew were the signs of approaching shores. Herbage carried out by the tide floated around the ships. Land birds, with flashing plumage as brilliant as the hues of the rainbow, circled in the air overhead; they perched on the topmasts and poured out their thrilling songs of welcome.

Lamartine tells us that a little bird's nest, built on a branch which the wind had broken off, and full of eggs on which the parent bird was sitting, gracefully floated by one of the ships, now rising and now falling upon the swelling waves. That, without a doubt, meant land, and land very close at hand. All these were voices from the shores. They put soul into the care-worn and exhausted sailors. The last night of sailing has come, and all the sails are tightly reefed. The ships draw near into a realm of intangible mystery. There is no sleep for a single soul; all minds are kindled with a fever of intellectual suspense. Columbus walks the upper deck and scans the horizon with his eager eye. It is pitch-dark. Suddenly he stops. What is it that gleams out yonder between sea and sky? He looks with all his might. What is it? As God lives, it is a light—a light! Yes, but what sort of a light? It cannot be a star; it is not diamond-pointed, as God's stars are; it is ragged and flickering, like every light of human kindling. Alas! it is gone; it was the illusion of an overwrought brain. No; there it is again; it moves—it waves; it is a torch-light upon some shore. Hark! a great boom sounds from the *Pinta;* her guns sound again and again. God be praised! Her crew, too, has seen the light on the shore. It is all settled, for that is land, and that is a light on the shore carried by an Indian hand. The voyage is a success. Columbus has won his greatest glory.

You know what followed—the landing the next morning, the setting up of the cross, the prayer to God, and the song of praise. You know the return to Spain—the reception by king and queen, the procession at Barcelona, with its American Indians in front, its American products, its gold and spices, and its treasures. You know, too, the enthusiasm for exploration which followed, and how quickly a new expedition was fitted out with a different type of fleet and crew. A sky-rocket of success had gone up into the sky, and brilliant showers of enthusiasm fell all over Europe.

We have passed in our narrative the zenith of Columbus's glory. There was nothing great after this. There were voyages, but they were fruitless; there were mutinies, cruelties, slavery, disappointment, displacements, sickness, chains, poverty, neglect, a broken heart, death. When Queen Isabella died Columbus lost his only influential friend. Ferdinand, the king, only trifled with him. Columbus had cost him more money than he had brought in. All his discoveries, from a monetary point of view, were failures; but money, riches, these were the things Ferdinand wanted and these were the things Columbus had promised to secure.

The story of Columbus's death is a sad one. He died neglected and forsaken; he died so obscurely that his death was scarcely known; he died in a little miserable room, bare and unsightly, the only ornaments being the chains which bound him when he was sent home from America as a prisoner. The priest was there and a few attendants, but that was all. These tell us that he said, "Father, into Thy hands I commend my spirit," and then all was over.

Do you wonder that he died unnoticed and forgotten? The reason was, others had pushed past him in the rush of the age. The exploits of other voyagers had caught the public ear and monopolized public attention. Americus Vespucius had returned from his second voyage and was talking to all Europe of things Columbus knew nothing about. The Cabots had been to North America and were talking about what they had found there. Columbus never set foot upon North America. Balboa and Magellan had already completed their apprenticeship and were on their way to the Pacific Ocean. Already the fishermen from Portugal were plying their vocation upon the banks of Newfoundland with profit, and Valasco, the Spaniard, was on his way to the St. Lawrence. The daring and the success of others overshadowed Columbus, and he was lost sight of by the great world. This was the reason he was allowed to die in the lonely and unnoticed way in which he did die.

Such is the story of Columbus told in a broken, fragmentary way. What now is our judgment with regard to him? He is not the Columbus who was the object of our hero-worship when we were children. The search-light of history has cleared his life of myths and has completely obliterated the Columbus of romance. It is shown that most of the thrilling stories about Columbus which have captivated us are to be regarded as apocryphal. The world hitherto has been worshiping an idealized man and not the real man. Columbus was not a saint. I say this in the interest of accurate scholarship. Such works as those of Henry Harriss and Justin Winsor, the librarian of Harvard, and Dr. Adams, the late president of Cornell, show that Columbus can never be canonized on merit of character. His character is a thing exceedingly problematical.

The works of these scholars which I have mentioned are all written in the interest of the truth and after the modern idea of fairness and impartiality in biography-writing. The old idea of the biographer was this: he must be the eulogist and apologist and advocate of his hero. The modern idea of the biographer is this: he must first and always seek the facts and tell the truth about the man whose biography he writes.

These are some of the facts in the story of Columbus. He was a pirate in the early part of his life; he sailed several times with the Portuguese slave-ships to the coast of Guinea to capture slaves. In his journal he admits that land was first seen and announced by Roderigo de Triana, of the *Pinta*, at two o'clock, October 12th; but on his return to Spain he set up the demand for himself that he first saw land, and claimed and received from the sovereigns the special money which had been offered as a reward to the man who should first see the land. His will shows that his son Fernando was born out of wedlock. His first letters glow with accounts of the gentleness of the Indians; he praises their hospitality. When his vessel was shipwrecked they gave him every possible aid; some of them even shed tears of sympathy. You know what followed, how he repaid this kindness and love of the Indians. I cannot speak of the horrors inflicted upon the Indian women. And there was no protest from Columbus; nay, he made excuses for the conduct of his brutal crew. Because husbands protected their wives and daughters and declared war to the hilt of the knife, he captured and enslaved the red men and shipped whole cargoes of Indians as slaves to

Spain. This he did in the face of the rebuke administered to him by Queen Isabella.

He advocated and prosecuted the slave-trade as a means of procuring riches for Spain. His chief aim in all that he did was riches. Above all things he was eager for gold and fame and titles and personal advancement. But was there no religion in his life? There was. It was not nineteenth-century religion, however. He always carried the cross with him, and he always said he would devote his gains to a crusade to take the Holy Sepulcher out of the hands of the infidel Moslems. That constituted religion in his day. Charles V. was religious; Philip II. was religious; they erected the cross everywhere, and in the name of the cross committed all manner of crimes. The religion of Columbus was akin to their religion.

One reason why we should be thankful to-day is that religion has grown since the day of Columbus. To be religious after his kind to-day would put a man behind the prison bars and blackball his character out of the fellowship of the true church of God. What I rejoice in to-day is this: the world has outgrown Columbus and the religion of Columbus, and demands an infinitely higher type of manhood.

When I put Columbus upon the background of 1892 I can find nothing in him to admire but his genius, and his faith in himself, and his push.

Following his faith and genius, he performed a work he did not know he was performing, and became a benefactor of the world by accident. If you wish to respect Columbus you must keep him back in 1492.

One act of this man is all that I celebrate, viz., his running the prow of the *Santa Maria* upon the American shore. I celebrate the period which follows that act; I celebrate the progress which God has evolved by means of the years between 1492 and 1892.

Farewell, Columbus. I honor you back there in 1492. You are better than Ferdinand; you are better than Bobadilla; you are better than Ovando. I deplore the treatment you received from these; it was unjust and cruel. You are better than Charles V. and Philip II., but I prefer the nineteenth century. I prefer liberty to slavery. I prefer the policy of William Penn to the policy of the bullet and the knife in dealing with the Indians. I prefer the virtue that respects the womanhood of all races to the virtue that can keep silent because the womanhood being trampled underfoot is that of an alien race. I celebrate the period; I celebrate the fact that we are four centuries away from Columbus. As an American I celebrate America, American progress, American opportunity.

Let me give you some of the points which I keep before my mind as an incentive to this Columbian celebration. We are celebrating the science of discovery and not the science of war.

This indicates a new epoch in history-making, and to me there is no better index of advance than this new epoch. What has history been hitherto? What has controlled history? Who have figured upon the pages of history, captivating eye and heart and making the future of mankind? These are leading questions. Tell me what history is, and I will forecast for you the future.

History has a power parallel to the power of fine painting. In the art salons in the palace of Versailles there are miles and miles of battle scenes. Any one can tell what the education gotten through the eye by these pictures means. It means the domination of France by the spirit of militarism. Put other pictures in that national art-gallery, pictures of the leading French scientists, pictures illustrative of their experiments, pictures showing their marvelous triumphs, and you will make the rising generation scientists and give the spirit of science the domination of the land.

I want to assert it here that, according to my thinking, it is a gross outrage upon all the principles of Christianity when Christendom is busy making swords and spears and Gatling guns and ironclads. When it is busy doing this it is clashing with God's pacific purposes and smiting the cross with lightning. War and the cross are as much in antagonism as were the cruel slavery of Columbus, forced upon the Indians, and the dying love of Jesus, symbolized by the cross which he erected upon American shores.

I hold history largely responsible for the existence of war. History is written in such a way as to make war popular. Who walk the pages of history? Warriors, and they are represented as the great heroes of the world—almost the sole heroes of the world. They crowd all others into the background. History must be rewritten. War heroes must be made to take a subordinate place in history. The world's thinkers and workers, the world's missionaries, scientists, educators, these must be crowned with laurels. The genius of industry must be exalted. When this is done men will aim at being missionaries, educators, explorers, scientists, philanthropists, workers. Such celebrations as this lead to this needed rewriting of the world's history, and of the exaltation of character and of life and of exploits that make for peace and for the triumph of mind and soul in the world.

Another point I keep before my mind for recognition and inspiration. It is this: we are celebrating the overrule of God in human history.

Columbus is nothing; God is everything. God could have discovered America without Columbus. It was discovered independent of Columbus and in another way. While Columbus was struggling with his rebellious colony in Hispaniola, Pedro Cabral, a citizen of Portugal, with a fleet of thirteen vessels, sailing on his way to Calcutta, was blown across the Atlantic Ocean to Brazil. It was because of this fact that Portugal afterward claimed Brazil. Portugal virtually owned it even down to the days of Dom Pedro, when it became a republic.

God works in long periods, and this is illustrated in the history of the discovery and population of America. Yet, while God works in long periods, everything is timed to the hour, and each event has its place and order. The compass must come to make navigation possible. The astrolabe and quadrant must come, so that the navigator can make out his exact distance from the equator by the altitude of the sun. These instruments make man perfectly at home upon the sea; they unchain the ocean from the old bondage of timidity and fear. Now men may learn that God intended the ocean not to be a dividing waste, separating continent from continent, but He meant it to be a highway between land and land, whitened with the sails of a universal commerce.

After the opening of the highways of the sea, the art of printing must come, and then the art of making paper. These give the Bible to the world. It is time now for the discovery of America, a new land for a new and a higher life, and America is discovered. But, mark you, while discovered, America is not at once populated. The time has not come for that. It must be explored first, and the world must be taught just what America is.

A century and a half passes before God lets the people in. A century and a half is needed for the Bible to work its way in Europe and prepare a people for the prepared land. At the right time the prepared people come to New England and build up institutions there according to the teachings of the Scriptures. The Atlantic coast is made a fountain of liberty and law and righteousness. When the Atlantic coast becomes strong enough to influence the whole land for God and truth, a Western pioneer finds a flake of gold in the Rockies, and in a single decade a whole nation pours out into the great West. But not gold, nor the glory of kings, nor the pride of power, made the discovery of America worth while. No. The tremendous impulse and opportunity which it gave to mental activity, and the wonderful loosening of shackles which it brought, and the field which it furnished for the American Republic—these only made the discovery of America worth while.

I can mention only one point more. It is this: we are celebrating the possibilities of the future. Whose future? Our future. For it is true, as Emerson says, "America stands for opportunity."

It stands for opportunity in the development of a magnificent patriotism and of magnificent ideals.

I am glad of one thing, and that is, this is a time devoted to the honoring of the American flag. The old flag is waved in our public schools and it floats from the windows of our homes; it is in the breeze everywhere. This week in Chicago it will be thrown in the form of pyrotechnics into the open heaven at midnight to blaze above the dedicated buildings of the World's Fair.

One of the promised attractions of the week in Chicago is a fiery simulation of our country's flag floating in the air. A vast cloud of smoke will be tossed high into the dome to form the blue field; into this forty-four mortars will discharge as many bombs, carefully timed to explode simultaneously, which will form forty-four stars; other mortars will fire shells at the same time, loaded with colored explosives which in bursting will throw out long streamers of red, white, and blue to form bars. The whole will produce a gigantic American flag, with colors harmoniously blended.

Americans, let this be the occasion when you shall run up the stars and stripes in your hearts and when you shall consecrate yourselves anew to the highest patriotism.

IX.

GEORGE WASHINGTON A FACTOR IN AMERICAN HISTORY.

IX.

GEORGE WASHINGTON A FACTOR IN AMERICAN HISTORY.*

My fellow-citizens, it is a grand thing for a nation to have grand men for ancestors; to have a history the opening pages of which are crowded with interest, the first chapters of which are filled with God and with human heroism, the product of man's alliance with God. Such a history will send a holy and an inspiring thrill through the body politic age after age. Such ancestors will stand as eternal sentinels, guarding the liberties of the nation and the principles of the nation and the faith of the nation. Such men will rebuke and commend and lead the nation perpetually.

You see the bearing of all this. It leads us directly to the topic of the evening, which introduces us to the great ancestor of the American Republic, George Washington. Our civil fathers,

* Delivered in the Academy of Music, Brooklyn, at the celebration of Washington's birthday by the Grand Army of the Republic.

whom George Washington led, were men fired by a world-wide purpose, which came from the heart of God. Guided and sustained by this purpose, they took possession of this continent for us, and they left us as a heritage the embodiment of their principles in our vast and honored Republic. They planted the seed which grew the national tree under which we live. The product of their life is grand, but, grand as it is, it is only a prophecy of what shall be. We have not yet reached ultimate America, nor even typical America. Typical America is yet in the future. There are prayers of our national fathers still before the throne of God awaiting an answer. The prayers of George Washington at Valley Forge were broader than Valley Forge, and these prayers are still before God. God feels their strong pulsations, which beat in unison with His own purposes for America, and He is keeping them constantly in sight for the coming of the right day. When that day comes they will be translated from divine decrees into human realities. George Washington is not yet through with the American Republic, and God grant that he never may be. When the Republic breaks with the father of our country the doom of the Republic will be forever sealed. Let the celebration of Washington's birthday go forward. It is in accordance with the mind of the great Ruler of the universe, who Himself crowns every true man, and who issues His decree that the righteous shall be held in everlasting remembrance. Let North and South be one in honoring the man; let music and artillery and pyrotechnics grace his memory; let mature scholarship praise the statesmanship of the eighteenth century; let burning eloquence depict the glory and advance of the nation for which Washington lived; let the voice of prayer reverently rise to God upon this day, and commit the nation's future to the God who made the nation's past.

In contributing my part to the celebration of to-night, I wish, in the presence of the brave men of America who fought for the life of the Republic which George Washington gave us, to tell the story of George Washington and then evolve from that story some lessons of American patriotism.

Owing to the limit of time, our picture of Washington this evening must be the merest charcoal sketch—an outline and nothing more. But in this outline we wish to see the *real* Washington and not the *traditional* Washington; the *historical* Washington and not the *idealized* Washington; the *prose* Washington and not the *poetic* Washington; Washington the man and not Washington the myth; Washington as seen in the clear, open sunlight and not Washington as seen in the haze of eulogy. We protest against every tendency to starch and stiffen and costumize this plain, honest farmer, who was faulty in his grammar and elliptical in his spelling. Let Washington be kept humanized. For my part, I am accustomed to take comfort from what Washington *was not* as well as from what he was.

He owed nothing to birth. The light of no ancestral glory haloed his brow. No bluer blood flowed in his veins than that which flowed in the veins of ten thousand other Americans. He was not a brilliant man, as men who rule and lead in the world of letters are brilliant; he was not possessed of brilliant parts, like a diamond which can be turned in the sunlight; his was not so much the genius of intellect, although he had enough of that, as it was *the genius of character*. I rejoice in this, because *the genius of character* is attainable by all. The man who lives in right relations with the truth and with the right and with God, and who deals in noble and honest and brave things, can and does build up a true character. True character-building is within the power of every mortal.

"But Washington was a providential man," you say. Yes; but so may you be a providential man if you will. Every man who absolutely yields himself up to God and to the call of the hour, and who explicitly and implicitly follows the openings of Providence, is a providential man in the full length and breadth and sweep of his life. And he is as necessary a man in his place as George

Washington was in his. I do not regret that Washington was not a brilliant man. A man of character is infinitely better than a man of brilliancy. Ninety-nine times out of a hundred he will excel. The majority of brilliant men in history remind me of a bolt of lightning. A bolt of lightning is a mighty power. Hurled out of the cloud-covered and storm-shaken dome, it sweeps along its course in dazzling and flashing grandeur. It is a magnificent thing; it holds us enrapt as we watch it, but at the same time it fills us with fear. We tremble, not knowing what is coming, nor how it will use its power, nor where it will strike. Brilliant human lives are often like the thunderbolt; they illumine, they dazzle, they show mighty power, but they keep the world in perpetual fear and anxiety as to what the result of their living may be. They are liable to be erratic and wickedly ambitious; they are liable to throw themselves against the right; nine times out of ten we find them to be Napoleonic and not Washingtonian. The difference between Napoleon and Washington is the difference between the iron heel and the helping hand, the difference between tyranny and freedom, the difference between a man living for self and a man living for broad humanity. Brilliant men are usually proud men, selfish men, tyrannical men.

History gives us a full record of Washington.

Its eye was on him from birth to burial. He came into life in a plain fashion and lived his boyhood days in a plain fashion. His early education was something like the education of Abraham Lincoln, the only other American who is able to stand life-size by his side and grandly hold his own. Neither of these men saw the inside of a university. Washington went to a low grade of private school, taught by the parish sexton. He learned the three R's, but he never studied grammar. In his brother's house he studied a little geometry. This sums up all that the schools did for him.

If this sums up all that the schools did for him, how are his wonderful state papers to be accounted for? They are models. His farewell address, like Lincoln's Gettysburg address, is nothing short of a national classic. I account for the form and power of his state papers just as I account for his wonderful career. I see here the result of great goodness. He wrote out of himself. His face was everywhere and always toward the light, so not a vocable rang false in his state papers. He spoke and wrote electly and directly, because he spoke and wrote from a pure character. He felt through and through his entire consciousness the beauty of simplicity. He did not know how electly he did speak and write. Such is always the case with goodness. He had something true and important to say, and this, too, was a reason why he struck a high level in literature. There is a relation between ethics and esthetics. Washington's thoughts were full of ethics, hence Washington's words were models of esthetics.

Deprived of school privileges, he trained himself out of school. As we see him train himself out of school, we see the man in the boy. As a boy he drilled himself in self-control, and in regularity of work, and in the art of politeness, and in respect for conscience, and in the fear of God. As a boy he was soulful and thoughtful and devout; he was of a meditative spirit. As a boy he studied the art of courteous, agreeable intercourse; he laid down rules to guide him in the avoidance of all that would offend refined taste, and in the culture of that which was pleasing in manner and in habit. Manuscripts found in his own handwriting show this. The majority of boys and men do not try to please or be pleasing, and they succeed: they are not pleasing. By ill manners they throw away half the power of their life. Decorum and politeness are greater forces in society than we imagine. They are the evidence of self-respect, and the man only who respects himself is respected by his fellows.

Here are some of the rules which he wrote out for himself at the age of thirteen:

"Never violate the laws of good society. Avoid everything that offends or annoys.

"Endeavor to keep alive in your bosom that little divine spark called conscience.

"When you speak of God or His attributes, speak seriously and in reverence."

These rules have come down to us in the handwriting of the boy Washington. Living under these rules I call putting one's self under the highest type of religion.

At the age of seventeen Washington earned his livelihood as a surveyor of public lands. He followed this occupation for three years. This was a wholesome discipline: it made him physically, and when, at the end of three years, he stood forth six feet two inches, he was broad-shouldered and full-chested, every inch of him a man; it identified him with the least artificial of human pursuits; it shielded him also from the perversion of his moral energies; it made him practical; it inured him to habits of keen local study; it made him familiar with fatigue and exposure; it taught him to accommodate himself to limited fare and to camp life; it made a soldier out of him.

At the age of nineteen he took a commission from the colony of Virginia and entered into the French and Indian wars. After this he went with his brother to the West Indies; while there his brother died, leaving him his estate. It was in this way that he came into the possession of Mount Vernon.

At the age of twenty-seven Washington married Mrs. Martha Custis, a widow with two children; she was noted for two things, wealth and beauty. No one could ever say that he married her for money, but her money came in good place during the Revolutionary times and enabled him the better to serve his country.

At the age of forty-two he became a member of the first general Congress of the colonies, and at the age of forty-four he was, through the influence of John Adams, selected as commander-in-chief of the American forces. He took command of the army under the old elm-tree which still grows on the common of Cambridge, Mass. America required as a leader a man reared under her own eye, who combined with distinguished talents a character above suspicion, and George Washington was that man.

He remained at the head of the army for seven long years, during which time his foot never stepped across the threshold of his home. The history of these seven years is familiar to you all; they were full of intense interest, from the raising of the siege of Boston by building batteries on Dorchester Heights, to the surrender of the British army at Yorktown.

Two battles at least during this period showed great military genius and would have been worthy of Napoleon—the battles of Trenton and Germantown. Washington showed a military genius in these, just as afterward, in reading the future of America and in creating our foreign policy, he showed a genius of statesmanship. Washington crossing the Delaware on a stormy night in midwinter, when the river was running high and full of ice, was like Napoleon crossing the Alps. For his services during the Revolutionary War he took no remuneration whatever; that showed where his heart was and for what he was fighting. He was ambitious not for self, but for country. He fought not for glory, but for a cause.

His services in this war illustrate his character and set forth his endowments. While he was constantly active and was full of untiring perseverance, he was also noted for his large passive virtues. These were the virtues which won the day. He was not able to meet the foe on an open field; he had not the army with which to do that; his only hope was to weary the British by long retreats, making now and then a daring attack and winning a brilliant victory, to revive his troops and his country and to keep the love of the cause of liberty alive. Only a man largely endowed with the passive virtues could have endured the gibes of foes and the suspicions of allies and the charge of incompetency by friends. We want to make more of the passive virtues than we do.

The war over, was Washington's work through?

No; it was only half through. Many more years of service were required from him upon the part of his country. The war over, the States free, a new era opened before America. God had brought the States through the great struggle, but danger was not over for them. War had united them, but, now that the war was over, they were in danger of falling apart and of entering into battle with one another.

The most perilous years in the history of our nation were the four years after the Revolution. This period was what John Fiske has called the "critical era." Each State began to look out for itself and to become jealous of every other State. The Articles of Confederation were too indefinite and too feeble. The Continental Congress, ruling under these, had but limited authority. A heavy debt rested upon the nation, and the soldiers who had won the freedom of the nation were compelled to go unpaid. It is impossible to magnify the ills of this period; yet the average American rests under the delusion that when the Revolutionary War was over our fathers had a political millennium. There was great financial distress. There was civil war in North Carolina and there was revolt in Pennsylvania. The times demanded efforts for a more perfect and permanent union, and for better articles of confederation, and for a wider central government. This demand originated the convention which framed the Constitution. Of this convention George Washington was the chairman and head. The Constitution framed and adopted, he was elected the first President, with John Adams Vice-President. It was not his wish to be President; the office sought him, he did not seek the office. Every office which he held during his long public service was forced upon him; he took and filled public positions only from a sense of duty and only to serve a cause. Let our politicians and statesmen take note of this fact. It is delightful to see how Washingtonian the men of our day are, especially the men in whose bonnets the presidential bee is buzzing. How much coaxing they require! How extremely modest they are! Not a single man is doing a single thing to get the nomination. They are so completely hidden behind their modest blushes that they can be discovered only by that new-found element of light, the X ray, which has such a penetrating power that it can photograph even our bones.

By the way, if you are searching for a candidate for the Presidency, what is the matter with Governor Morton? or what is the matter with Speaker Reed? or what is the matter with the major? Major who? Why, Major McKinley.

Gentlemen, the most effective way to kill your candidate is to hurrah for him ahead of time. We are six months away from nomination day, so now is the time to hurrah for the men you don't want. If there is a candidate you are afraid of and would like to kill, present his name to the public at once and at once begin to hurrah for him. This is what some men in our State are charged with doing today. If that charge be true, if any man or any set of men are trifling with our venerable governor, or are making game of him, or are insincere in asking him for his name, or are using him for the purpose of ignobly trading him by and by, they ought, to use a military figure, to be immediately court-martialed and in disgrace be drummed out of the political camp.

But I must return from these pleasantries to our subject. The day of Washington's inauguration was a great day; he himself felt it to be such; for if the gigantic enterprise upon which the Republic enters prove a failure, "government of the people, and by the people, and for the people" will be set back centuries, and the tyrannies of the Old World, with their monarchical ideas, will receive a new lease of life. But if the enterprise prove successful, the cause of civil freedom will bound up in every land, and the whole world will begin its march toward constitutional liberty.

The day when it dawned found the whole nation, so far as possible, assembled at New York. Multitudes with thrilling hearts witnessed the administration of the oath of office; and when George

Washington, with great fervor, said, " I swear, so help me God," the chancellor who administered the oath turned round to the living throngs and cried with a loud voice, " *Long live George Washington, the President of the United States of America!* " That shout the people echoed all through the city and all through the Republic, and then a thousand chimes pealed forth in musical notes of joy, and a thousand guns answered with their voice of hearty salute.

Having served his country for eight years, the limit of presidential rule for any man, Washington retired to the privacy of his home at Mount Vernon and lived in quietness until death called him to take up his march to the throne of God. When he died all America mourned him, and the nations abroad joined America in the mourning. The flags of France were craped, and even the flags of Great Britain floated at half-mast; for, as Goldwin Smith says, " England felt that he had only fought against the government of George III., and not against England."

Washington is now before us, and we see him as he is and as he reveals himself in his life-work. He impresses us as a man whose manhood is pure and simple ; he is self-possessed ; he is temperate ; he is methodical ; he has the power of carrying with him all details ; he is prompt, filling each day with the duties of the day ; he is a man of deeds more than of words; he gives us a life by which to know him—a life full to overflowing with works, a life full of pathetic gravity and seriousness, which comes from a sense of duty, and from seeing and dealing with eternal realities, and from carrying the burdens of the human race. His life is a continued exhibit of unselfishness; it is an eloquent and an immortal oration on liberty. To repeat a phrase I have already used, *his was preëminently the genius of character.* It is his character that sets up his statue in our public parks and that hangs his picture in our legislative halls. It is his character that holds for him the attachment of a continent and the personal loyalty of the whole Anglo-Saxon race. It is his character that fires the guns and pulls the bell-ropes and inspires the orations. It is his character that makes his grave at Mount Vernon a mightier power than the presence of any living statesman. *The genius of character!* That is the greatest known power in the universe.

The man who admires the genius of intellect stands by me and asks, Do you make genius of character outrank genius of intellect? I reply, I do. Unless a man have love and devotion and self-sacrifice and self-control and honesty and truthfulness and manliness, he is lacking in the very pith and beauty of manhood; he is not a great man, no matter what else he may have. *He is not a great being.* He may have written a matchless poem, he may have arranged the marvelous plots of a striking play; his meters may run like the music of the flowing brooks, and his metaphors may shine like the green fields and the blue seas and the golden clouds from which they are drawn; the personages in his dramas may be grand men doing grand things. Pointing to these, the admirer of the genius of intellect asks me with confidence, And is not this glory enough for the man? Has he not reached the acme of greatness? I answer, No; this is not glory enough for the man; he has not reached the acme of greatness. There are great heights beyond him still. He must himself *be* the best character he can represent; he must himself enact in real life the highest qualities he can paint; he must do, and love to do, the noblest deeds he can abstractly conceive and beautifully describe. His intellect must not overtop his character nor his lips outboast the achievements of his hands. *The genius of character!* There is no power like that. That was the power possessed by George Washington. It was that which gave him his clear and unerring insight into things; it was that which crowned him and the cause which he espoused with success; it was that which carried the blessing of almighty God with it. We might truthfully describe this man, whose power was *the genius of character*, as Tennyson describes one of his heroes; he was

> "Rich in saving common sense,
> And as the greatest only are—
> In his simplicity sublime;
> Who never sold the truth to serve the hour,
> Nor paltered with eternal God for power;
> Whose life was work, whose language rife
> With rugged maxims hewn from life;
> Who never spake against a foe.
> Let his great example stand
> Colossal, seen in every land,
> Till in all lands, and through all human story,
> The path of duty be the way to glory."

Such is our Washington. To-day we stand in his presence and feel his power. We do this as part of our education. It is one of the most hopeful of our human attributes that we have the capacity to be touched and thrilled and inspired by those who are above us. It is the germ and promise of progress. We are educated by our admirations; nothing, perhaps, educates us more. I rejoice that this is so, because I remember that Washington calls out the admiration of all America. He educates the American citizen; he refines him; he elevates him. Do you not hear his voice? Do you not see the civic precepts shining out of his life in letters of gold? Let me read you some of these and in this way give you the lessons which, at the beginning of my address, I promised to evolve from his life.

I hear the father of his country uttering three precepts to-night, all of which are practical and are necessary for the making of ultimate America. The first of these is this:

1. *Americans, give your country a true manhood.*

This, and this alone, is true patriotism. This alone will make our country strong. As a chain is no stronger than its individual links, so the character of the nation is no higher than the character of its separate citizens. There is no getting away from the individual man; he must be made right if the world is to be made right. There is only one effective process of regenerating society, and that is to regenerate the atoms of society. It is only the citizen who has a true manhood who can do manly things and build into our civil institutions manly virtues. The night cannot emit the light; it takes the day to do that. The citizen is never better than the man; your patriotism cannot rise higher than your morals. Hence the vital question is, *What are you?* Are you a man of truth, a sober man, an honest man, a generous man, a loyal man, a man of God? Show me a nation of such men, and I will show you a magnificent nation, a nation that is a model of civil and religious liberty, a nation with grand popular institutions, a nation full of commercial prosperity, a progressive nation, a nation whose laws are righteous and whose career is one of exaltation.

I am in search of good men for our nation, because, in this latter and better age, which Washington has inaugurated, goodness is greatness. The great man of the future will be the good man of the future. I know that goodness has not always been considered the equivalent of greatness, but Washington by his great American life has changed our estimate. It was not so considered when the race was young, but it is so considered now; for the human race has reached its maturity.

As we review the history of the world, we see it dividing itself into three stages: in the first stage power is magnified; force is deified; the great man is the strong man. In this era Nimrod is the hero after the world's heart. Strength receives the homage of the many. In the second stage power is pushed a step or two back, and intellect comes to the front; the great man is the intellectual man. In this era Homer is the favorite idol before whom the populace delight to bow. Genius receives the homage of men. Christianity has inaugurated the third stage. In this era the world is pointed not to Nimrod, not to Homer, but to Christ, who goes about doing good. Ever after this it is not power, it is not genius, but it is goodness. The great man of the future will be the good man of the future.

What seems strange, these three stages of the world's history which I have just mentioned are paralleled in the individual experience of man as he admires the forces operating in the world. What causes the heart of the boy to respond in admiration? David slaying Goliath—*power*. Cæsar leading the Tenth Legion—*power*. Napoleon at the head of the Old Guard—*power*. Let the boy pass into young manhood; what causes his heart to respond in admiration as a young man? Shakespeare creating his wonderful characters—*genius*. Macaulay writing his history—*genius*. Goethe throwing off the marvelous products of his pen—*genius*. Let the young man reach his full maturity and become able to sift and analyze and judge things by the most approved standards; what calls out admiration from the heart of the mature man? John Howard at work among the reeking prisons—*goodness*. Livingstone in the heart of the Dark Continent, struggling for the elevation of Africa—*goodness*. Abraham Lincoln calling into existence the Grand Army of the Republic and writing the Emancipation Proclamation—*goodness*. *Goodness is greatness.* The great man of the future will be the good man of the future. Above all things, then, let the coming patriot give his country a manhood which shall be the incarnation of goodness.

My fellow-citizens, our country first of all wants men—good men; national men *versus* local men; apocalyptic men, men of prevision, seeing a sublime future for the Republic; men of progress, men who are not afraid to improve upon their ancestors; men of powerful pens; men of executive ability; men who are genuine through and through; men like Washington, who not only had the genius of intellect and the genius of war and the genius of statesmanship, but who had preëminently, above all these, *the genius of character.*

> " God give us men! A time like this demands
> Clean minds, pure hearts, true faith, and ready hands.
> Men who possess opinions and a will;
> Men whom desire for office does not kill;
> Men whom the spoils of office cannot buy;
> Men who have honor; men who will not lie;
> Tall men; sun-crowned men; men who live above the fog
> In public duty and in private thinking;
> Men who can stand before a demagogue
> And denounce his treacherous flatteries without winking.
> For while base tricksters, with their worn-out creeds,
> Their large professions, and their little deeds,
> Wrangle in selfish strife, lo! Freedom weeps,
> Wrong rules the land, and waiting Justice sleeps."

The second Washingtonian precept which I wish to present is this:

2. *Be intense Americans.*

It was to found an *American commonwealth* that Washington gave his life It was for *American ideas* that he fought. When his soldiers wanted to crown him as a king, he refused, because he believed that every man in the Republic was a king. A free manhood, carrying in it the necessity of the consent of the governed, free thought, free speech, free schools, with the American flag in them for our boys and girls to salute, a free ballot, a free press—all these are American ideas; and Washingtonism, which is the highest type of Americanism, consists in standing for the defense of these.

I am not ashamed to stand here and advocate intense Americanism, for there is nothing grander under the sky. A fine Americanism is the equation of the highest civilization, of the broadest humanity, of the purest and simplest religion, of the largest liberty, of the grandest personal and political principles, and of magnificent manhood and a holy womanhood.

Intense Americanism requires us, above all things, to look after the integrity and the wholeness of our nation. We must see to it that there is no division of loyalty upon the part of its citizens. We have opened the gates of our nation to all the world and have dispensed the right of franchise freely; we must see to it that all who accept our gift understand what they are doing and give to us in return what we require by the oath of naturalization. GUARDING THE OATH OF NATURALIZATION IS FUNDAMENTAL. Guarding it means guarding our American principles and our American institutions; for if we keep out of citizenship the unworthy, and let into citizenship only those who positively love our principles and institutions, we conserve these. Let us tell all foreigners the moment they step upon our shores that we mean that this Republic shall be practically and ultimately American. The

American Republic exists for the purpose of becoming supreme. In Europe there is Ireland for the Irish who will not consent to become reconstructed, and Italy for the Italians of the same type, and Rome for Romans, and Germany for unworkable Germans, and France for fussy Frenchmen; but on this continent, from Plymouth Rock in the East to the Golden Gate in the West, from the Alaskan snows in the North to the tropical waters of the Gulf of Mexico in the South, *there is room only for Americans.* Now it is not illiberal in us to push Americanism to the front. No; for in Americanism there is room enough and breadth enough for all the races which are willing to unify with us. America exists for the world, and it is axiomatic that America can serve the world *only as it is American.* Americanism is the broadest kind of humanitarianism and the widest type of cosmopolitanism.

When our Republic was organized and our institutions were introduced and our future was outlined, it occurred to American patriots that it would be a generous thing to invite others to the enjoyments of civil wealth. So our Republic unfurled its flag of welcome and waved an invitation to the nations far and near; it opened its door of citizenship to the wide world. But were there no conditions of citizenship? Were not people of all nations invited for a special object? Oh yes; they were invited for this object, viz., to build up the institutions which our fathers had founded and for which they had shed their blood. *They were invited to work out Americanism.* It was the distinct understanding that each one who accepted the invitation accepted also the object of the invitation. Anything else would have been suicide upon the part of our Republic. A strict oath of naturalization was built up at the door of entrance; by that oath every man who became an American citizen was required to renounce forever and entirely all allegiance to every other civil power.

Now all this is easily understood. No honest man dare take that oath with a mental reservation; if any man dare, he steals his citizenship and no more owns it than the thief who plucks your watch from your pocket owns your watch. How do you treat such a thief? You take the watch from him and you legally and lawfully do something more.

When a man is born into our Republic by naturalization, our institutions receive a new defender and the nation an additional element of strength. The oath of naturalization says to every man seeking citizenship, You must subordinate everything to America. There is no class here; there is no union of church and state here. If your creed specify that such a union should exist, you must give up that creed. There is nothing here but Americanism. *And you swear that there shall be nothing here but Americanism.* The oath of naturalization is an oath of purgation whereby all foreign allegiance is renounced. The man who takes it in its spirit is born into a new civil life. Acting in loyalty to that oath, let us see to it that we make public sentiment so true and so American that every foreign thing, man, school, church, shall be completely absorbed and assimilated by republican principles and purposes, *or else shall be openly and unequivocally rejected as un-American, and treated as akin to treason.*

There is only one legal way of transporting the waters of the Danube and the Rhine and the Seine and the Thames and the Tiber, that they may flow by right and peaceably in the channels of the Hudson and the Charles and the Connecticut and the Merrimac and the Columbia and the Mississippi. That way is by evaporation and condensation. The evaporation takes place in Europe; the condensation takes place here in the American atmosphere. Let us see to it that the process which takes place in our American sky-dome is so complete that each drop of water distilled shall be so American that there shall not be in it the least taint or tinge of Danube, Rhine, Seine, Thames, or Tiber. On American soil race should merge into race, as crystal water merges into crystal water, to flow on as a sparkling river of life. Let there be one country for all, one standard of loyalty for all, one system of free State non-sectarian public schools for all, one sacred ballot-box for all, one type of citizenship for all, one Declaration of Independence for all, one national language for all, one flag, Old Glory, the stars and stripes, for all, and one sovereign for all, and that the sovereign will of the people, exercised according to the spirit and purpose of the national Constitution.

The last Washingtonian precept which I stop to present is this:

3. *Patriots, see that America holds her leadership among the peoples and nations of the earth.*

This is a precept which I feel I can confidently urge upon the men of the Grand Army of the Republic, the successors of George Washington in the military life of the nation. No class of men are more willing to see that America leads than you are. There are no men who have done more for their country than you have. You purchased the country with a second and a great price, and you own it as no other class of American citizens own it. Your voice on behalf of the right will be heard when no other voice can prevail. There is no plea like the plea of the empty sleeve and the bullet-scarred body of the veteran soldier.

My fellow-citizens, you won the victories of war; your country now calls upon you to win the greater victories of peace. There remaineth yet much to be done; we are still in our formative period. The clothes of the boy will not answer for the clothes of the man. Growth brings new problems and new battles for ideas and principles. We need men who will fight for honest money, and who will fight for a common-sense measure of raising a sufficient revenue wherewith to run the government. We talk of the old colonial and Revolutionary times as times that were big. Times are always big to earnest men. Our times are big to us if we are earnest; they are crowded with problems which can be solved only by men like Washington and his compeers. There is the money problem and the labor problem and the emigration problem and the race problem and the educational problem and the problem of our foreign policy; and these must all be met and solved, because our solution of these will touch and influence for good or for evil every nation on the earth.

Then there is the great problem of our relations to broad humanity. The oppressed in all the nations of the globe are looking toward America for light and for ruling principles and for certain guidance and for an uplifting hand. We have a mission to all the nations of the world as well as a mission to our citizens at home. Our national experience gives us that mission, our progress gives us that mission, and our holy ambition to reach the highest civilization gives us that mission. It is our mission to lead humanity on all continents, and it is our mission to lead just because civilly we are ahead of humanity.

My task is finished. This is our ideal. When our patriotism matches our ideal, then, with radiant faces, we can turn to our beloved native land and address it in the well-known words of our honored poet:

> "Sail on, O ship of state!
> Sail on, O Union, strong and great!
>   Humanity, with all its fears,
>   With all its hopes of future years,
> Is hanging breathless on thy fate!

> "We know what masters laid thy keel,
> What workmen wrought thy ribs of steel,
>   Who made each mast and sail and rope,
> What anvils rang, what hammers beat,
> In what a forge and what a heat
>   Were shaped the anchors of thy hope!

> "Fear not each sudden sound and shock:
> 'Tis but the wave, and not the rock;
> 'Tis but the flapping of the sail,
> And not a rent made by the gale!

> "In spite of rock and tempest roar,
> In spite of false lights on the shore,
>   Sail on, nor fear to breast the sea!
> Our hearts, our hopes, our prayers, our tears,
> Our faith triumphant over fears,
>   *Are all with thee*—ARE ALL WITH THEE!"

X.

THE CHURCH AND THE REPUBLIC.

X.

THE CHURCH AND THE REPUBLIC.*

I HAVE in my library a volume bearing this title: "Historical and Patriotic Addresses, Centennial and Quadrennial." The American flag forms its frontispiece and American history constitutes the contents of its pages. The book has over one thousand pages. It was issued last year under the editorship of Frederick Saunders, librarian of the Astor Library. It is the intention of the book to give the steps of American progress and set forth the elements of our Republic's strength. In the book are national odes by Whittier and Holmes, and orations by Webster and Adams and Evarts and Curtis and Depew and Winthrop and kindred spirits, and patriotic sermons by loyal divines, closing with a sermon delivered in this pulpit. When I took up this book and turned its pages, this was the one thing which I noticed:

* Delivered in Lafayette Avenue Presbyterian Church, Brooklyn, on Home Mission Sabbath.

looking through the book was like looking over an American landscape or over an American city; the chief thing which caught the eye was the Christian church. In every ode and oration and sermon of the book rises the tapering church spire, tipped with a glittering cross or with a blazing star. Here is a book composed of the deepest thoughts and observations of America's foremost thinkers,—poets, jurists, statesmen, merchants, ministers,—and it represents all classes of Americans as saying, The Christian church has been one of the most potent factors in the construction of the American Republic and one of the greatest bulwarks of its magnificent principles and institutions.

That book set me thinking. It gave me also my topic for this morning. It started such questions with me as these: Is its teaching true? Ought the church spire to shoot up in every patriotic ode and oration and sermon? If the Christian church be the national power which these patriotic men represent it to be, what constitutes its power? How does the church serve the Republic? If the teaching of this book be true, then is it not also true that in the power of the church we have one of the grandest arguments in favor of pushing the great work of home missions in our land? The ultimatum, the objective point, of every American home missionary is to plant a Christian church on the frontier of the Republic, and to make it an elevating, saving, spiritualizing, patriotic power in the wild life which men live on the outposts of our civilization.

I affirm that the teaching of this book concerning the Christian church is true. The church spire is in every American landscape and in every American city, just as it is in every ode and oration and sermon of this historic volume. Without the large prevalence of the church spire jutting from its pages the book would be untrue to American history.

The very first house of any importance which our Pilgrim fathers built on this continent was the house of God. To use the poet's phrase, they made New England the land of " templed hills."

> " I love thy rocks and rills,
> Thy woods and templed hills."

Like the Jews of old, they looked upon church-building as an unmistakable proof of a love of country. " He loveth our nation, and he hath built us a synagogue " (Luke vii. 5). The synagogue was the one democratic institution of Judea, the one institution in the land wholly free from any touch of priest, an institution " of the people and for the people and by the people."

The *Mayflower*, which brought our Pilgrim fathers to Plymouth Rock, was simply the old church of Scrooby Manor afloat and heading its way to a great future. And Plymouth Rock, where the prow of the *Mayflower* touched and where the Scrooby church landed, was simply a fragment of the Alps, broken off at Geneva, the home of John Calvin. Plymouth Rock stands in history as the symbol of Calvinism. The covenant of the *Mayflower*, which every American should write in his memory, shows all this. It shows the play of religion in the origin of American national life. Before the Pilgrim fathers set foot on American soil they took America for God and the Christian religion, and entered into a religious compact with one another. This is the way that covenant opens:

"In the name of God, amen. We whose names are underwritten, having undertaken for the glory of God and the advancement of the Christian faith, do solemnly and mutually, in the presence of God and of one another, covenant and combine ourselves together into a civic body politic."

Do we wonder that, in beginning to construct our nation in accordance with this *Mayflower* compact, the first building of note which the Pilgrim fathers constructed was a Christian church? There was no other way of beginning for them, and as there was no other way of beginning for them, there is no other way of continuing for us. In taking possession of new territory we must run up the church, and we must run it up in the very beginning. The Christian church must be there in the new territory to help formulate the character of its institutions, and to breathe the soul of Christ into its gathering society, and to incarnate God and conscience in all its history and in all its progress. That is the way it was in the beginning. That is the way Plymouth Rock was taken possession of. It is good to keep near to the Plymouth Rock type of life. Take Plymouth Rock out of the Republic, and the Republic will fall to pieces in the very first storm upon the sands of infidelity.

So imbedded in the life of our early civic fathers was the Christian church that we cannot think of them apart from the Christian church. The church was the real morning of the state with them. They saw to it that every infant settlement had its sanctuary, until ten thousand spires pointed upward to the Source of their national prosperity. With them this was the method of their political building: the people made the laws, and the churches made the people. Their churches were local democracies, and of each one this was the motto: "One is your Master, and all ye are brethren." Their churches were the incarnation of federalism and so prophecies of the coming American Union. They built into New England general intelligence, reverence for law, and faith in God. These were the triple foundations which they put underneath the young Republic. When, in after ages, the sons of New-Englanders moved out of New England and sought the West in the conquest of new territory, they belted this whole continent with a zone of New-Englandism and built this triple foundation under our whole political fabric. Into the great West they carried with them their churches, and these continued what they were in the beginning, centers of political intelligence and of patriotic devotion and of hope for the future. The holy and everlasting principles taught in the churches wove new stars and stripes to float over new homes, and added new State luminaries to the galaxy which dotted the blue in our national banner. Some one has said, " Education and religion are at home wherever our flag shakes out its folds," and this is true; but there is a truth prior to this and greater than this, and that truth is, the stars and stripes are at home wherever Christian education and the Christian religion pioneer and take the land and fill it with churches.

I am endeavoring to-day to construct an argument for the establishment of Christian churches in the American Republic for the Republic's good. But in doing so allow me to define the type of a church the multiplication of which I ask. I would not multiply all religious entities which call themselves churches. We have too many of certain

types of church already. I do not argue for a
church with a hierarchy; such a church is too far
away from the people. It is too dogmatic; it
carries too much human authority; it savors too
much of aristocracy. I believe that the authority
of the truth is the only authority which belongs
to any church. I do not believe that the church
should have thumbscrews or racks or dungeons or
swords or bayonets or muskets or cannons of any
kind. There is something better than a military
religion and something more effective than a police
Christianity. There have been churches whose
sermons have had back of them the sword and
whose prayers have had behind them the musket,
but these churches have had their day. There is
room in our Republic only for churches whose influence comes from their goodness, morality, justice, charity, reasonableness, weight of argument,
and amount of truth. The argument which has to
be supported by any kind of human authority is
no argument at all. Every true argument is its
own authority. A prayer which must have a cannon behind it had better never be offered. A truth
which has not force enough in itself to push itself
and gain for itself acceptance is truth which had
better sink out of sight and be allowed so to sink.
A church which demands or claims anything more
than the simple authority of the truth is a church
in which liberty is crucified, and of course it is not

expected that I should argue for churches in which liberty is crucified. Such churches are the enemies of our Republic. I argue for churches of an altogether different spirit. I argue for churches which teach equality, which are large-thoughted, which broaden a man, which know no class distinction among men, which treat capitalist and wage-earner alike, which preach the same law to all, which hold up a lofty ideal on all lines of life, which teach that nothing is politically right which is morally wrong; churches which believe in God and assert God's truth, which believe that God's opinions ought to be our opinions; churches whose theology is axiomatic and which push self-evident truths; churches which eschew speculation and unworkable hypotheses, and put their strength into the affirmation of essentials, which ask no more questions than they can answer; churches which strike at all things that debauch public sentiment, which touch the entire life of the community, which never discuss great and living issues in a whisper, but openly; churches which talk right out against all evil, which believe that the moral law should throttle everything unjust, which believe in man at his climax and which will not rest until he reaches his climax; churches which will not only allow men to think for themselves, but which will teach them to think for themselves; churches which are practical and which stand for accredited and applied Christianity; churches which refuse to be controlled by gold, submitting only to the rule of principle; churches which are up to God in their aims and plans, and not behind God; churches which believe in real Christians and not in nominal Christians, which believe in men and women with the kingdom of heaven built into them; churches which are pillars of fire in dark places, which humiliate men before their own consciences when they do that which is mean and low and vile; churches which preach a full salvation through Jesus Christ, which guide the thought of the community, hold the balances of judgment, inspire the motives of the heart, and in God's name give decision to the will of the multitude; churches which, under God, lead in truth and in duty. Such are the churches I argue for, for such churches will build into the American Republic the elements of perpetuity.

Have such been the churches of the past which have led the American Republic? Not wholly, but in a measure—in a large measure. While I say in a large measure I make no effort to hide facts. I do not screen the churches. I admit that in many regards they have been unworthy and have deserved the rebukes and the philippics administered to them. For example, I remember their guilty silence when negro men and women and negro boys and girls were sold at ten dollars and twenty dollars and thirty dollars a pound, and when African slavery, under the reign of a just God, was forging the thunderbolts of war to smite the Republic. I remember when such men as Wendell Phillips and such women as Lydia Maria Childs refused to sit down at the communion-table of the churches of Boston, because the churches refused to throw themselves on the side of the oppressed. These lovers of liberty met together by themselves and observed the Lord's Supper in their quiet upper room; and in this they were right. Churches do not exist for a contemptible silence, or for a detestable neutrality, or for a masterly inactivity, when there is wrong in the air and when it is the duty of the hour to utter the protest of almighty God against a debasing iniquity. I admit the delinquency of the Christian churches of America in the days of slavery, but this also I must claim for the churches: by and by, under the leading of God, they finally came up to the performance of their duty, and when the great crisis was reached they were loyal to the cause of liberty. Let justice be done all around. When the time came to sustain the Emancipation Proclamation and make its principles a part of our federal Constitution, it was the vote of the Christian churches that carried the day. When that crisis came, if the churches had not done their duty African slavery would have remained the curse of the American Republic to this day.

I have pictured the character of the churches for which I argue to-day and whose multiplication I seek. Give me such churches and you give me so many fountains of national life for the Republic —fountains which will send crystal tides of purity and vitality through every artery and vein of our national and sectional government to cleanse and sweeten and heal and vitalize our government.

I wish to say just here that very few of us have any adequate conception of the power of a pure and holy and loyal Christian church. It is the parallel of irresistible might. It can carry any good cause to triumph in this land when it unitedly and fully asserts itself and when it marches to the music of old "Coronation." We underestimate it, because when we think of the church we think simply of the pulpit and make that stand for the church. The pulpit is not the church; the church is far more than that. The church includes in itself all the agencies which it creates and supports and mans. The religious press, the religious platform, Young Men's Christian Associations, Christian Endeavor Societies, Sabbath-schools, Christian colleges and seminaries, the vast missionary societies, the consecrated gold and silver in the bank vaults of Christians, the millions of devoted men and women who keep step to the purposes of heaven, and the millions who are in its grand membership and who form the hosts of God's elect—these are the church, and not merely the pulpit with its single voice here and there proclaiming the gospel. Now when all these personalities and agencies and influences give themselves up to the work of God on earth, and to the pulling down of the strongholds of sin and Satan, what can successfully resist them? What cannot they accomplish? They can build churches by the thousands, mold nations, and govern the world. If this be true, then the thing our Republic wants is the church of God everywhere throughout its broad territory, creating and supporting its redemptive agencies and forming and leading public sentiment.

At this point I imagine you ask me to particularize. You say to me, "You are asking for more Christian churches, and that in the name of the Republic; tell us wherein the Christian churches benefit the Republic." In responding to this request I will indicate two ways in which the Christian church serves the American Republic. The first way is this:

1. *It protects and fosters those institutions which have proved a blessing to the Republic.*

I will center my thought here upon one institution, viz., the Christian Sabbath. The rule is, where there is no church and no church-going there is no Sabbath, and where there is no Sabbath and no Sabbath-keeping there is no religion, and where there is no religion there is no God, and where there is no God there is no conscience, and where there is no conscience there is no respect for the rights of men, and where there is no respect for the rights of men there is no security for life or property. Now take religion, God, conscience, respect for the rights of man, and protection of life and property out of the American Republic, and just how much of what is left would be worth having?

How are men to be made good and honest and trustworthy and upright without a time for religious culture? That population which habitually neglects the pulpit or its equivalent can ultimately be led by the merest charlatan, and will be. Look abroad over the map of popular freedom in the world and you will find that it is not accidental that Switzerland and Scotland and England and the United States, the lands where the Sabbath is best observed, are almost the entire map of safe popular government.

The Sabbath is the starting-point of great good in our land, and any instrument which will guard and protect that is of incomparable value to us and our country. I ask no stronger argument for the Sabbath than this, viz., the finest type of our American men are its Christian Sabbatarians. They are first in morals; they lead in all the great humanities; they project the highest and most practical ideals; they build up the noblest and most enviable lives; they leave behind them gifts redolent with blessings and beautiful with hopes and aspirations for the progress of their fellow-men and their country; they leave Pratt Institutes and Packer Institutes, and beneficent homes and asylums. Their Sabbaths are their most telling days. Sabbath rest makes them steady-nerved and clear-brained and strong-hearted and sweet-tempered and tender and broad in their sympathies.

There is a myth concerning an old painter that by a happy chance he compounded one day a certain mordant which, colorless itself, possessed the power of heightening every color with which it was mixed. By the help of his discovery, from being a common artist he rose to the position of a noted master. His works were renowned for the marvelous brilliance of their tints. On his canvas was produced in exactest hue the waving emerald of the forest, the silver gleam of the river, the swimming light of the sunset, and the infinite azure of the sky. Everywhere and always the charm of the picture was due to that colorless nurse of color, which by its strange alchemy transfigured the crudeness and coarseness of the common tint.

My fellow-man, it is not mere ecclesiastical prejudice which asserts that our American Sabbath has silently and similarly wrought vigor and attractiveness and power into our American life.

All fair-minded judges pronounce it our social mordant. The student of legislation, the observer of our domestic and social prosperity, the inquirer into the excellences of our educational system, one and all find everywhere the influence of national reverence for the Lord's day. Unrecognized in its workings, the Sabbath is the element that has wrought out the choice beauty of the best things of which we boast. To it, and largely to it, we are indebted for juster laws, better schools, happier homes, greater security of social order, than can be found in any other land.

There is a second way in which the Christian church serves the American Republic. It is this:

2. *It keeps before the people the true idea with regard to national greatness and national strength.*

This point leads right into the midst of one of the burning questions of the day, viz., What are the strong pillars of our Republic? What elements do we need to give our nation perpetuity? Even scholarly men, like the president of Harvard College, have brought their minds to bear upon this question and have felt the importance of trying to correct wrong views, which are so largely the popular views. President Eliot has an elaborate article in a recent issue of the " Forum " on this subject, " Some Reasons Why the American Republic may Endure." The things which he enumerates he calls the new principles and forces which make for the permanency of the Republic. In his article he first reviews the history of all the boasted republics of time and shows wherein their strength lay. But none of these republics proved permanent, and yet they had all of the things which, the casual observer imagines, constitute our greatness. They had broad lands, great wealth, luxurious living, large inter-commerce, fine military equipment, fine architecture, great achievements in sculpture and art, and vast population. These did not save the republics of Rome and Greece and Italy and France and Mexico, and alone, with no other possessions, these cannot save the American Republic. It ought not to be the destiny of the American Republic to repeat the history of these ancient powers. But make New York a second Carthage, and Boston a second Athens, and Philadelphia a second Antioch, and Washington a second Rome, and our Republic will simply repeat the old experiment of history. When he has set forth this fact President Eliot proceeds to enumerate and elaborate the elements in which our strength consists. They are such as these: toleration in religion, general education, better domestic relations, publicity of life (secured by the morning and evening issue of the daily press), platform discussion of everything that pertains to the public welfare, increase of mutual dependence of man on man and the growing sense of brotherhood and unity, and, finally, the greater hopefulness of men as they deal with God and with man and with the broad world.

There is much that is tonic in this timely article of the president of Harvard. But my point is this: all that he presents, which is true and which is in harmony with history and with facts, the church of God has been presenting from the very beginning of our national life. The church has been asserting all along that it is not material wealth, but moral wealth, that makes a nation; not broad acres, but principles. It is not gold, but men—men of God. It is the things of God that make a nation strong and keep it strong. It is character, personality, ideas, that make a nation.

The church, in teaching American citizens, begins with God. The first essential is to get into right relation with God, to get His law written on the heart and incorporated in the life. Institutions must harmonize with His will, and so must rulers, and so must voters. The church, in instructing American citizens, sets Jesus Christ before men as the pattern after which to model. His views of man, man's dignity, man's rights, man's needs, must be held. His principles and His views of doctrines concerning God must be adopted. The divine love which shines out of His cross must be allowed to dominate all the affairs of human life. His hopefulness must be granted an entrance into the souls of men. His manhood must be reproduced in our citizens, and the nation must wheel itself into line with the purposes of His coming kingdom of righteousness and peace and love. It is the mission of this nation and of every nation to prepare the way, so that the pure, white, and unsullied feet of the Christ may be able to ascend the steps that lead to His millennial throne.

> "In the beauty of the lilies Christ was born across the sea,
> With a glory in His bosom that transfigures you and me;
> As He died to make men holy,
> Let us die to make men free.
>   Our God is marching on."

The church of God is laboring, and has been laboring, to make our nation a Christian nation in the highest and truest sense, and to my mind there is nothing equal to that. That is the only road to perpetuity. There is a grand glory in a Christian nation. It is the greatest known living force in the world. Take England, for example. "Not alone with drum-beat," as Webster has put it, "has she encircled the earth." She has carried civilization and Christianity wherever she has carried her flag; and she has carried also with her flag her noble language, with its treasures of literature and science and religion. She has planted great institutions and principles in every latitude of the globe. Even we have inherited much from her. All that is grand and good in our national life we have inherited from the Bible she gave us and from the Christian churches which Englishmen, and men kindred with them, have planted on our soil.

Do I properly magnify and represent the Christian church, this institution of God which announces the law of God, and which guards the day of God, and which labors to make the nation Christian? Is it the power in this land of ours which I have represented it to be? If so, then duty is plain, and there is no escape from duty. What is duty? It is duty to give the Republic Christian churches. Build a church in every valley and put a bell on it, build a church on every hilltop and put a bell on it, build a church on every prairie and put a bell on it, build a church on every ranch of Texas and New Mexico and put a bell on it, build a church amid the snows of Alaska and put a bell on it. When you have done all this, then set these bells a-ringing, singly and all together. Let them ring out everywhere a "Hosanna to the Son of David!" and call all the people to Sabbath rest and Sabbath worship and Sabbath fellowship and Sabbath instruction. Keep the air vibrating with the ten thousand thousand chimes until, in the language of the Hebrew prophet, our land may rightly be called "Praise." When we have church bells everywhere, from Alaska to New Mexico, and from Maine to California, then we can challenge them to do their God-assigned work for the American Republic. We can say to them:

> " Ring out the old, ring in the new;
> Ring out the false, ring in the true.
>
> " Ring out a slowly dying cause
> And ancient forms of party strife;
> Ring in the nobler modes of life,
> With sweeter manners, purer laws.
>
> " Ring out false pride in place and blood,
> The civic slander and the spite;
> Ring in the love of truth and right,
> Ring in the common love of good.
>
> " Ring out the darkness of the land;
> . . . . . .
> Ring out the narrowing lust of gold;
> Ring out the thousand wars of old,
> Ring in the thousand years of peace."

But let me get a little nearer the duty of the morning, a little nearer the collection basket. We have found that the churches of God are blessings to our Republic; the questions now are, Where shall we plant them, and how? The great cause of Home Missions, which knocks at our door this morning, answers both questions. Plant them at the strategic points which we have chosen in the North and West, and which form our field of labor, and plant them by contributing of your gold to replenish our treasury. Let there be no footsteps backward in giving and in sending. Brethren, a great field is open to us in the great West—fields as large as Germany, as large as England, as large as France. You could take the whole of France and put it into the State of Texas and then have a border of twenty miles all around uncovered.

San Francisco is only the center point of our territory west. It is as far to the end of Alaska from San Francisco as it is from here to San Francisco. The six States recently received into the Union have nearly one fifth of the entire area of the United States if you exclude Alaska. And all this is our land.

And remember the gigantic growth of population in these frontier States. It is just as gigantic as the land. The question of the Christian guidance of this our Titanic growth is the grave question which confronts us, and it is a question which touches the very life of the nation. The gigantic work to be done out there calls for gigantic giving here. We must give the great West Christian workers and Christian gold. We must give the great West Christian churches. We must not let the growth get ahead of the cultivation. Chicago is an illustration of the growth we may expect in Western fields. In 1830 the Chicago directory was not a very portly volume. The commercial and business section of it stands thus; I will read you the whole of it: " Taverns, two; Indian traders, three; butchers, one; merchants, one." The poll list for the county election embraced thirty-two voters. To-day the directory of Chicago is larger than that of New York. To-day Chicago requires Lake Michigan as a goblet to satisfy its thirsty lips. If that be an index of Western growth, soon the shanty or umbrella towns of to-day, with a great deal of outdoors to them, will rapidly become teeming centers of life.

Although our task is great, there is one thing in our favor: our dominion is not fractional and therefore not hard of access. With the exception of Alaska, it lies in one undivided body and is animated practically by one blood, one national language, and it is living under one law, enacted at one common center. This is a great advantage and a help in evangelizing the Republic. In this regard it contrasts with the British empire. Her cosmopolitan dominion is scattered over the world in forty-five parcels.

When I look at the great work to be done, I thank God for the Home Missionary boards of the different denominations, who are so alive to the needs of the hour and so willing to push the work. These boards have done grand service for our country. I want to tell you this: I have found out by investigation that the first churches in Cleveland, in Sandusky, in Galena, in Beloit, in Dubuque, in Burlington, in Leavenworth, in Omaha, in Cheyenne, in Tacoma, and in other important centers, were Home Missionary churches. The Home Missionary societies have founded over five sixths of all the churches in the great Western States. In view of this I am ready to-day to affirm that if you subtract the Home Missionary societies from our national history, you subtract the freedom from our Republic. Since this is so, we cannot be too liberal with our Home Missionary Society; we cannot make our collection too large.

Here I am face to face with the collection. I have mentioned that obnoxious word "collection." And the times are hard; and I want more than usual, for more is needed. When I call at your homes to see you socially, you show me your palatial mansions, and your treasures of art and of beauty which you have brought from abroad; a word now and then drops out about some successful business enterprise; and then there are hints of gain and of financial ability. But these are not the things we hear of, talk about, or think about when we are in the presence of the collection basket. We forget all about our palatial houses. We talk about going to the poorhouse. We canvass the cost of living. We figure up the school bills of our children. We lament our large tax bills. We look at how we are swindled by political corruption. We figure how much the city was cheated in the erection of the Soldiers' Arch. Then we come back to the point we started with: the times are hard, **very hard.** Do you know that in all this you only show me the debit side of the ledger, and not the credit side—your liabilities, and not your assets? What about those corner lots, those mortgages, those stocks, those dividends, rentals, that interest, those accumulations of past years? Oh, that debit side of your ledger, with taxes and debts! I sympathize with you. It is an awful burden and plague and worry. I come to your relief. I have a generous proposition to make. Let me tell you what I will do. I will take the debit side of the combined ledgers of this great church if you will give me the credit side of the combined ledgers, and I will pay your taxes and your children's school bills and the necessary expenses of your households—eliminating the superfluities, of course, i.e., the debts which you incur by bowing down to and obeying a godless, carnalizing fashion. More than this, I will not only pay all necessary bills,—necessary from a Christian standpoint,—but I will abolish all collections for home missions and foreign missions and city missions, and all missions, and I will contribute to all these grand essential causes, without a collection, from the credit side of your ledgers, and I will contribute so largely as to raise the name of this church in the estimation of the community and of all church boards and all deserved charity organizations. I am not through yet. And then, out of the remainder of the funds left, I will pay all the expenses of the church and of the chapels, and I will generously double the salaries of all the salaried workers, and add a third to the salary of the choir, and give a trifle of a dividend to my faithful elders and deacons and trustees to encourage them and make them more faithful. And when I have done all this I will guarantee to show you a large and a respectable balance. That is my offer. If it is accepted on the spot, the contribution of this church to-day to home missions will be the largest ever known in its history.

If you reject my proposition, then forever cease talking about hard times on collection Sabbath, or of school bills or taxes, or of the debit side of your ledger. If my proposition is rejected and you think you can do better for the home mission cause and for the reputation of this church than I have proposed to do, I submit to your decision and step out of the way and give you your golden opportunity. The collection will now be taken up.

XI.

AMERICA FOR CHRIST.

XI.

AMERICA FOR CHRIST.*

In one of his glowing letters Paul the Hebrew writes to his fellow-countrymen, "Brethren, my heart's desire and prayer to God for Israel is, that they might be saved."

These burning words introduce Paul as a citizen. They photograph him as he appears in a supreme patriotic moment, and the result is a magnificent personage—a Christian patriot. The camera of inspiration catches the picture just as an intense prayer leaps from his intense soul. Although the prayer is condensed into one brief sentence, yet it is a prayer of magnificent sweep. It seeks the grandest display of the glory of the true God and the greatest good of a whole nation. The patriotic prayer of the apostle at first sight seems like a chance thing, the creation of a second, the outburst of a passing emotion; but it is not; it is far more than that. It is not a meteor sentiment, a

* Delivered in Park Street Church, Boston, Mass.

flash in the sky followed by the usual darkness. It is a burning, soul-absorbing desire; it is a regal passion; it is a well-considered purpose wearing the robes of a prayer; it is the climax of a long train of thought.

Paul had before him two great objects, Christ and Country, and these he had been contemplating with all the powers of his giant faculties. These had for some time absorbed his whole being. He had been contemplating Christ: Christ's wonderful and transforming character; Christ's holy and regenerating doctrines; Christ's world-wide principles, which carry in them life and power and perpetuity for nations; Christ's crown rights and royal prerogatives; Christ's enthronement in heaven; Christ's investiture with the universal scepter; Christ's name, which is written upon His vesture and on His thigh, "King of kings and Lord of lords;" Christ's coming future, with the marching hosts of truth sweeping on to victory and trampling underfoot all resisting foes.

He had also been contemplating his country. He knew his country well, and it was vividly before his mind. All its beauty and greatness passed before him. Jerusalem in its glory, the joy of all the land; Eshcol with its clusters; Lebanon with its majestic cedars; the temple of marble and gold with its sacred memories; Gilead with its healing balm; the rolling Jordan with its baptismal waters;

Hermon with its sparkling dew; Sharon with its blooming roses; and the valley of Esdraelon with its waving crops—all the history of his country passed in review before him, and we hear him recapitulate to his heart the shining facts in its record. "To my people," he says, "pertaineth the adoption, and the glory, and the covenants, and the giving of the law, and the service of God, and the promises; whose are the fathers, and of whom as concerning the flesh Christ came, who is over all, God blessed forever."

You see the contemplation which had been holding the soul of the apostle, and in it you see the origin of his prayer. Christ and country were united in his deepest thinking, and this was the reason that when he came to pray Christ and country were united in his most ardent supplication. He saw his country's antagonism to Christ, and the doom which inevitably awaited it if it continued its antagonism. It had just crucified Jesus. He saw also the glory that awaited Israel if it would only repent of its crucifixion of Jesus and bow in loyalty to His scepter. Standing before these things, his patriotism burned at a white heat. He was like John Knox, the Scottish reformer, of whose patriotic agony history gives us such a vivid picture. Casting himself prostrate in prayer before the God of nations, Knox's cry to God was, "Give me Scotland, or I die!" "Scotland for Christ!" Paul's cry to God was, "Give me Israel, or I die!" "Israel for Christ!"

From Paul we wish to learn our duty to our country. We wish his patriotism to relive in us; we wish to bring before our souls the two objects which he brought before his soul,—Christ and Country,—that we may pray as he prayed. It is our privilege to see Christ as Paul saw Him; more than this, it is our privilege to look at the march of Christ through nineteen centuries. The centuries transfigure Him and give Him an added glory. They reveal Him as the mighty force in history. History reveals that the ruling nations of the age are the nations in which He is honored.

It is our privilege to see a country equal to Paul's country. We look at our country after a century and a quarter of progress, and what a panorama of grandeur do we see in our native land! What broad acres full of the bread of life for the hungry! There are millions and trillions of acres. What magnificent mountains and rivers and lakes! what inland and what shore-land! what salubrity of climate, the best of all zones! From lake to gulf, and from sea to sea, there is salubrity. There is a happy mean of temperature, neither too rigorous nor too luxurious, but a temperature demanding healthful activity. What a country! A country abounding in wood and stone and coal and cotton and iron and oil and precious metals and all the staples of the world. It is a country whose resources are so distributed as to require an extended commerce and the varied activities of agriculture and manufacture and trade, all of which are blessings to any nation, giving it work and vitality and strength. It is a country in itself calculated to keep the many States of our Union one and united. The very configuration of our land demands national unity, while the lakes and the St. Lawrence and the Mississippi, with its vast network of tributaries, tie all indissolubly together. Antagonistic nationalities could not occupy our land. To them it would be a vast plain of perpetual war. They would require chains of forts from Boston to San Francisco. To a united people it seems purposely laid out for a grand civilization. It requires one people, one language, one literature, one religion. Pervaded and controlled by the same language and institutions and sentiments of brotherhood, it becomes a splendid school for humanity's higher education, a workshop for the grandest of achievements, and a home for all beautiful graces and brotherly fellowships.

Not only have we a great land, but, like Israel of old, we have a grand history. We started with the past as our inheritance. Our historian Motley tells us that American democracy is the result of all that was great in the bygone time. All leads up to it and it embodies all. Mount Sinai is in it,

Greece is in it, and so is Rome, and so is Egypt, and so is England. All the arts are in it, all the reformations are in it, all the discoveries are in it. As it fronts the future it carries in it glorious prophetic eras eclipsing all. As we look back we are like Paul; we cannot refrain from enumerating the providential things in our past. What providential things? I consider this as providential. Our land was colonized, not by effete despotisms of church and state, not by the Romish Church with its antiquated ritualism and ecclesiastical tyranny, not by despotic Spain, and not by gay and flippant France, but by Britain, whose people had grandly battled their way to constitutional liberty, and who had the richest language and the grandest literature and the most solid progress in all the line of European nationalities. Nor is this all. Our land was colonized by the very flower of England, the God-fearing few who would rather die than be false, and who were willing to brave the unknown perils of an unknown land in order that they might have freedom to worship God. The choicest heroes and saints of the Old World became the pioneers and leaders of the New World. When we stand amid these things and contemplate, when we recall the sufficiency of Christ for a nation and even for a world, when we recall the past of our nation with its attainments, and when we think of the far greater future with its possibilities, as patriotic

Christians there is only one cry in our souls, and that is, " America for Christ! Christ for America!"

I mean to push this motto; I push it on three grounds: for America's sake, for the world's sake, for Christ's sake.

1. We demand America for Christ for America's sake.

We know what Christ does for an individual when he yields himself up to Him; He fills him with His own life and makes him one of the luminaries of the world. He lifts the apostles out of the fishing-boats and places them upon the thrones of thought which rule the ages; He makes Paul a leader of mankind; He makes Luther a reformer of a whole kingdom. We know what is the result of treason to Christ. The doom of Judas shows us this. Contrast Judas and John, Judas and Peter, Judas and James. Contrast Christlessness with Christfulness. The difference between them is the difference between day and night, between success and failure. Now, what Christlessness and Christfulness are in the individual man, Christlessness and Christfulness are in the nation. A nation is only an aggregation of individual men. Christ deals with nations. In His sight nations are moral personalities. They perform all the functions of a moral person, and He treats them according to their character. Divorce your nation from Christ and you ring its death-knell; you link its fate to the fate of Judas. Marry your nation to Christ and you open for it a door into a new future and secure for it a place among the nations of the world like that which Paul occupied among men. Tell me how the American Republic will treat Christ and I will tell you the future of the American Republic. Because the destiny of this nation depends upon its relation to Christ, I stand at the portals of the nation and as a loyal citizen cry, "Lift up your heads, O ye gates; and be ye lifted up, ye everlasting doors; and the King of glory shall come in."

We are not willing to dwell upon this fact at which I have hinted, viz., the very life of our Republic depends upon its loyalty to the King of kings. But as patriots it is our duty to read this fact from the sacred page of God's Book, and act upon it, rather than wait until God compels us to read the fact in the ashes of our Republic when it is too late to act.

The whole story is told us in the Second Psalm. In this psalm we have a complete treatise with regard to the duty of a nation Godward. It teaches us that civil government is of God and that God is the Ruler of the nations. He rules nations through "the Anointed," i.e., the Christ. He has put all authority into the pierced hands, and nations must acknowledge the Crucified One or meet the traitor's fate. There is a wonderful and an expressive picture in the Second Psalm. In it we see God walking among the nations on a tour of inspection, just as a potter walks among the newly finished vessels that have been brought out of the kiln. The potter has an ideal for every vessel which has been shaped in the pottery, and burned, and given permanence. The potter has a reputation to sustain for ideal and for skill of execution, and in every vessel which he shapes and finishes his reputation is at stake. He examines every vessel minutely. In his hand he holds an iron rod, and when he comes to a misshapen, defective vessel, he deals it a crushing blow and strikes it into dust. Why? Because a misshapen vessel is a slander and a slur. It maligns his reputation and falsifies his skill. Even so God has a reputation to sustain in the business of nation-making; and in His tour of inspection among the nations and kingdoms of the earth He must shatter with His rod of iron and cast out of sight all those nations which by oppression and godlessness slander His reputation and misrepresent His civic ideal. The only wisdom of a nation is to wheel into line with God and accord with the divine ideal. History is only a transcript of this psalm, a translation of the printed page into actual life. The highway of history is right through the shattered fragments of nationalities which have been broken under the stroke of God's rod of judgment. Nations mightier than ours have been shivered.

As American patriots we should not allow ourselves to be blind to facts by a foolish optimism. We should not be puffed up with Yankee conceit, as though danger were an impossible thing to us. With all our greatness, the God of nations could break us in pieces with a single stroke. Our only protection is loyalty to Christ. We must make our land and keep our land a gospel land. Whenever America becomes a Sahara of infidelity it will be as worthless as any other moral sand-heap. Whenever the citizens of our Republic allow the sirocco of atheism to sweep it, then, so far as I am concerned, farewell, Republic; whoever wishes may claim the old, withered, shriveled, blasted, lifeless thing which the sirocco leaves.

But is our view on these matters the view universally held? No; men who have no practical interest in Christ and His religion ignore Him and His as factors in the upbuilding of nations. For example, an infidel science sees the elements of a nation's destiny solely in its physical environment. Buckle writes the history of civilization as if character were the product of outward circumstances. Following in his wake, but without going to his extreme, Humboldt and Guyot, and students of physical geography, show how soil and climate, rivers and mountains, have mightily affected the people's life. What science teaches is the truth, but at best it is only part of the truth. The highest truth and the largest truth and the fullest truth is this: the element of religion is the one element above all elements that determines destiny. Religion has made grand men and grand nations in all climates and upon all territories.

The majority of men attribute our greatness as a nation to our natural resources and to the width and richness of our land; the *Mayflower* and Plymouth Rock are ignored. But that is not the true explanation, and facts show it. The North American Indian possessed these natural and material resources ages and ages before our Pilgrim fathers set foot on this continent. There is not a river nor a mine nor a field that was not here when they owned the land. Why did not God unlock these natural resources to them? This is the reason: He kept them that He might give them to those who were in true relations with Himself. Our Pilgrim fathers came to these shores for His glory, and gave themselves to Him in the *Mayflower* covenant as a preparation for taking possession of the land. They were consecrated to His cause, and this is the reason He opened the treasures to them and to their children. My fellow-countrymen, it required the magic inspiration of spiritual life to transmute the natural resources of the United States into wealth. Our territory, every inch of it breadthwise and lengthwise, is in the hand of God, and He can lock up its mines, and stop the flow of its rivers of oil, and blight its most fertile soil. Canaan was once fertile, but it is not fertile to-day, and you know the reason; Paul's ideal for Canaan was not realized; had it been realized, had his nation accepted Christ and His gospel and lived by these and maintained its loyalty to these, we should have Judea as a ruling power in the world to-day. The poet would still be able to find the Twenty-third Psalm on the very fields where David first picked it up, and Jerusalem would still be flourishing in its glory, and the old temple doors would be open on this very Sabbath that the nations might enter in and worship.

I wish, in treating this point that America needs Christ, that the nation should be taken for Christ for America's sake—I wish to hew close to the line of history and to build only with historical facts. History shows that the Christ-men and the Christ-women have always been the loyal men and women of the land, and the men and women who have inaugurated great and beneficial movements. Our national liberties were bought with their blood. This is an open and fearless statement, but it has as many verifications as there are races in our American nationality. Each race has contributed its heroes. Some of you have come down the line of the Pilgrim history, and you have the verification of the statement on that line. Some of you came to America in the loins of the French Huguenots, and in the history of these noble refugees you have a verification of the statement. Some of you are Dutch, your ancestors were the true-minded Hollanders who gave America primitive New York, and you have a verification of the statement on that line.

I know the verification which the statement receives on the line of the history of the Covenanters of America, and I am proud to be able to speak of this verification. Scotland is not the only land of Covenanter heroism. America has its stories of Covenanter heroism. The Covenanters were here before the American Republic, and they held the principles of the American Revolution long before the American Revolution was inaugurated. Bancroft tells us that two years before the American Declaration of Independence was issued in Philadelphia, 1776, the Covenanters in Mecklenburg, N. C., in 1774 issued the Mecklenburg declaration, and it contained the very same principles which are in the Philadelphia Declaration. Two years in advance? Yes. All honor to the Covenanters of America. When the Revolutionary War was declared that old church almost to a man fell into rank, and the report of the Covenanter's rifle was heard in the very forefront of the battle. But why single these men out? To show that wherever there were true Christians there were true warriors for American liberty. Through Christian men and women of all races the gospel worked itself into our civil life. The Pilgrims of Massachusetts, the Covenanters of the Carolinas, the Huguenots of New Jersey, the Hollanders of New York, the Episcopalians of Virginia, all were loyal. The story of their loyalty to country and of their sacrifice for country is one. The type of men who built the nation in the past, and the principles with which they built, are the men and the principles which alone can develop and preserve the nation.

Allow me to push this point just a little further. Give our country men who fear God and God only, and who live perpetually in His sight, and who feel that God has commissioned them to carry on reform and incorporate Christ into the national life, and you give it the men who become the heroes of the country. They are the men of courage. If I were allowed to mention the name of one man as an illustration, I would mention the name of John Brown. What John Brown? John Brown of Osawatomie, the man whom Wendell Phillips eulogized in eloquent oration, and of whom Whittier sang in thrilling poem. Whatever you may think of him, you must admit that he acted up to his light and that he thought he was doing God's service. It was this thought which filled him with courage and sustained him to the last. The men who executed him hoped to break down his courage, and this was the method they followed:

when they put him on the scaffold they kept the poor old man standing full twenty minutes on the death-drop, with the black cap drawn over his eyes, expecting every instant to be launched into eternity. They thought that they would subdue his heroism by the awful suspense and compel him to die as a trembling weakling. They were afraid that he would die the hero, which he did, and that after his death the story of his heroism would be a power, which it was. He bore the suspense without the least shadow of flinching. John Brown died on the scaffold as he fought at Harper's Ferry, a man of unyielding pluck and a witness to the power of what a thought of God can do by way of breathing manhood into a man. That old Christian man gave to the nation the war-song of America, the Marseillaise which put soul into the Northern army and which did more than any one thing to preserve the Union and carry the forces of Grant and Sherman and Sheridan to victory. America needs Christ—the rule of Christ, the truth of Christ, the spirit of Christ, the gospel of Christ, and the men of Christ.

2. We demand America for Christ for the world's sake.

It is well known that America is the great cosmopolitan nation of the world; it is a fusion of nationalities. Hence the eyes of all nations are upon it; hence all the nations claim kinship with it.

We can best see the relation of America to the world by putting it in contrast with England. England and America are the great unmeasured Christian powers to whom God has largely committed the evangelization of the nations. What we wish to notice as we put them side by side is the different ways in which, under the providence of God, they find their opportunities and their duties.

England has comparatively a small territory and a full and overflowing population crowding her small territory. As a natural result she throws out her people from her overcrowded territory; she sends out colonies upon colonies into other lands. For three hundred years colonization has been a marked feature of her foreign policy. She has made her presence felt by her colonial possessions and by her arms in every part of the globe. In America, as well as in Asia and Africa, she has her English-speaking settlements; while the uncivilized tribes and races around have felt the beneficence of her protection and power. Wherever she has planted her standard she has carried the fruits of a thousand years of progress and liberty and learning and religion and law. This she has done in British and Central America, in Sierra Leone, in Natal and in the Transvaal Republic, and especially in British India. For the hundreds of millions of people thus brought under her sway, she has assumed the direct responsibility of their temporal and eternal weal, and if she gives to these good government, and the means of education, and the true religion, and the Christ of God, she will do her fair share toward the evangelization of the world. This it seems under God is preëminently her work and a work which she accepts and is ready to do.

The work of America, on the other hand, is different. Instead of sending out her colonies to distant lands, and bringing other peoples under her sway by conquest, she has opened her vast territory to be colonized. She has invited all nations and races to meet and mingle here and make one composite family, thus forming a world's republic, and thus illustrating the world's humanity. In view of this, America becomes to the world what the normal school is to the State. On her own soil she gathers the children of the nations, and in her homes and churches and schools she trains them to be the teachers of the world. This is an opportunity such as is given to no other nation on the face of the earth. These polyglot populations are thrown upon her to be fused into one nationality by one culture and one faith and one liberty and one civilization and one religion.

The responsibility laid upon her, therefore, is a double one: first and supremely, to keep the fountains of her own intelligence and virtue and religion pure for the sake of the native-born in the land; and second, to ply with all the forces of Christian learning and religion the thousands of the unevangelized who have come to her shores, that they may send back to their old homes, in the form of letters and newspapers and earnest appeals, the blessed gospel of the Son of God to work as a regenerating and converting power in the different fatherlands across the sea.

All this being true, it is the veriest truism to say that America taken for Christ means the nations of the world far and near taken for Christ; America a Christian nation means a mighty witness for God among all lands of the earth.

I would like to arouse an enthusiasm on behalf of our grand nationality. Let the enthusiasm of other nations over nationalities infinitely inferior to ours teach us. Let us gather a stimulus from the enthusiasm which others have relative to nationalities that are as yet only in the air, that have as yet taken no better shape than a dream. We had an illustration of such enthusiasm a few years ago, during the days when the name of Parnell was untarnished and when the character of Parnell was a masterful and rallying power. Men of the Celtic race, colleagues of Parnell, crossed the Atlantic to plead in this land the cause of a nationality which existed only in human hope. You remember how these men were received. The largest auditoriums in our largest cities were crowded to suffocation to receive these delegates of the National League of Ireland and to express sympathy with constitutional liberty and Home Rule and national right. The green flag with the harp was unfurled and waved ; great audiences were thrilled and lifted into rapture by the simple idea of an Irish nationality. If such be the treatment of an unattained thing, if such be the enthusiasm that can be created by an unrealized dream, how great should be our enthusiasm over our American nationality, purchased by the Revolution and then purchased again by our long Civil War! It is not a thing of dream, but a thing of glorious reality, sending its genius and its spirit to the ends of the earth.

My fellow-men, our country is the battle-ground on which the conflicts of the ages are to be fought and decided. It is the valley of decision, filled with multitudes and multitudes. Every instinct of our being ought to say, " Let that nation be saved, and saved at once, which carries the world's largest hopes and the world's final destinies." In the Christianizing of our nation the Republic has its life at stake, society its order, labor its reward, home its happiness, and the world its future.

What are we going to give the world as it pours in upon us on every side? With what are we going to Americanize and Christianize and utilize these multitudes, these millions from the different nationalities? That is the burning question of the hour. How are we going to unify our citizens? There are certain things we must eliminate from them, which are alien to our history and our faith and which are deadly in their effects. There are imported treasons which would throttle the Republic, and against which we must not adopt halfway measures, but measures which will destroy them root and branch. How are we going to fuse into our nationality and make good citizens of the incoming masses, the men whose personality will be as great a political power in a very few months as is the personality of the native-born octogenarian?

I am told that we must educate them. Pass that on, for that is true; we must educate them. We must educate them by our national days, which lift up as on a pedestal the great historical facts and doctrines of the nation. We must educate them by righteous laws, clearly proclaimed and rigidly enforced. We must educate them by preserving intact our blood-bought institutions which are the embodiment of the essential truths of our nationality. Especially must we educate the children of these incoming multitudes. There are fifteen millions of school-children in this land, who in a few years will receive the Republic into their hands; as Christian patriots we must stand by the rights of these children, and we must stand by that institution, that great unifier of the nation, which the fathers built for them and which has been in the nation from the very beginning, viz., the free public school. Paralyzed be the hand, foreign or native-born, Protestant or Catholic, that dare fire a murderous shot against that strong citadel of American unity and American intelligence. Such a man should be treated as we treat the man who fires on the flag.

But something more is needed. We must give the incoming masses the pure, simple gospel of Jesus Christ. This is our only bulwark against moral evil and intemperance and social impurity and atheism. When we take away the false religions and the deadly isms from our new-made citizens we must give them something in the place of these; and we must give them something positive. The gospel is that positive something. It brings man positive models, positive views of himself and of his destiny, positive commandments, positive principles, and positive duties. We must overcome their evil with our good; we must give them something better than that which they have. We can learn from Boniface just here. He was a brave and conquering missionary of the middle ages; he plunged fearlessly into the dark and tangled forests of Germany and conquered thousands of the savages for Christ. Near Gossamer, in Upper Hesse, there stood a vast and venerable oak, sacred for ages to Thor, the god of thunder. St. Boniface tried in vain to win the Germans from the superstitious adoration of the thunderous oak. At last he seized an ax, and the pagans stood around in breathless wonder and alarm. He sent stroke after stroke ringing on the gnarled trunk. The priest of Thor implored the deity to avenge himself, and the pagans thought that each moment the scathing lightning flash would smite down the sacrilegious monk. But no flash came, and then at last with thunderous fall the mighty oak crashed down. But Boniface was wise. He knew that if he did not put a better worship in the idol's place the old idolatry would reënter and another oak would be chosen. So he built out of the fragments of the fallen splintered tree the chapel of St. Peter's, and in the room of the worship of the thunderer left the worship of the Crucified One. This kept Thor forever out of their hearts. While we take from America's incoming multitudes their evil isms we have only done half our work, and the least half. The isms will come back again and rule them if we do not fill them with Christ and His Word.

3. We demand America for Christ for Christ's sake.

As Christians we are zealous for the glory of Christ. We are anxious that He shall be known in a grand way, a way accordant with His greatness. We demand our nation as a medium through which He may operate and show His wonderful and redeeming love. So great is His heart that there is room in it for every American citizen. This nation with its seventy millions cannot do more than fill the smallest corner of His heart. The world does not know how He can handle nations and what His ideals for nations are; so we must put America into His hand that through it He may teach the world. Nations seem mighty to us, but before Him they are as drops in a bucket and as the small dust that gathers upon the balances, which the weigher brushes off. He who works through constellations and suns and systems has great thoughts for the nations of the earth. He would have them become reflections of the principalities and powers and thrones and dominions amid which He walks in the celestial world. He would have their characters as grand and their loyalty to Him as true. He would have all their laws and institutions and controlling principles shine with righteousness and purity and love. If America would put itself completely in His hands He would make it a model among the nations and the admiration of all.

Give America to Christ as you give the canvas to the artist. Meissonier took a canvas twenty inches square and by his colors and creations and genius worked out upon it that which commanded as a price ten and fifteen and twenty thousand dollars from lovers of art. Christ can do a grander work than that on and in and through a nation as an immortal canvas. Give Him the canvas. He took that little bit of canvas, Palestine, a plot of ground no larger than one of our smallest States, and see what He gave to the world through it! It takes the full Bible to tell the beauties of that canvas. Paul's nation was a small canvas in comparison with our nation. Oh, that Christ might have our nation to work upon as He worked upon the Jewish nation! My soul thrills to think what a masterpiece He would produce. He would portray upon it a perfect and mammoth gospel, visible in all its glory and beauty to the ends of the earth. He would produce such results that the world on seeing His finished work would break forth into one long and loud and enthusiastic anthem of praise. Then would begin that grand day whose sunrise glory and whose noontide splendor are painted upon the page of prophecy—the day when the whole earth shall be full of His glory, and when voices in heaven shall join with voices on earth, and all shall sing, " Hallelujah: for the Lord God omnipotent reigneth. The kingdoms of this world are become the kingdoms of our Lord, and of His Christ; and He shall reign for ever and ever."

It seems like a hopeless undertaking to capture America for Christ when we look at it in an isolated way; but when we look at it in union with all the branches of Zion there is no peradventure with regard to the accomplishment of the task. There are ten millions of evangelical church-members in the United States. Let these ten millions, with their constituency, become aroused and united, and there is nothing which the church of God cannot do in America. It can push every needed moral reform on to victory; it can restore the American Sabbath; it can grind to powder every evil traffic; it can frown down all abuses and live down all skepticism; it can secure all needed moral legislation and give the gospel to every soul in the land; it can do this and yet have resources unused ready to take up Christ's work in foreign fields. Are you willing to do your share? Are you willing to pray for your country and put your prayers into gold? This is the hour when we can use American coin and American bills for America's regeneration. If we do our duty to our country, then we can trust God to do His duty to our country. Then we can trust our country to do its duty to the world.

XII.

THE HONOR DUE TO OUR PATRIOTIC DEAD.

XII.

THE HONOR DUE TO OUR PATRIOTIC DEAD.*

VETERANS of the Grand Army of the Republic, we welcome you to-night to this temple of God. The story of your patriotic service and the story of this patriotic church match. It is fitting that loyal men should celebrate loyalty in a loyal place. This temple, reared while the smoke of battle was rolling over the land, rose to its splendid proportions with the American flag floating from yonder turret. A flag was raised the very moment the turret was strong enough to support it, and, without being lowered a single time, it floated there day and night during the whole of the nation's perilous crisis. Its continual waving in mid-air wore it into shreds, until it passed out of sight and lost itself in that great victory which we celebrate to-night,

* Delivered in Lafayette Avenue Presbyterian Church, Brooklyn, on Memorial Sabbath, to the Grant Post of the Grand Army of the Republic.

whose coming it had been signaling for weary years. Not only was yonder turret loyal, this pulpit was loyal. The man in the pulpit was himself an American flag, starred and barred through and through with a patriotism that was seen and felt the broad land over. The story of your life and the story of this temple match; both are full of patriotic reminiscences.

In entering upon this service, let us keep clearly before our minds its definite object; let us sweep away all misunderstanding. The object of this Memorial service is not the glorification of war. It is to hold up the horrors of war; it is to talk of tattered ensigns and decimated regiments and soldiers' graves and disfigured bodies and broken hearts and shattered homes, that in the presence of these ghastly things we may magnify the moral worth and heroism of the sons of America and the grandsons of the Pilgrims, who could easier meet and endure these horrors than allow the right to be trampled underfoot and the nation rent and dishonored. It is not the design of Memorial day to cultivate the brutal in man, or to represent human life as cheap, or to fire the minds of young America with a love and admiration for a barbarous business, which drenches the world in blood and makes widows of wives and orphans of helpless children.

America has never been a warlike nation; she

has never prided herself upon her standing army or her navy or her military academies. Our army has been, and is now, nothing more than a mere police force reduced to the smallest possible peace minimum. We are a nation of citizens, and not a nation of soldiers; we are a republic of men after the Washingtonian type, and not a republic of men after the Napoleonic or Cæsarean type. Washington, who was the father of our country, ceased from war as soon as it was possible to cease, and this is what his sons have always done. In history he is noted not only as " first in war," but also as " first in peace." In our Civil War the army of the North, like the army of the nation in Revolutionary times, was an army of men mustered directly from the workshop and the farm and the store and the court-room and the college and the pulpit. Our troops were rallied by a magnificent outburst of the moral sense of the people. They rallied that they might stand up for God's cause and for freedom, and for the integrity and the wholeness of the nation, and for the future good of the States, and even for the best interests of their fellow-citizens who drew the sword against them and turned their guns upon them. When this moral sense, which was the echo of the mind of God, was satisfied, when secession, with its national curse and crime of African slavery, became a lost cause, when the nation came from the furnace a new moral person and prospectively a united nation, beautiful and pure as the shining gold of the seventh refining, then our soldier-patriots dissolved themselves into the ranks of civilians. That day which brought the close of the civil strife found the American Republic again out of sympathy with the blood-stained Napoleon and the despotic and armor-clad Cæsar. We were then, and we now are, Washingtonian inside and outside, lengthwise from head to foot, and breadthwise from finger-tip to finger-tip. The American Republic is one grand peace society believing in and advocating arbitration for the nations of the nineteenth century *versus* war.

In speaking thus against war I am speaking the mind of the members of the Grand Army of the Republic. Old soldiers never desire war; they are the truest peace-men on earth. Abraham Lincoln said to the South, "There shall be no war until you compel it." And there was no war until the South compelled it. It was Grant, the great soldier, who established national arbitration. Washington, Jackson, the Harrisons, Taylor, Grant, had no war during their administrations, and they were all old soldiers, the nation's veterans. All of our wars have begun under politician presidents.

I find among my excerpts this vivid picture, which I keep because of its striking character. It teaches us how our veterans regard war per se. It is a sketch from the experience of a Vermont veteran. The man's feelings could be duplicated a hundredfold in the Grand Army of the Republic. Describing a battle in which he fought, he writes: "The enemy are going to charge us. Orders run along the lines that every bullet fired must hit a man. I select my man while he is yet beyond range. Soon our volley shall prove a veritable flame of fire. On comes the foe. My man is still before me; I have eyes for no other; he is a tall, soldierly fellow and wears the stripes of a sergeant. As he comes nearer I imagine that he is looking fixedly at me as I am looking at him. I admire his coolness; he looks neither to the right nor to the left. The man on his right hand is struck and goes down, but he does not falter; he moves right on. I am going to kill that man. I have a rest for my gun, and I cannot miss him; he is living his last minute on earth. The order to fire is given, and there is a billow of flame and a billow of smoke and a fierce crash, and four thousand bullets are fired into that compact mass of advancing men. There is not one volley, but another and another, until there remains not a living man to fire at. The smoke drifts slowly away, and our men cheer and yell. All we can see is a meadow heaped with the dead and the dying. As our line advances I look for my victim; he is lying on his back, eyes half shut, his fingers clutching the sod. He gasps and is dead, and I pass on. He fell by my bullet, and I am entitled to all the glory. Do I swing my cap and cheer? Do I point him out and expect to be congratulated? No, no; I have no cheers, I feel no elation. That man's agonized face is in my soul, and it looks out at me in the daytime and in the darkness of the night; and it will haunt and torment me all through life, and I am in dreadful terror lest it haunt me all through eternity. Carrying that agonizing picture in my soul, I for one say, 'A thousand curses on war.'"

We believe in war only as a stern necessity; but when it does become a stern necessity, when divine logic can get utterance only by the mouth of the cannon, then we enter it as a part of our religion. This nation of ours has never accepted of war except when it has been assured that war was a God-assigned duty, and only when it has been able to carry its conscience with it into battle. Did this Republic ever fire the first gun in any war? In the Revolution, which blood was shed first upon the streets of Boston? The blood of the soldier of Britain, or the blood of the citizen of Boston? In our Civil War, was it Sumter which opened the fire, or was it Sumter which was fired upon? From the standpoint of the North the Civil War was a stern necessity, to flee which would have been treason upon the part of our fathers and brethren, who bravely fell and whose graves deserve the brightest laurels of earth. From the Northern standpoint our Civil War was a divine dispensation whereby, according to the method of heaven, our nation was first made pure that afterward it might be made permanently peaceful.

Memorial day is not devoted to the art of war, which our American soul abhors; it is devoted to the praise of peace and liberty, which, our fathers found, could be purchased only at the cost of their lives. They were not fond of being shot at or dying; being shot at and dying were accepted as stern necessities; such was the price of liberty. This is the day on which we give God praise that the sword has been beaten into the plowshare and the spear into the pruning-hook. This is the day given up to symposiums upon patriotism, to find out what patriotism is and what it will do and how it can be cultivated. This is the day given up to the study of history, that in history we may see the rule of God, and the play of the human, and the operation and the issues of moral principles in national life. This is the day dedicated to the men who patriotically sacrificed their property and their lives that we might have civil and religious liberty. They fell, but the Union lives, and the power of their sacrifice will forever circulate in the life of the nation. The hour is to be used in thinking of these men who are in the silent tent of green. Name their names with respect and reverence. Repeat their deeds and describe their battles. Crown their graves with the beauties of earth, and proclaim by symbolic flowers the moral beauty which you see in their deeds. This day gives to every soldier's grave a voice. Every grave declares that our national privileges are blood-bought. These graves are the price of liberty, equality, fraternity, and unity. They are a testimony to this fact, that our land and laws and institutions are worth dying for. They are a witness to the value of American citizenship.

The period of the war is not an empty period; it is full of revelations and lessons; it declares the strength of our Republic. Not another nation on the globe could have stood such a strain and have come forth a whole nation. Out of our terrible conflict there comes an assurance of a long and a strong future. A nation which at most will only reel and rock, but will not rend nor break, under the greatest possible pressure and strain, will certainly not collapse under minor stresses. Our war was a crucial test, and it has shown that America can always count upon great men for great crises. Greatness is slumbering in the North and in the South; it only needs opportunity to awaken it. Let necessity create another war and Illinois will give the country another Lincoln, and Ohio another Grant and Sherman and Sheridan and Stanton, and Indiana another Logan, and New York another Seward, and Pennsylvania another Thaddeus

Stephens, and Massachusetts another Charles Sumner and another Henry Wilson.

But let us keep to the main thread of our subject. The occasion which has brought us together calls us to honor our patriotic dead. The practical question of the hour is, How can this best be done? How can loving Americans honor the great American dead? To this question you will allow me to offer several answers.

1. *We honor our heroic and patriotic dead by simply naming them and making their names household words and national powers.*

To pronounce the name of a man is a very simple thing, but it makes the man who is named known, and where the man is a hero knowledge is power. Why is Paul such a power in the world? Because he is talked about and named and known. The same thing explains why Shakespeare is a power and an influence. It is our duty to talk about those men who saved our nation and stood between us and national humiliation. We owe it to them as a debt of gratitude, and we owe it to ourselves. We owe it to them and to ourselves to conserve their influence for the good of the nation. Let this nation cease talking of Abraham Lincoln for a single generation, and what power will Abraham Lincoln have in the future of America? By naming him and talking about him we give him an earthly immortality and also a power to repeat himself in our sons. Talk, then, about the heroes of the war! Talk about Ellsworth, who, though a mere lad, was the first hero to fall a martyr to the flag. His death was a blast from the silver trumpet of liberty which brought a hundred thousand men to the defense of the flag he loved. Talk about Mac-Pherson, who died at the age of thirty-five. Talk about Sherman, the great soldier, the leader of the campaign from Chattanooga to Atlanta. Talk about Sheridan, the hero of Winchester, and about Hooker, whose name will never cease to be linked with the clouds of the precipitous Lookout Mountain. Talk about Meade, whose fame is enshrined in the famous Gettysburg, and about Burnside, who will never be forgotten so long as the story of the defense of Knoxville is told. Talk about Logan, who founded Memorial day. Talk about Grant, to whom all the comrades willingly give the palm for greatness, whose name is the synonym of victory. Talk about Farragut, the sea-king of Mobile Bay; and about the unsurpassed Admiral Foote of Fort Henry and Fort Donaldson and Island No. 10. None of these are living. How rapidly the roll of the Grand Army of the Republic is shortening! It will not be long until these graves must be handed over to the sons of veterans for decoration and safe-keeping.

But I would not have you stop the roll-call

when you have named these conspicuous names to which I have referred. There are thousands upon thousands of names, inconspicuous, but just as noble. Like the soil at the foot of Mount Washington, they are of the same stuff as that which crowns the summit that overlooks the continent. The summit of Mount Washington towers because the soil at its base upholds it. It was these thousands on thousands of unnamed ones that made Grant and Sherman and Sheridan. Let every man who did his duty be honored, whether his shoulders bore the stars of a general, or the eagle of a colonel, or the bars of a captain, or the stripes of a sergeant, or the simple blue of a private.

It is a legend among dwellers by the Rhine that on a certain night every year, when the moon is at its full, the imperial Charles leaves his tomb and visits the scenes he loved. Walking upon an arch of light, he crosses the river, calling down a benediction upon the land, blessing fields and flocks, vineyards and cities, the hamlets and the sleeping people, and then softly returns to his dreamless slumbers. The legend is a vehicle of fact. The nobly true of our land, who have nobly lived and who have nobly died, can never be imprisoned with the dead. Their lives are grafted upon the immortal life of God's conquering and reigning righteousness. They pour down light upon us and breathe inspiration into us; they plant thoughts of power in our sterile brains; they are the pulses in the earthquake that is gathering power under the thrones of iniquity. Our Republic will live so long as it reveres their memories and emulates their virtues. The occasion to-day calls us to live with these men of the historic past, that we may be blessed by them and taught by them.

There is in the Corcoran Art Gallery, at Washington, D. C., a striking picture of old colonial days which serves me as an illustration. It is a scene from the battle of Monmouth. An aged fifer, his gray locks streaming in the wind, leads his company into the battle. By his side there is a drummer-boy looking anxiously into the old man's face and catching from him the tune and the step of the music of liberty. So from the lives and deeds of the men who fell in our Civil War, and from the cause for which they died, and from the results which they achieved, we take our step and learn the lesson of the cost of our institutions and liberties, and how to perpetuate and build up our nation. Over seven thousand miles of our country were swept by the tide of war; over two millions of men marched in solid phalanx in the army of freedom; over five hundred thousand men filled a soldier's grave; and every mile in the line of march, and every man in the ranks, and every grave, is fraught with a blessing if we only keep ourselves familiar with these and hold them in honor. In this broad land of ours, with its teeming millions, not a single name of a single loyal soldier should be allowed to lapse into oblivion. Somebody somewhere should be found able to name and able to tell the sacrifices of the least-known member of the Grand Army of the Republic. This is the very minimum of honor which we owe to all.

My fellow-men, there are healthful memories which carry in them healthful feelings—memories of our sorrows, memories of our sacrifices, memories of our conflicts. It is helpful to cherish these once in a while and to allow the old feelings which they carry in them to thrill through us again. A strange feeling swept through you when the first rebel gun sent its iron ball over Charleston harbor to strike with fatal impact the walls of Fort Sumter; a thrill of patriotism shot through you like a bolt of fire and set you all aglow with loyalty. Feel that thrill of patriotism again—feel it to-night. There are syllables, grand and loyal, which when pronounced are like the striking notes rung from old liberty bell on old Independence Hall. You know these syllables; they are such as these: Major Anderson, Elmer Ellsworth, the Massachusetts Sixth, the New York Seventh, the Brooklyn Fourteenth. Ring out these grand and loyal syllables again—ring them out to-night. There are names, sacred names, which have the power to cement our national Union. They were great when they were pronounced away back between '61 and '65, and they are great now: Abraham Lincoln, Ulysses S. Grant, William T. Sherman, Philip H. Sheridan. Pronounce these names again—pronounce them to-night. With them still keep binding our national Union. Memories, victories, successful causes; armies marching to the defense of the oppressed and battling for the conquest of the right; great and living principles; the great men and the true men and the holy men of the nation—my fellow-men, these are the great liberty bells of the Republic; keep ringing these and ringing these, and by their ringing call the Republic up to its high destiny. By these

> " Ring out the old, ring in the new;
> Ring out the false, ring in the true.
>
> " Ring out a slowly dying cause
>   And ancient forms of party strife;
> Ring in the nobler modes of life,
> With sweeter manners, purer laws.
>
> " Ring out false pride in place and blood,
>   The civic slander and the spite;
> Ring in the love of truth and right,
> Ring in the common love of good.
>
> " Ring out the darkness of the land;
>   . . . . . .
> Ring out the narrowing lust of gold;
> Ring out the thousand wars of old,
> Ring in the thousand years of peace."

2. *We honor our heroic and patriotic dead by keeping in the light the ideas for which they fought.*

The Civil War was a battle of ideas. It was not a conquest for spoils; it was a conflict of opinions. There was a thinker back of every rifle, and a thousand thinkers under every regimental flag. So far as the North was concerned, the war was waged for preservation and not for destruction.

The first idea for which the men of the North fought was this: this Republic is a Nation, and the word "Nation" is spelled with a capital N. It is not a confederacy, it is not a social compact, which can be broken by the States at will. The national government is supreme; it was not made by the States, therefore it cannot be broken by the States. If our national government was not made by the States, by whom was it made? The very first words of the national Constitution answer that question: "We the people do ordain this Constitution and government." If the Constitution had been made to read, "We the States do ordain," the South would have been right and the North wrong. The people are supreme, not the States. Besides this, by far the greatest part of the territory which was carried out of the Union by the Southern secession was territory bought and paid for by the federal government, and not by the Southern States. Florida, Texas, Louisiana, who purchased and paid for these? The United States government.

The idea of the American nationality in contradistinction from an American compact which could be broken at will first presented itself to Alexander Hamilton. He saw that national union was essential to growth and strength, so he applied all his power and used all his resources to give supremacy to that idea. He introduced it to the newly independent States back in the times of the American Revolution. He lodged it in the minds of the newly emancipated people. He lifted it into some power, but he was unable to make it the sovereign idea in the political life of his times. Jefferson saw in Hamilton's idea, as he thought, the return of the people to monarchy. He beheld in it a return of the domination which the colonies had just cast off, and the loss of the freedom which it had taken seven years of war and famine to secure. State rights seemed to him, and to many others of the earlier statesmen, another name for liberty. Hamilton died with the gloomiest forebodings as to the future of this country. He doubted whether it would ever rise into the consciousness of a great nation. After Hamilton came Webster, his great successor, the greatest man of the second period of our government, as Hamilton was the greatest man of the first period. The idea on behalf of which Webster put forth his whole strength was the idea of Hamilton, the idea of American nationality. All of his principal speeches are full of it. His famous senatorial triumphs were won on its behalf. He secured a new place for Hamilton's thought in the minds and in the hearts of his fellow-citizens; he clothed it in the language of reason; he set it forth in all the attraction of patriotic imagination; he sent it home to the soul of the whole North with the authority of his matchless eloquence. Nevertheless, in one half of the land, the Southland, his ideas were rejected and his doctrine scorned. Jefferson had an able and desperate successor in John C. Calhoun. He held the South loyal to the idea of State rights. Under the faith in State rights the Southern States seceded from the Union, and hence the Civil War. The intellectual contests of Hamilton and Jefferson, Webster and Calhoun, were repeated on the battlefield. They were hotly debated at Shiloh and Antietam, at Gettysburg and in the Wilderness. For a long time the battle was even, but finally it was won by the army of the North for the preservation of the Union. This was the result of your service and of the service of the men whom you commemorate to-night. You and they lifted into sovereign power the idea of the American nationality. You purchased for us the right to spell "Nation" with a capital N. The flag which to-day floats over every city from Maine to the Gulf, and from the Atlantic to the Pacific, is a symbol of the union and strength and national grandeur which you and your comrades achieved.

But the war was not only intellectual, it had a moral side. Patriotic men began to feel that the nation could not be half free and half slave. Slavery began to appear in its true light, a monstrous sin, and the guns of the nation were pointed against that sin. The cry rent the air, "Free the slaves! Strike down the nation's curse and shame!" My fellow-men, it was not until this cry was raised, it was not until the great moral principle of freedom for all was brought into the war and the Emancipation Proclamation was issued, that victory began to perch upon our banners. Prior to this it was one continued Bull Run. Then it was that God took our side, because then it was that we took God's side. Then it was that away above the crimson surge of conflict was God, holding in His mighty palm the stars of our flag, which, though dimmed, were not to be allowed to fall as dying meteors down the sky. Up to this point the African slave had been an incarnate sarcasm upon the boasted liberty of the Republic; but after this, with limbs unfettered and sword-arm free, he fought for the Republic, and the Republic won. Soldiers of the Grand Army of the Republic, you made the black man free; now stand by him and make his freedom a thing of value. Remember that the genius of liberty is an equal chance for every man to rise and enrich himself and be a man among men.

3. *We honor our heroic and patriotic dead by exalting the influence of their deeds.*

The battle of the heroes of '61 for liberty blessed the North, but it did more. Like every battle fought for liberty, it blessed the world. William Tell did not live for Switzerland only, he lived for all nations. In all lands where his story is told it stirs to action the innate instinct for liberty. The heroism of the Hebrews fighting their way from Egypt to Canaan has been a seed which has produced many a like uprising and which has given the world many a land of promise. When, in the heroic period of our national history, the period between '61 and '65, our armies fought down African slavery, they fought the battles of liberty for the kingdoms of the Old World. The cannon-balls and hot shells fired into and through the ships of the slaveholders of America were also fired into and through the slave-ships that plied the Mediterranean. They were long-range shots, but they sank the Mediterranean slave-ships out of sight. The American war told for good even in the heart of Africa, where black men were sold by black men. The world has been a freer world ever since. The American Civil War tells to-day. This very hour it is putting heart and hope into the would-be freemen of

Cuba, whom may the God of battles bless and crown with an everlasting victory. Every battle for liberty has been a blessing, and a blessing for those who have fought against liberty. This is the impartial verdict of history. Take an illustration.

American independence was the best thing which ever happened for England England did not think so at the time, but history has proved it. It is said that when Lord North heard the news of the surrender of Cornwallis, it was like receiving a cannon-ball into his bosom. The hope which he had cherished for twelve years had gone. He paced the room wildly, and, waving his arms around in mental distress, he fairly shrieked, " It is all over! It is all over!" He thought England's greatness had been permanently injured; but what do facts say to-day? This is the record: England of the present is England in its greatest glory and power. This Republic has kept the old mother-country from falling asleep or napping. It has been a friendly, stimulating rival; it has been a check and a safeguard against England's tendency to tyranny; it has sent through England a modifying and liberalizing influence. For a whole century England has been becoming Americanized and has been growing decent respect for the rights of the individual man.

Both England and America are satisfied now with

the Revolutionary War and with its results. This was demonstrated at the celebration of the one-hundredth anniversary of the surrender of Yorktown, the event which brought that war to a fitting close. During that celebration, by a happy inspiration, the officer in charge gave the order to the United States troops to run up the old British flag on the spot where it had been hauled down a century before and to salute it. The British flag was thrown into the breeze and it was saluted by American guns. This is what took place on our side of the Atlantic. On the other side of the Atlantic London spoke for old England. London answered back in a grand crash of drums and in the clear ringing notes of the royal band, which sounded down the Strand playing "The star-spangled banner, long may it wave!"

While bitter wars seem in the course of human history to be necessary, God be praised that time brings a reconciliation in which the old contesting foes can rejoice together.

As we have spoken of England, so we may speak of our own sunny South. The South by the war has lost nothing, but has gained everything. True, it has talked about "the lost cause," but the cause lost is infinitely better lost than gained. When we understand what "the lost cause" is it loses all its glamour. That cause was defined by the vice-president of the Confederacy to be "African slavery as it exists among us." "The lost cause" was a secession to enable one set of men without interference or remonstrance to own a weaker set of men as chattels, and the doctrine of State rights was used as an instrument to secure this end. That is the whole case in a nutshell. I think perhaps I can illustrate "the lost cause" still more plainly by relating just here a scene in the South which took place at the close of the war. It was given me by a friend who was there and saw it. In a Virginia town occupied by our troops, a Virginia gentleman beyond the age of military service was summoned to answer to a complaint of assault and battery. He was an urbane and courteous gentleman of expansive waistcoat, who most blandly declared to the court that he was utterly unconscious how such a mistake as his summons could ever have been made. It appeared, however, that the complainant was a colored man upon whom the gentleman had applied his horse-whip. The astonishment of the accused cannot be described; he looked at the black man and at the officer alternately and said in a half helpless way, "Assault and battery! Walloping a nigger assault and battery! Great heavens! what have we come to?" There, that is "the lost cause." "The lost cause" is simply the loss of a white man's right to wallop at pleasure a black man. "The lost cause" has long ceased to have any respectability. With "the lost cause" has passed away the foolish assumption that the South lost any property or became any poorer by the emancipation. It used to be said that four thousand millions of property were destroyed by freeing the four millions of slaves; but this ridiculous assumption is now abandoned. There was no destruction whatever. The only change which took place was this: instead of one man owning a hundred men, each of the one hundred came to own himself. The white man's loss was the black man's gain. The property was all there. The columns of profit and loss balance. The South was not robbed of the black people; the black people are there still. And they should stay there; that is where they belong. They are the children of the tropics, and their mission is to work in the tropics. They are worth more to themselves and to the world in the tropics than they can be anywhere else. No man ever rendered the South a greater service than did Abraham Lincoln when he issued his war Proclamation of Emancipation. By that one act he turned aside the curse of the liberty-loving God from the South and opened the land to free industry, which always carries with it a prosperity blessed of God. I do not hesitate to say that in a generation's time the loudest praises of Abraham Lincoln will be the praises spoken by Southern lips. That time is already here. There is no finer eulogy of our martyred President than that pronounced by Henry Grady of Atlanta. Publicly to-day the South proclaims that she is glad that slavery is no more. The Grand Army of the Republic has made our land free and prosperous.

4. *We honor our heroic and patriotic dead by exalting the humane way in which they closed the war.*

Our soldiers who fought were the very first to forgive the foe when the Rebellion grounded its arms. It was they also who taught the men at home to forgive. It was veterans who first decorated the graves of Confederate prisoners buried in our Northern cemeteries. They led the country in forgiveness. I rejoice in this, because it is a grand exhibit of the power and advance of Christian civilization. It magnifies Christianity. Compare the customs of war in the past and in the present, and see how Christianity has mitigated the horrors of war. Go back a few thousand years. There you see a great army gathered about the city of Troy. Out from the city comes the brave Hector, one of the Trojans, to meet the dread Achilles. The champions stand face to face, and Hector falls before the blows of Achilles. What then? In accordance with the savage usages of those times, Achilles the conqueror drags Hector's dead body, chained to his chariot, three times around the walls of Troy, and then throws it mutilated at the feet of his broken-hearted wife,

Andromache. That is the civilization of the past. Look now at the scene of Appomattox Court-house. There stands the victor, and you hear him talk to the defeated hero. "How many men have you?" asks General Grant of General Lee. The number is told. "Are they in need of rations?" "Yes." Rations are ordered immediately. "Have they horses?" "They have." "Let them keep them, for they will need them to till the ground in support of their families, and I will give them seed-corn that they may have a harvest the coming season." My fellow-men, there is a long distance from Achilles dragging the dead Hector around the walls of Troy to General Grant sending the conquered Confederate army back to the Southland to live in their old homes, to enter again into the Union, and to enjoy again their State and federal rights. The long distance is accounted for, because Grant and his men were Christians and forgave like Christians. Does any one say, "Oh, but the North took the property of General Lee and turned it into a national graveyard in which to bury the Union soldiers with honor. There it is at Arlington, the Mecca of America. It was nothing short of the finest irony of history to sow the acres of his dooryard with the bones of his victims and make his home a cemetery. The Arlington soldiers' cemetery was the old homestead of General Lee"? Wait! give the facts. The facts are these:

the North paid for that ground; the United States government paid the Lee family one hundred and fifty thousand dollars for those acres. There is not a single stain upon the magnanimity of the free people of the North in closing up the war and in dealing with their brethren of the South. No; the Republic, bleeding though it was at every pore, held no State trials, closed no prison doors upon political offenders, and reared no scaffolds amid the ashes of the Rebellion. Andrew Johnson tried to do this. In his early frenzy for revenge he determined to try to execute all of the rebel leaders. He had General Lee indicted and brought before the civil courts. General Lee appealed to General Grant, to whom he had surrendered and by whom he had been paroled. Grant claimed Lee as his prisoner, and declared that so long as he refrained from violating his parole, no court in the land should try or condemn him. He took Lee out of the hands of Johnson. Johnson would have ruined and spoiled the generous and conciliatory treatment of Appomattox. His conduct was a breach of faith, and if it had prevailed it would have undone Appomattox and have at once inaugurated another war. Because of Grant's magnanimous stand, because he threw himself between the raging President and the Confederate general, not a single scaffold was erected and not a single execution took place.

I am here to say that this is absolutely unmatched in the annals of civilization, ancient or modern. Our heroes of '61 to '65 followed nature, and went so far as to put flowers upon the graves of the Confederate dead. Nature, when the war ceased to plow her valleys with cannonballs, healed the scars which these iron bolts made. She even ordered wild roses to bloom through the broken drumheads, and she commanded the daisies to look out of the shattered shells with eyes of gold. Under her benediction battle-fields to-day are harvest-fields. The heroes of '61 to '65 followed nature and covered over everything which should be forgotten, and in the place of the Minié ball gave the right hand of brotherhood. We have just as much reason to be proud of the manner in which our hero soldiers closed the war as we have of the manner in which they conducted the war.

5. *We honor our heroic and patriotic dead by being true men, and, as true men, by faithfully fighting the battles of our day as they fought the battles of their day.*

The flower of a beautiful and true life is the flower to put upon the soldier's grave. Trueness to our country is the best way to honor the soldier who fell in the defense of our country. The best citizen, the best patriot, the best son of his country, is he who gives the best manhood to his country. He is the man who writes upon his nature the ten commandments and the eight beatitudes. You can have a Grand Army only when the ranks are filled with grand men. Soldiers of the Grand Army of the Republic, recognize the call of the hour! Our nation calls for hundreds and thousands of true men. There is treason still to be put down. There is the treason of a cowardly silence when patriotism and duty call us to cry out against the destructive sins of the land. This must be put down. There is treason in the Senate hall; there is treason in the political caucus; there is treason at the ballot-box—the selling of votes and the manipulation of votes and the intimidation of votes. There is treason in office which shows itself in the acceptance of bribes and rewards. It is your duty to put down treason in all of these forms. The traitor in the time of peace should be shot just as the traitor in the time of war was shot. He should be shot with the black ball. He should be shot with the cannon of public indignation and execration. He should be fired out of office and out of citizenship, and he should be buried in everlasting oblivion.

Soldiers of the Republic, the battles of the present are morally identical with the battles of the past. The form of warfare only has changed. The moral conflicts waged in our nation are as truly battles as were the conflicts of Gettysburg and Lookout Mountain. You have a duty in these as you had a duty in those. What are the moral conflicts whose roll-call you should hear to-day? They are such as these: the battle for temperance, for social purity, for the rights of the red man and the black man and the Mongolian, the battle of labor against capital and of capital against labor, the anti-poverty battle. Besides these there are battles against the deadly isms which have been imported to our land and which are warring against the very life of our nation. Our country is the land where the battles of the future are destined to be fought, and where they have already opened. In the push of discovery and of civilization there is no land beyond this. The fields of America are the outermost fields of the earth, and here the nations of the Old World crowd together and meet, and here the great problems and questions of the ages must be debated and settled. Rally around the true flag in these moral battles. Fire no blank cartridges, but pour hot shot into every form of evil. Deal not in feeble negations, but in strong positive statements, and fire these with the power of propelling conviction. Present a solid phalanx of true steel against every untrue and false thing. For example, let no one run the red flag of anarchism over the stars and stripes, neither let any one run the stars and stripes over the red flag. The two flags must never have any sort of union. Anarchism must not take the American Republic under its protection, neither must the American Republic take anarchism under its protection. We are living in a day when our country needs, above all things, intense Americans, who will Americanize every foreign thing, and will on no account allow America to become foreignized. Our fathers and brothers died for our country; it is our duty to live for it. We must pay a price as they paid a price. The price which we must pay for liberty is a pure manhood and an eternal vigilance. The monument which I would place by the grave of our noble dead would be, not a cold marble statue, but an honorable, wide-awake, honest, intelligent, moral, God-fearing American citizen.

Fellow-Americans, I have great hopes for our country for which our soldiers died. To me it is the great Niagara in the landscape of the nations. What roar and dash and tumultuous rolling and wild hurricane there are in the waters of Niagara! There is devouring, perplexing, fermenting, bewildering activity. But out of this roar and dash and wildness and fury there rises a silvery column of spray, which the sunshine penetrates and tints into loveliness and rainbow splendors. Niagara is the type of our Republic, and the type becomes clearer and clearer as we ponder our nation's history. What see we in America from the platform of history! Changes, revolutions, strifes, sects and factions pitted against sects and factions, wars, foreign and civil, cruel slavery, confederacies of evil; but out of the turbulence and conflicts of opinions rises the Republic, purified from slavery, and with a hundred institutions for the free development of mankind, and with a welcome to the oppressed of all lands. Only one thing is needed, and that one thing is that we shall be true. America, honor the right and the right will honor you. America, honor God and God will honor you. Credit Him with your liberty, and praise Him for your civilization. In the North and in the South make His unerring law the law of the nation. This and this only is solid patriotism; this and this only is a patriotism fit to match the patriotism of those who fell upon the battle-field.

An Illustrated Christian Monthly.

MAGAZINE OF RELIGIOUS AND CURRENT THOUGHT.

Undenominational, 13th Year; devoted to Applied Christianity, elegantly Illustrating the same; Sermons, Questions of the Day, Sunday-school, Mission Work. By best writers on Theology, Christian Life, and Work. $2.50. It fills a niche, meets a want not supplied by any other periodical. Sample, 10 cents.

HELPFUL BOOKS THOUGHTS for the OCCASION

1. PATRIOTIC AND SECULAR. A Repository of Historical Data, Facts and Beautiful Thoughts for Patriotic and Holiday Occasions, to wit: Arbor Day, Fourth of July, Flag Raising, Decoration Day, Washington's, Lincoln's and Grant's Birthdays, Labor Day, etc. 578 pages. **$1.75**

2. ANNIVERSARY AND RELIGIOUS. Occasions in Historical Outlines, Anecdotes, and Incidents, suggestive Thoughts for Timely Occasions to wit: Christmas, Communions, Children's Day, Lenten Season, Easter, Thanksgiving, New Years, Young People's Service, etc. 600 pages, 12mo. Edited by F. Noble, D.D. **$1.75**

3. MEMORIAL TRIBUTES. A Compend of Funeral Addresses and Sermons, for all ages and conditions, Best thoughts from eminent Divines. An aid for Pastors. Introduction by John Hall, D.D. Cloth, 12mo, 500 pages. **$1.75**

4. THE BOW IN THE CLOUD; or, Words of Comfort for the Sorrowing. Over 200 contributors in Poetry and Prose. Introduction by Wm. M. Taylor, D.D. 452 pages, square 12mo. **$1.75**

5. REVIVALS. How to Secure Them. As Taught and Exemplified by the Most Successful Clergymen. A helpful volume to all commissioned to "Go and Preach." Edited by Rev. W. P. Doe 444 pp. **$1.75**

6. CURIOSITIES OF THE BIBLE. (10,000) Prize Questions pertaining to Scripture, Persons, Places, and Things, with key, Seed Thoughts, Bible Studies and Readings, Prayer-meeting Outlines, etc. By a New York Sunday-school Supt. Introduction by Rev. J. H. Vincent, D.D. 610 pp. **$2.00**

Sent postpaid, on receipt of price. Agents Wanted.

E. B. TREAT, Pub., 5 Cooper Union, N.Y.

www.ingramcontent.com/pod-product-compliance
Lightning Source LLC
Chambersburg PA
CBHW030404230426
43664CB00007BB/749